RETRIBUTION

A scathing story of mandatory minutiae, softening students, pretentious parents, too much testing, common core conundrums, and the slow death of a noble profession.

Frank Stepnowski

outskirts
press

Also by Frank Stepnowski
Teaching Sucks; But We Love It!
A little insight into the profession you **think** *you know.*

"Why do I get up and do every day? Why do millions of other educators do the same? It's because we love what we do. "Teaching Sucks—But We Love It" is written from the heart of a teacher. Step's stories will make you laugh, get angry, cry but most of all expose the heart of teaching. The greatest message anyone can hear is that you are not alone. Step takes us on journey many claims to understand yet few are willing to take. His story is our story. It doesn't matter if you are an angry parent, confused student or frustrated teacher; Step speaks to us all in this book and helps us all see we are not alone."

"I stumbled onto this title on the BAT page and ordered a copy, simply for the title. Little did I know I would not be able to put this book down. It is the most accurate accounting of teaching in today's world. There were times I thought Step was a male version of me because of so many similarities. It's not just for teachers. It's also for people who LOVE teachers, so they can understand our quirkiness. If you're a teacher, you will see yourself and your students. If you're a student, you will now understand why your teachers are the way they are and why they love you in spite of you. Read it! You won't be sorry."

"While there are plenty of great books out there that expose what is wrong with education, very few speak in a language that the average person can easily digest. [Mr. Stepnowski] sheds a clear light on the dangerous trend towards one-size-fits-all education, and reminds us that—very often—Teachers are the ones on the front line PROTECTING our kids from it. Filled with euphoric highs and tear-jerking lows, "Teaching Sucks" is the 'Blackboard Jungle' for this generation."

Step's latest offering follows the hero's journey through the trials and tribulations, and ultimate reward, of being a teacher. He puts into clear and concise language what teachers wish they could say when confronted by those who are quick to put down our profession, call it "glorified babysitting," or somehow doubt that there is artistry and craftsmanship in the art of teaching. His narrative voice makes this book a pleasure to read. Teachers are often confronted by forces that get in the way of our desire to teach "our kids" and help them grow both academically and socially. Step's book is informative to the non-classroom-initiated and cathartic to those in the trenches every day. Yes, Teaching Sucks—but oh, how we do love it!

S.C.R.E.W.E.D.; an Educational Fairytale

"For all its fierceness, the message of the book is surprisingly gentle: 'Find out what our kids need to know. Understand that they won't all learn the same way (not should they). Care about each other enough to be honest...Embrace the idea that real teaching and learning do require hard work. Don't quit. What most of the time sounds like a primal scream turn out to be a cri de coeur." — Philadelphia Inquirer

"This hilarious and (at times) scathing satire dissects our educational system from the bottom up, holding accountable clueless politicians, spineless administrators, lazy teachers and absentee parents for its shortcomings. Although allegorical in nature, Step's ideas seem not too far off the horizon, given our current educational climate and state of the country as a whole. The education of America's youth is a complex, multifaceted endeavor, with no easy solution for its problems. In S.C.R.E.W.E.D., Step makes a valiant and skillful attempt to address all of these facets, all while keeping the reader thoroughly entertained, from start to finish. This book is a must read for anyone in the educational spectrum."

"A total page turner, S.C.R.E.W.E.D. voices ideas that many people may have on their mind but don't have the stones to say. Teachers aren't always to blame and students need to take responsibility for their actions... Too many students graduate high school without truly earning it, which will screw (pardon the pun) us all eventually. Think about it."

"I'll take my hat off to Step on having the guts to put to paper what most people who want to say but can't. Well done. Get this book read it and open your mind to the new way of the world."

"I am left wondering why schools aren't being run this way. Then the reality of the world we live in creeps back into my newly awakened mind and I realize what country I live in. Having spent most of my adult life mired in one form of government bureaucracy or another, I fully realize why the powers that be will never let go of their control of the people. If schools could be empowered (again) to hold children responsible for their actions, just imagine how much more productive we could be as a society. S.C.R.E.W.E.D. really is a fairytale, because we as a society are not ready to take that cold, hard look in the mirror and see who really is at fault. Nor are we prepared to go the distance and let others hold our precious child[ren] accountable and point out their faults. Our fragile egos and feelings will have us hiding behind an archaic system that is dumbed down to the lowest denominator. But, if only it could be ..."

Why Are All the Good Teachers Crazy?

"As a teacher, I'm a tough critic, and very cynical about books written about the teaching profession. I find most of them cute and heartwarming—deserving of a "chicken soup for the teacher's soul" award, but I rarely find them realistic in nature. "Why Are All the Good Teacher's Crazy" was a breath of fresh air. I am grateful to read a book that tells the true trials and tribulations we, as teachers, go through everyday just to maintain some sort of order. Of course, I don't have nearly the battle scars that the author has (I teach middle school mainstreamed classes,) but I can admit that I am crazy and feel proud to be after reading this book."

"In order to understand and enjoy the book, you need to relate deeply to where step is coming from...His methods are all based on surviving in that environment and loving those students that no one else cares to love. His candid crotch-wetting chronicles are thoroughly entertaining and often have to be read twice to get the full effect. I was laughing out loud on many an occasion. Thank you for writing this book, which truly IS a breath of fresh air. Step has brought jeans and [a] Motley Crue t-shirt approach to teaching where the tweed jacket and pressed chinos used to exist. I know which one I prefer. I salute you!"

"I can't tell you how many times I turned the pages back to laugh again and again at parts of Step's journey and relate it to my experiences as a teacher. (Isn't that what we English teachers want our students to do...make a "connection" to what they read?) The humor, and the ability to relate to Step's experiences with his students, personal life, and outlook on that life, is what truly makes this book hands down a book that all those in education should read. For all those teachable moments, and the not so teachable moments, Step's drive and humility in caring for his students as human beings is what makes this book a life lesson for all. To all those teachers who teach in tough schools, or have had a student you can't get through to, perhaps it will remind you of those students whom you will never forget... this book will bring back memories of your own!"

"Why Are All the Good Teachers Crazy? is a profanity laced book filled with hilarious stories of one person's struggle to stay sane in the midst of insanity. (Spoiler alert, I don't think he was ever really sane to start with;)This book is full of thoughts usually reserved for happy hour booths and spouse's ears. It's dirty, jaw-dropping, angering, and at times, unbelievable; it's just like teaching school!! Thanks Step, for making this teacher laugh so much that I bought it for a friend! Definitely a book for any teacher you know as long as they don't mind a little swearing and chest thumping. **Definitely** not for your book club."

"I had ordered this for our breakfast book club. The language was so vulgar that I sent all the books back! Don't waste your money on this book! It is not funny, but disgusting!"

Retribution

A teacher strikes back

A scathing story of mandatory minutiae,
softening students, pretentious parents,
too much testing, common core conundrums,
and the slow death of a noble profession.

"Nothing haunts us like the things we don't say."
—Mitch Albom

This book is for my living children: Samantha, Mason, and Frankie.

I lived a good portion of my life with a misguided sense of fearlessness, and that kept me insulated, cold, and unable to fully enjoy the wonders of the world and the finite amount of time I was given to enjoy them; then, the death of your brother Cain threatened to solidify the self-imposed walls around me.

Your arrivals, each in their own beautifully unique way, made me afraid: afraid of wasting one moment, afraid of not *spending* each of those moments making this world a better place for you to live, afraid of not living to see the inexorable evolution of you all as human beings, afraid of not being there with your mother to guide you up close and admire you from afar.

I thrive on the fear, the urgency and passion that loving you brings, the unapologetic approach to life that comes from, to quote Elizabeth Stone, "having your heart go walking around outside your body."

You did that to me.

You gave me life every bit as much as your mother gave it to you.

Don't ever forget that.

Some may question dedicating a book of this decidedly non-delicate nature to one's children...but they don't know our connection, nor do they understand the strength and resiliency of our clan.

I am afraid of living a life without purpose, afraid of allowing old age to seduce me into weakness and irrelevance. I am afraid of being loved for being silent, being compliant, and being like everyone else.

That won't happen because, above all,

I am afraid of disappointing you.

That fear was your *gift*, and I love you all for it.

—Dad

*"Better to write for yourself and have no public,
than to write for the public and have no self."*
— *Cyril Connolly*

*"What are you waiting for?
What do you think you were created for?*

*Show us, you care, show us you dare.
You don't know what happened, not if you weren't there.*

*Born to raise hell. Born to raise hell.
We know how to do it and we do it real well."*
— **Motörhead** *(Born to Raise Hell)*

AUTHOR'S DISCLAIMER

"Truth, uncompromisingly told, will always have its ragged edges."
-Mark Twain

For those of you unfamiliar with me or my previous works, I curse a lot when I'm angry (it's a character flaw, to be sure, but there it is.) Also, I'm fairly iconoclastic, so don't expect a lot of deference to any of your cherished beliefs or institutions.

Yes, I'm an English teacher, and yes, I'm one of the most loving people you'll ever have the pleasure to meet; thus, the paradox. I have never intentionally tried to hurt anyone innocent without provocation, but if you hear my rattle and choose to tread on me anyway, you're going to get bit, *hard*, and I'm not going to apologize for it. Speaking of which, I'm far too enlightened to get caught up in the bullshit "divide and conquer" nonsense that pervades our society, so if you're in my crosshairs, it's not because you are gay, straight, black, brown, white, purple, conservative, liberal, fat, fluffy, alien, canine, bovine, wealthy, poor, Christian, Jew, Muslim, illiterate, illegitimate, illegal, inbred or a porn-loving, cross-dressing, vegan hippopotamus…

it's because you're an asshole.

And, at times, so am I.

Got that? Profane, iconoclastic, confrontational, unapologetic, and maybe a little ugly on the side. If that sounds like fun to you then, in the immortal words of Macbeth, "lay on, Macduff, and damned be him who first cries 'Hold! Enough!'" (V.viii.31-32).

If not, <u>if you're one of those politically correct, easily offended people, you should put this book down now and save yourself an unpleasant experience. Go find another book. Know that I wish you well and appreciate your self-awareness.</u>

You should know that these are but a small handful of stories that, over the course of more than two and a half years, made me rethink why I stay in this profession. I am acutely aware that most teachers could easily echo or trump my stories with those of their own; (you should see the letters and emails I get, from the hilarious to the downright chilling,) but many of my brothers and sisters remain silent, for a variety of reasons. I bear no malice toward any of them; whatever their motivation, they remain dedicated to their students.

As do I.

However, I will not remain silent any longer. As a teacher, I've heard what the corrupt politicians, enabling parents, cowardly administrators, misguided "education reformers," and anonymous online trolls have to say about me.

Now it's my turn. If you're interested in hearing the **truth**, raw, unedited and unvarnished, from an actual teacher and his students, with no ulterior motivation but to open your eyes and your minds, read on.

Join me, if you will, for a little full-frontal honesty.

A legal note: I probably don't need to tell you this, but I mixed up the genders, races, ages, grades, species, etc. of my "characters" like a 5,000-piece holographic jigsaw puzzle in a Ninja blender to create what my wickedly efficient legal team lovingly refer to as "plausible deniability." They also asked me to inform you that everything contained herein is true except for the parts I made up.

Table of Contents

PART I:
STANDARDIZING TEACHING
+ PRIVATIZING EDUCATION
= SCREWING YOUR KIDS

RETRIBUTION vs. RESIGNATION

*"Sometimes people don't want to hear the truth
because they don't want their illusions destroyed."*
—Friedrich Nietzsche

ret·ri·bu·tion—retrə'byo͞oSH(ə)n/ *noun*—punishment inflicted on someone as vengeance for a wrong or criminal act.

Ex: "Teachers generally do not speak up in the face of injustices heaped upon them because they fear **retribution**."

Synonyms: punishment, penalty, one's just desserts, revenge, retaliation, vengeance, *lex talionis*, retributive justice, redress, reparation, recompense, repayment, atonement, indemnification.

I am sure I'm not unique in that, like most educators out there, I get lots of teacher-related pictures, articles and videos sent to me via social media, and I'm getting a little tired of reading stories about teachers that have left the profession for any number of perfectly justifiable reasons.

These are, almost always, **good** people—people that *loved* their students, people that were, to borrow from the world of memes, "in it for the outcome and not the income." Nonetheless, they were beaten down and emotionally gutted by a system that made them feel like (and I'm paraphrasing now) they were losing little pieces of their soul every day by staying.

This angers me.

Deeply.

Sadly, that's a pretty good amalgam of the countless anecdotal stories I have absorbed. I read one today by a woman named Elona Schreiner entitled *The One Reason I Quit Teaching*, which was shared with me by a fellow educator named Priscilla Sanstead, whom I greatly respect. I don't know why this one particular teacher's story was the proverbial last straw, but it was. Maybe it was the fact that her love for her students resonated off the page, as did her heartbreak at having to leave "her kids"[1] to keep her soul and sanity intact. Maybe it was how close to home her words hit during this particular time in my teaching career: 25 years in and trying desperately to convince our young, once inspired, now deflated GOOD teachers to stay. I don't know, but it galvanized my intentions behind the writing of *this* particular book.

I am tired of hearing stories from teachers—good, well-intentioned people—that were forced to leave a very important calling because:

- they have been told it's a second-class profession,
- the pay to responsibility ratio is inconceivably unfair,[2]
- every loud-mouthed asshole in this country thinks that because they went to school they know how to teach;

or just because they've left too many pieces of their own hearts and souls on classroom floors *at the expense of their own loved ones* that they feel the need to evacuate their profession before they lose EVERYthing that is precious to them.

Yes, I know about that, too.

And, again, I'm tired of hearing these stories; they make me angry. Angry enough to say—a 'la Peter Finch in *Network*—"I'm mad as hell, and I'm not going to take this anymore!" We have a ton of these heartbreaking stories, and the pile grows every day, but you know what we *don't* have?

---

(1) A term I still use for ALL of my students, past and present

(2) I'm guessing you know better if you've read this far, but if you are one of those "teachers get off on weekends and all summer" people...stop, don't make me throat punch you. I work more hours OFF the clock than I do ON the clock and, unlike "respected" professionals like lawyers and accountants, I don't bill for those hours.

We don't have any books from teachers <u>that are still actively teaching</u> that take these repeated assaults to our character, our significance, and our self-worth, crush them into small pieces, and use them to forge a weapon to smash our detractors right in their sanctimonious faces.[3]

I'm resigned to the fact that someday, on MY terms, I'll move on from my calling as a teacher, but it won't be until I have, in the words of my graduate professor Mr. Amato: "pissed off the right people." So…

For the people that have been forced to walk away from the profession they love,

for the people that are suffering the thousand indignities of being a teacher in silence,

for the people at a crossroads just waiting for someone to speak up for them,

I'll choose retribution over resignation.

And if that gets me fired, maybe then I'll grow my balls big enough to finally open the school I've always wanted to open. My promotion will be simple:

"We do just about the **complete opposite**
of what your kid's normal school does"

I figure I'll have an enrollment line almost as long as the list of people trying to sue me; and maybe I can "Jerry Maguire" a few of the really good, really frustrated teachers I know to come on board.

Stay tuned.

In the meantime, join me now for a highlight (or lowlight?) reel covering almost three years of teaching as seen through my eyes. Three Superintendents, three principals, and too many changes in vice principals, supervisors, curriculum and pedagogies to count.

But one thing remained consistent:

I, like so many of my peers, remained as dedicated to the kids I was asked to teach as I remained angry at the idiots messing with my ability to teach them.

And with righteous anger like the wind in our sails… away we go.

---

(3) Well, we've got one now, don't we?

THE PARCC AND PRISON RAPE; A LOVE STORY

"Welcome my son, welcome to the Machine.
What did you dream? It's alright, we told you what to dream.
— Roger Waters

WARNING: This chapter will begin in a lighthearted manner but will quickly descend into an unprecedented level of rage and loathing (even for this book.) Think of it like marriage![1]

With apologies to Midnight Star, please sing the following to the tune of the 1983 classic *No Parking on the Dance Floor*:

Academic violations are easy to fix
  Just tell your parents to opt you out of the mix
    Shake up (the system,) and shake it on down
      Let me hear you refusin', make them Pearson people frown
No PARCCing, baby!   No parccing for a bad score (Beep! Beep!)
No PARCCing baby!   No parccing for a bad score!

Ok that was stupid but fun, and, if you're like me, you just added *No Parking on the Dance Floor* to your iPod, so go ahead and shake your groove thing for a minute.

But I digress; yes, we're talking about the PARCC test, although I suspect that if you're NOT from Colorado, Illinois, Maryland, New Jersey,

---

(1) He said from the couch, after his wife read that line over his shoulder.[2]
(2) Oh, OK, you don't read ANY of your husband's books, but you'll read THIS and get mad?[3]
(3) #permanentlyonthecouch

New Mexico, or Rhode Island (the only states left that are PARCCing on the dance floor) you could insert whatever state mandated test **your** state inflicts on its kids and this would still be relevant. Where I teach, it's officially three school days from the tests, and the automated calls home have begun in earnest. These calls ominously remind (some would say *intimidate*, but who am I to judge?) parents and guardians that "this is a State mandated assessment and there is NO option to 'opt out' of the test."

And I was told today, at a staff meeting, to "please encourage kids to just take the test" in the same tired, half-hearted voice that a parent uses at the end of the day to beg the kids to "please just keep it down."

Meanwhile, my copy of NJEA magazine just arrived in the mail, and the cover story is all about the burgeoning Opt Out movement and how "Our Family Refuses the PARCC" signs have started multiplying on people's lawns faster than seagulls at the sound of a potato chip bag.

As an educator, I am conflicted, consternated and, to be honest, professionally compromised.

So, I can only imagine how John Q. Public feels. Honest questions like *"Why are these tests so 'important?'"* and *"Why are they still pushing these tests so hard when it's clear nobody wants them?"* start to be heard everywhere. Who will answer these questions?

I said WHO WILL ANSWER THESE QUESTIONS!?

The sad truth is that students and parents are being forced to buy a product (let's call it the PARCC, shall we?) that the teachers are being forced to sell, even though almost NONE of us believe in it. To amplify the figurative fascism of this phenomena, many of the administrators that are forcing the teachers to sell the product *don't believe in it either.*

Got that?

Some million-dollar corporation created a test that administrators **know** is bullshit, but local politicians are in bed with the companies that created the test, (AND the test practice materials AND the practice books AND the...well, you get the point) so they **pressure** the districts to **strong arm** the Superintendents, who then **threaten** the principals to **coerce** (euphemism for threaten) the teachers to **inflict** the tests upon the students and parents, almost none of whom give a rat's ass for a variety of reasons, all of which are either well informed and/or purely emotional.

Your public educational system at work.

So anyway, I was taking a lengthy break from the one-size-fits-all curriculum[4] and covering an article about—wait for it—*Why Public Schools Don't Teach Critical Thinking*[5] and, as I teach them to do, one of my students questioned me:

"Step, why do we have to take these stupid ass tests?"

(This is me frowning slightly, but gesturing my head in a way that says: "Try again.")

(Student exhales loudly:) "OK, Mr. Step, are these tests the *only* thing we need, as a requirement, to graduate?"

Having been 'called into the office' on more than one occasion for indoctrinating the youth of America with my radical ideas, (aka: teaching my kids to actually think critically and question everything,) I knew how to handle this inquiry. *"Ask me a specific question."*

"OK, do we need to pass these tests to graduate?"

"Nope, there are a variety of scores, on different tests, that you can use as per New Jersey graduation requirements."[6]

"Then why are some teachers like Mr. Flagg saying we gotta take them?"

Frown, head gesture

"Grrrrr…OK, why would ANY teacher tell us we gotta take them?"

"Because they've been pressured to imply that."

"But who wou—OK, that's a stupid question…"

"There are no stupid questions, only stupid students." (Class laughter)

"Funny. But seriously Step, why are ya'll pushing these tests on us? I heard you don't even get to see the scores, and we KNOW y'all don't like wasting class time on giving them."

"That's a question, an implication, and an assumption, so I'll simply

---

(4) I know; I'm hyphenating a lot in this section—must be the Death Wish Coffee kicking in.

(5) By Frank Breslin—check out Parts 1 and 2, you'll be glad you did; they're eye openers.

(6) As of the writing of this chapter, that is true for NJ graduating classes 2016, 2017, 2018 and 2019.

say—I'm not, we don't, and you're correct."

The conversation continued in earnest. Young minds inquired, a significantly older mind responded, we debated, we attempted to understand a variety of possible answers to a progressively evolving set of questions, and we *all* learned something.

Kind of like how education

is

supposed

to work.

So, let's get to the titillating title of this chapter, shall we?

One of my well-informed cherubs posed a very specific question:

"Step, I heard that they announced at the beginning of the year that they're only giving the PARCC once this year,[7] is that true? And if it is, how do *you* feel about that?"

I thought that a well-constructed inquiry such as that deserved a well-constructed metaphor, and the smile on my face must have indicated as such, because 48 eyes looked back at me with intense focus and anticipation—a rare sight in a High School classroom, I can tell you. Never one to blow an opportunity of this rarity, I began metaphoring in earnest, with some rhetorical questioning to whet the appetite:

"How do I feel about these tests being offered ONLY once a year? Well, if you were to go to jail, and your big bully cellmate prison-raped you twice a day for a year, (much laughter) NO, stay with me here— so you got some prison lovin' twice a day and then he came in one Monday morning and said 'Hey, I'm only gonna violate you once a day from now on,' (uproarious laughter) would you be all like 'Whoo-Hoo! Only ONCE a day?' How would you feel? Well that's how I feel."

Of course, the class settled down and they all pinkie swore (the equivalent of a notarized contract in our class, because we're big on honor) not to refer to the PARCCs as prison rape, at least within earshot of anyone that could fire me.

For the record, now that I went public, anyone who has a problem with my admittedly sodomistic simile? (Rolls eyes and says in a

---

(7) As opposed to two sessions of testing the previous year.

tone of boredom) *"Piss off; First Amendment and all that. And don't ever tell me, if you support tests like the PARCC, that you're interested in the kids' welfare again, because you aren't, period."*

Ah-kay, now that we got that out of the way, let me not bore you with the yawn-inducing details of the PARCC (or any other standardized test for that matter) but instead, try to summarize, quickly, exactly why I ***loathe*** these tests. Anyone who was lucky enough to grow up and experience *Schoolhouse Rock*[8] knows that "Three (sing it with me) is a magic number," so I'll keep my vitriolic onslaught to three reasons. Here goes:

The people who design these tests don't know our kids.

Not that any of the uber-wealthy pricks I'm referring to are reading this book, but if you are, before you spill your latte on your suit, I know what you're going to say: "data collection is the key to understanding what these kids need to learn!" "How will we know what to test if we don't collect data?" etc. and you're ***wrong***. Stick your beloved "data" up your ass and understand that you collected that data with—oh, sweet mother of ironies—MORE one-size-fits-all-fill-in-the-circles tests and instruments that do NOTHING to address the uniqueness of our LIVING, BREATHING CONSTANTLY EVOLVING student population; which brings me to my second point,

Teachers are constantly hounded to differentiate their instruction, yet these tests standardize their questioning.

Listen, I am a big fan of rigor, (legitimate, realistic rigor,) so much so that I spend an inordinate chunk of my year in offices fighting with parents who think I'm "too hard" on their delicate dirty snowflakes. *However,*

---

(8)   Absolutely amazing series that used to be shown in fast, 3-4 minute songs between Saturday morning cartoons, Schoolhouse Rock taught everything from proper use of conjunctions, to how bills got passed in Congress, to the skeletal system. We could use more of this type of genius today with our predominantly visual/auditory learners, for sure.

there is an Indominus Rex-sized difference between pushing kids that I have worked with, methodically over the course of many months, past their comfort levels, and just dropping a four-hour (standardized/ computerized/dehumanized) monster test that sometimes costs upward of a hundred bucks, filled with arbitrarily designed questions (that just happen to be easy for machines to grade,) onto our kids.

It should also be noted that tests like the PARCC, in very many cases, set our kids up to fail and—infinitely worse—retard ANY progress we, the teachers, may have made in repairing their already massively damaged self-esteem. Which takes me screaming into my third point,

These tests set certain kids up to fail.

I'm going to say it, in print, because somebody that is still actively teaching needs to. These tests are inherently biased against kids from low income families. They are. Before you start, let me qualify something—I am the guy who, for YEARS, when students, parents, administrators, etc. cried "racism," "sexism," or any other "-ism," usually told them (in one variety or another) to shut the Hell up and get their facts straight, mainly because most of the aforementioned people were wheeling out those terms in the hopes of distracting/ intimidating/ digressing from the actual issue at hand, which usually involved some degree of personal accountability on their part.

So, when *I* tell you that there is an *institutionalized bias* built into these tests, you know I'm not just whistling Dixie.

Want an example of what I'm talking about?

I thought you might.

Just this year alone, I have 56 Juniors and well over HALF of them are reading on a 6th grade level or lower (*much* lower in some cases.)

Got that?

11th graders, that would struggle greatly, possibly give up, when faced with a 1-2-page story written on a 9th grade reading level.

Now do me a favor, go grab a PARCC or SAT or ACT practice book from your local bookstore and look at the reading test section. Maybe even take one *yourself?*

Mm-hmm.

Five lengthy, low-interest (the effects of pollution on 1960s London, anyone?) passages written on 11th grade levels, with about 52 questions to answer, *in 65 minutes?!?*

My students would be lucky to get through two, maybe three of those passages in the time provided. In the interest of validity and solidarity, I spoke to many teachers out there in cyberspace,[9] *even some of the ones that teach kids in affluent, two-parent communities that value investment in education and have state of the art technology (and standardized test prep) built into their schools*, and they all agreed that both the amount of material, the random nature *of* that material, and the time provided to response *to* said material, all combine to facilitate a surgically efficient screwkidsectomy.

> By the way, if any of you "educational reformers" out there are going to imply that my kids' inability to breeze through any of these arbitrarily designed confidence and creativity Terminators is somehow a manifestation of my subpar teaching ability, put this book down, drive to Home Depot, and get the biggest assistant in the place to kiss you on the cheek with a 12lb. sledgehammer—that ought to closely approximate me punching you in the face.

Violent home repair fantasies aside, the harsh reality is that these tests are just a giant racket designed to make a small handful of testing corporations (yes, Pearson, I'm talking to you, among others,) a shitload of money while simultaneously making sure certain school districts bend over and obey, which simultaneously assures that certain demographics never do well on these tests.[10]

So, upon reflection, I DO apologize for calling the PARCC prison rape.

---

(9) Thanks to my publications, I collaborate pretty regularly with a small army of educators, nation-wide.

(10) Which, simul-simul-simultaneously ensures that those kids never get the opportunities afforded to those who DO manage to perform well on these tests.

That's an insult to prison rapists.

While the rapist might threaten you to get what he wants, *like how certain districts and schools with high opt out (parents who choose not to subject their kids to the tests) numbers are threatened with having federal funding withheld,*

...and intimidate you to comply *like certain school districts that demand parents opting out to come in and "explain themselves" to administrators*

...or turn the blame around on **you** *like how schools force parents/kids to call it "refusal" instead of opting out*

...or threaten to kill you if you tell anyone *the way teachers in certain districts were going to be* **threatened with misdemeanors** *and having their* **licenses revoked** *for simply talking about Common Core standardized testing,*[11]

one thing that a prison rapist usually DOESN'T do is **profit** from their sodomy, *UNlike the corporations that create the tests, charge districts for the testing software, then change the tests—and with it, all of the test prep books, materials, software, etc. etc. etc. until your ass is bleeding and your eyes are crying.*

Oh, and before I wrap up this little ray of sunshine of a chapter, I feel I would be remiss if I didn't mention that these tests **almost never** measure anything remotely applicable to what the test taker wants to DO with her/her life; and no, I'm not talking just about the kids that want to be beauticians or auto mechanics or police officers, I'm talking about the kids that want to be doctors and engineers, too.

My children are as unafraid of accountability as their father, so allow me to use them as examples: Samantha went to college to major in Biology in the hopes of going into medical illustration, so WTF does reading charts and graphs about the dominant rodent species and successional time on plots of abandoned fields in Alabama have to do with that?[12] Mason attends Philadelphia University, majoring

---

(11) Not kidding. "Where?" You ask, Oh I (ho) don't know...

in construction management/ engineering, so why is he answering questions about the tone of Sylvia Plath's *The Bell Jar?*[12] Frankie is in the nursing program at Duquesne University, so why in the name of all that's French does he have to read and juxtapose excerpts from 1700s political pieces from Maximilien Robespierre and the Marquis de Lafayette?[12]

Utterly ridiculous, and completely irrelevant to their immediate future. And while I'll acquiesce that it'd be impossible to design a standardized test to measure what kids specifically want to do with their lives (especially given that the kids themselves are generally in a state of flux regarding what they want to do,) you can't tell me these tests couldn't be made both a little less arbitrary and a tad more contemporarily relevant

To conclude, I hate these standardized tests (and the Common Core that spawned many of them) with a white-hot passion, and I don't respect any of the people who created them or any of the powers-that-be that bent over and allowed themselves to be...well, you know, ***in the name of selling out our kids in favor of convenience and the almighty dollar.***

By the way... On the SAME DAY we [allegedly] had the prison metaphor conversation in class, the yawn-inducing Power Point at the center of our staff meeting after school was about—you guessed it!—The PARCC tests, how shitty our scores were, and how many kids "refused"[14] to take them.

"But hey," swear the people 'in charge,' "we're not ***blaming*** anybody, we're just ***sayin'***"

In the immortal words of my friend Pete's 3-year-old daughter Lena: "Puppet fucking assholes."

Anyway, three of my students happened to be walking by the auditorium and saw, (as teachers lined up to sign in) the PowerPoint title page 2015 PARCC DATA ANALYSIS and they...how can I put this delicately?

---

(12) ALL based on very real questions from the ACT, SAT, and PARCC. (13)

(13) "Based on," not actual questions, so chill out with your potential lawsuits.

(14) Students were not ALLOWED to say they "opted out" of the tests; they—and their parents—HAD to use the term "refused."[15]

(15) If that kind of borderline-censorship shit doesn't concern you greatly, I give up.

...simulated the act to which I had previously alluded in my colorful comparison, then ran away laughing.

It was one of my proudest moments.

But hey, maybe I'm being needlessly harsh on the ol' PARCC. Testing begins next week, and we're only ~~wast,~~ er, ~~sacrific,~~ I mean *spending* nine days (instead of two weeks like last year) on PARCC testing, and I'm just spiffy diffy sure that things will go as smoothly as the Silver Surfer sliding safely into home on a saturated Slip & Slide,[16] but let's see, shall we?

---

(16) Alliteration is fun.

PEARSON GOES DOWN ON ME.[1]

"Arbitrary power is like most other things which are very hard, very liable to be broken."
—Abigail Adams[2]

"...and I'm just spiffy diffy sure" he said, "that things will go as smoothly as the Silver Surfer sliding into home on a well lubricated Slip & Slide, but let's see, shall we?"

Yes, let us indeed see how it goes.

Today, on April 20th, all PARCC testing (which is already, I think I may have mentioned, a colo$$al wa$te of time guinea pigging our kid$ through a te$t with no di$cernible advantage for reaon you can probably gue$$) had to be postponed because...drum roll please...the ENTIRE PEARSON WEBSITE WENT DOWN.

Yes. The entire site. Down faster than a groupie at a Mötley Crüe concert. But hey, they *were* sorry. Laura Slover, CEO of Parcc Inc., patronized that "[they were] disappointed by the disruptions" adding dramatically that "these kinds of mistakes are unacceptable."

Hmmm...please define "unacceptable" for me, ma'am. **Unacceptable** as in "we're going to pay for the tens of thousands of dollars lost to substitute teachers [hired to cover classes] that weren't needed?" **Unacceptable** as in "we're offering financial remuneration for the transportation issues created?" **Unacceptable** as in "we're going to offer compensatory education for the hour and a half these kids sat in front of useless computers waiting for our site to become accessible?"

Or **unacceptable** as in "we'll just say-gosh darn this sucks and then resume this bullshit testing tomorrow as if nothing ever happened?"

---

(1) Only now do I realize, how bad that sounds.[2]
(2) That's a total bald-faced lie, because Pearson can suck me sideways.

16

THAT kind of unacceptable?

Yes, I thought so.

Apparently, the error occurred after a [nameless but you can bet your ass currently unemployed] Pearson employee tried to improve the computerized testing system Tuesday night; however, instead of making it better, the employee unwittingly unleashed some bad voodoo— otherwise known as a *technical glitch that shut down the whole system*. Nothing like tampering with the engines of an airplane soon to be filled with schoolchildren the night before an intercontinental flight. Well DONE, sir!

I can't imagine what other teachers throughout the Garden State were going through, and I'd ask our current governor, but he's never actually *in* New Jersey (too busy *these* days following Donald Trump around like a sycophantic lapdog and hiding from "Bridgegate,") but in my little slice of Heaven I, along with another teacher, sat in a room with 45 disgruntled teenagers who weren't allowed to do ANYthing (testing protocol, you know) except stare—for an HOUR and a HALF— at computer screens that told them they were "unable to connect to PARCC testing," only to then be told, along with us (the teachers,) that "you've been successfully circle jerked all morning, go back to your normal classrooms, effectively nuking this week's lesson plans, and we'll waste another day later this week doing this the right way, assuming Pearson gets its shit together."[3]

Another day in paradise.

EPILOGUE: SHUT UP AND EAT THE PEANUT BUTTER!

So, your Mom and Dad get divorced and you and your siblings (and Mom) move in with your grandparents. It's hard, but Dad was kind of away all the time anyway, and your grandparents, while slightly out of touch, are very loving, and they take care of Mom. Eventually Mom gets her feet back on the ground and starts dating a new "Stepdad."

Let's call him David C. Pearson.

---

(3) Ok, that's not exactly what was said, but what's a little paraphrasing between friends?

He's a dick.

There are myriad reasons why DCP is a dick: he doesn't listen to your Mom, he thinks YOU are little robots born to do his bidding, he manipulates the shit out of Mom Mom and Pop Pop and—the thing that makes you 100% quantifiably certain of his dickdom—is the issue with the peanut butter.

David makes his own peanut butter, and it sucks.

No, really, it sucks harder than a methamphetamine fueled groupie at a 1985 Def Leppard concert, and nobody likes it.

You hate it, your siblings hate it (well, your baby sister doesn't HATE it, but she prefers just about any other kind of peanut butter, but your older brother has a *well-documented*, and **serious** peanut allergy,) and your Mom doesn't like it on general principle simply because Davey boy screams at you guys to "eat it or else!"

Mom Mom and Pop Pop have tried to talk to him about it, but prickly Mr. Pearson? He tells them—*in their own house*, mind you—to:

Shut up and step aside because they're old and he knows what's best for their daughter and their grandkids, and besides he's got more money than they do, so they should just get the hell out of the way, because he knows what he's doing, dammit, so just eat the frickin' peanut butter; why don't you understand that you need to eat the peanut butter, I mean, godDAMN, I made the peanut butter, and I know what I'm doing, and besides, I can't afford to admit I'm wrong because among other things I (and my investor friends) would be embarrassed and go broke, SO EAT THE MOTHERHUMPING PEANUT BUTTER!!!!!

You'd probably kick Dave out.

I mean, just for his run-on sentencing alone, right?

No, seriously, Mom would certainly have had enough, your Grandparents would righteously want this tool out of their home. And you guys? C'mon…you know you love David about as much as a root canal without anesthetic.

Yeah, when you put it like that, it seems obvious. Why would any group of people [supposedly] committed to the happiness and progress of one another put up with a foreign invader that forces his shitty (and potentially harmful) product, created almost purely for his own profit, onto you against your wishes?

I don't know. Maybe—please don't get mad, I'm just throwing it out there—just *maybe*, Mom Mom and Pop Pop really *ARE* out of touch with you guys. Or mmmmaaayyyyybeeeee the BANK (the ones that still, technically OWN the house) *told* your grandparents to keep Dave the dick and his pesky peanut butter because—and this should be obvious—they really don't give a shit about any of you.

I don't know, maybe you could ask the New Jersey School Board Association, who are considering making the PARCC test a graduation requirement for all classes starting with the class of 2020.

Despite massive controversy and resistance from students (you guys,) teachers (Mom,) and school districts (Mom Mom and Pop Pop,) Pearson Corporation (Dave) got what they wanted and now ALL of the children in my home state—yes, even the ones that have "peanut allergies"—will have to take this unproven, formulaic, problematic, one-size-fits-all computerized clusterfuck

because

they

said

so.

Keep in mind, folks, PARCC = Common Core, and the more you know about Common Core,[4] the more I **guarantee** you'll be ready to get out your torches and pitchforks.

In hindsight, we really need to drop a [purely metaphorical] bomb on everything with two Cs: Common Core, PARCC, Chris Christie, Corporate Control,[5] Colon Cancer, Nicklebacck…

Or, you could just shut up and eat the peanut butter.

---

(4) I'll tell you a little about that biblical plague upon public education two chapters from now.

(5) So sorry; Chris Christie = Corporate Control, sorry for the redundancy.

...AND SPEAKING OF TESTING, YOU CAN'T SPELL SATANIC WITHOUT SAT and ACT.[1]

"What was educationally significant and hard to measure has been replaced by what is educationally insignificant and easy to measure. So now we measure how well we taught what isn't worth learning."
—Arthur Costa

At the risk of massive redundancy: I don't like standardized testing.

I get it. You want some sort of "universal" test that all the kids take so you "know who belongs in certain post-secondary institutions." Translation: we're gonna design these tests here, (and you're gonna pay a pretty penny to TAKE 'em) but we're gonna make damn sure they reinforce the *certain-kids-will-qualify-for-certain-colleges-or-Universities* hierarchy that's been in place for a long time.

What's that you say, test designers? Every kid has the ability to do well on these tests if they would just—oh, I don't know—get tutored, or do online practice, or take the tests multiple times, ALL of which benefits YOU because YOUR materials must be purchased to do so?

Nice racket you've got going there, College Board (architects of the SAT) and ACT Inc. (creators of…well, I'll give you three guesses.)

Oh, and just in case you think the aforementioned materials will be reusable…

Uh, no. They're not, not for long. Why?

Pretty much for the same reason your current version of Windows

---

(1) No offense to Satanists, most of whom, I believe, are more honest than David Coleman.

20

becomes obsolete shortly after you purchase and upload it onto your computer, because PROFIT is priority.

You thought it was **education?**

Oh, that's cute.

If you don't believe me, ask ANY kid you know that's ever been subjected to one of these torture devices if he/she felt like the material on those tests, (the tests they need to score well on to get into the schools of their choice,) was ANY kind of reflection of what they learned in school. Ask as many kids as you can and see what they say.

OK, so now that we've quasi-established that these costly, massively time-consuming tests DON'T really reflect what your kids are learning in school, then I feel compelled to ask a question, with the "Caps Lock" button depressed, so as to impart both the frustration and urgency of my inquiry:

WHY THE $#@!&? ARE WE, AS TEACHERS, ACCOUNTABLE FOR WHY THESE KIDS DON'T KNOW THE STUFF ON TESTS THAT ARE DESIGNED BY PEOPLE WHO DON'T CARE WHAT'S GOING ON IN THE CLASSROOM AND DON'T LISTEN TO THE COLLEGE PROFESSORS WHEN THEY TELL THEM THAT THE TESTS DON'T MEASURE WHAT **THEY** WANT THEM TO KNOW EITHER?!?!

Go ahead, re-read it, let it sink in. Seriously, is it asking too much to simplify things for these kids? Assuming, Mr. & Ms. Testing Corporation that don't give a flying monkey turd about these kids, that you're not willing to abolish these tests altogether, can we at least make a few basic accommodations so as to not screw these kids often and expensively? I'll get into why teachers shouldn't be held accountable for these marathon exercises in motivational assassination in a minute, but first—

UNCLE STEP'S SUGGESTIONS FOR OVERHAULING THE SATAniC Test PREP EXPERIENCE!

1. Let's start by NOT changing the books the kids need to study for these tests all the time (and subsequently gouging them to

the tune of $20+ *for* those books.) I shit you not, the ACT book, at one point, went up $5 *because they changed the cover and added a CD to access online tests.* Really?

Then, once tutors, teachers, parents and big brothers and sisters across the country went through those books so they could help the next wave of kids, the book changed again, lazily mixing some of the old book with newer stuff, and (in a move that infuriated legions of us,) the old book was discontinued immediately. Oh, and they cut down from 5 practice tests to 3, all with a shiny new (and more expensive) price tag. Any person that has experienced the *shrinking* of the size of your food (potato chip bags anyone?) while the price *increases* knows this feeling.

And the SAT books? Well, we'll get to that little conundrum in just a minute.

2. Find a way, you mercenary cocksuckers, to work together and forge ONE test so the kids won't be torn and confused and forced to…

Never mind, I might as well ask the Democrats and Republicans to engage in bipartisan decision making for the good of the American people; I'll take the "L" on this one in the interest of brutal honesty.

3. Let's stop confusing the kids by offering more choices for prep material than you have in the shampoo aisle at the supermarket. (Damn it, I want the coconut verbena with split end control but that honeysuckle with built in conditioner is pretty luscious too!) Only a few of these materials are created by the companies that actually *make* the tests. While I unabashedly hate the devils that make these tests, I also know that if you absolutely, positively needed a map through Hell, you'd want the one drawn by Satan himself, right?

And speaking of the Lord of all things abominable and unnatural, let's talk about David Coleman, the newly appointed president and chief executive officer of College Board, the group that creates the SAT. In Coleman's Brave New World, the 'old' SAT that everyone was familiar with got the scorched Earth treatment and a new, very confusing and [apparently] "evolving" thing sprung up in its place. (I'm talking entire sections and question types were *fundamentally* changed. New styles of reading passages were added while other were removed, etc.) Of course, ALL of the materials you used to use to study for the SAT are...

Yes!

You guessed it! Gone the way of the dinosaur and replaced with shiny new books and materials with shiny new price tags. Does that sound suspiciously like "they're learning how to get the right answers so we'll change the questions?" Well, who am I to tell you otherwise?

But I digress.

4. Oh, and **you might want to let the students actually have an opinion.** I'm not kidding here; in fact, the *Official SAT Study Guide* (published by CollegeBoard) states: "your essay should not explain whether you agree with [the author's] claims but rather explain how the author builds an argument to persuade [his/her] audience," (page 177) "and "you will not be asked to take a stance on the issue. In fact, if all you do is express your own feelings on the issue, you won't receive a strong score" (page 176).

Forced compliance, anyone?

But don't worry, you'll have TWICE as much time to forcibly agree with what you're told to read. Yes, the benevolent dictators at College Board have **doubled** the time for the essay from 25 to 50 minutes. Such nice people, until you consider that they made the length of the passage the students have to read **six times** longer (from 80-100 words to 650-750 words.) Got that? 6 times the length in only twice the time, and you HAVE to agree with what you're told to read.

That, folks, is downright dystopian.

Lest you think I'm being too hard on douchebag Davey and his

23

minions of monopolization, let me quote **directly** from a reading Workbook for the new SAT.

INTERACTIVE READING FUN ALERT!

1. Try reading **the bold "teacher-made reading tests" parts in a serious, scary voice.**
2. Then *read the italicized SAT test stuff in a lighthearted, I'm-Carney-the-Common-Core-Dinosaur-and-I-love-you voice*
3. Then, feel free to read the TRUTH in your voice.

Comparison #1

SAT Prep book: **"School reading tests are almost always closed book,** *[whereas the] SAT is open book… you can go back to the passage as often as you need."*

TRUTH: We very often give students open book tests, especially now that we know revision, collaboration and the ability to discern pertinent from irrelevant information are becoming increasingly important in the global workforce. Oh, and as for being able to "go back to the passage as often as you need?" 52 questions, based on FIVE reading passages (3,250+ words) in 65 minutes; yeah, I'm sure they'll have **plenty** of time to go back and work through those passages. Liar liar, your pants are most *certainly* on fire.

Comparison #2

SAT Prep book: **"School reading tests are often about specific facts, so it is vital that you memorize details and definitions as you read,** *[but the SAT] test questions are more often about inference, purpose, and big ideas…"*

TRUTH: We, as English/Reading teachers, are often told, explicitly, to make our questions "specific" so as to avoid confrontations and confusion; however, most of the teachers I know focus intensely on "big idea" questions (we call these text-to-text, text-to-life, etc. questions) because, again, we understand that these type of reading skills are what will best prepare our students for the world they're entering. At this point, every fiber of my being wants to call these people and say "Why don't you stick to what YOU know, making arbitrary tests based on your out of touch approach to education, and stop making generalizations about what goes on in the classrooms you're afraid to visit, you self-congratulatory pieces of shit?"

But I'm busy writing this book, and hey, if you just wait long enough…

Comparison #3

SAT Prep book: **On school reading tests, "Occasionally, there are mistakes on a test with a couple of right answers to a question. It is easy for a teacher to simply give everyone a free point if there is an error,** but *SAT questions are very* (they actually italicized 'very') *well written, and there will be **just one correct answer*** (yes, they wrote that in bold type) *to each question…"* and then they go on to talk about how they invest tremendous resources into ensuring blah blah blah…

TRUTH: There is so much I could say here, and if I had the clown that wrote this within arm's reach…But let me focus on you, the readers, so you can truly understand the hypocrisy of this comparison.:

First, these self-righteous tools just talked shit about teacher tests in comparison #2 for being too specific, AND THEN PRAISED THEMSELVES FOR THE SPECIFICITY OF THEIR OWN QUESTIONS IN #3?!?

Secondly, let's address the assumption that **"it is easy for a teacher to simply give everyone a free point if there is an error."** How the fuck would YOU know? And if I want to give my students a few points for a question that, in hindsight, after an intelligent discussion, we determined to be unfair, then that is a valuable life lesson in accountability and respectful discourse, which I reserve the right to exercise.

As for it "being easy," you mean easier than a corporation quickly and discreetly changing a few questions on a three hour long, 150+ question standardized test from which they profit considerably? That kind of easy?

Yeah, I thought so, the only difference is we teachers don't change the prep materials and then charge our students for them, you sanctimonious twats. But I shouldn't really waste my time looking for these kinds of hypocrisies, because, as the SAT prep book tells me, verbatim: **"do not waste your time and energy taking the SAT looking for flaws in the test. Instead, give the SAT reading section the benefit of the doubt..."** You mean the kind of benefit of the doubt you gave the teachers of America with your insinuations and overgeneralizations?

I'm getting angry again, so let me fast forward to the fact that I have found more than a few grammatical, punctuation, and clarity errors in my review of the SAT's *very* well written questions. Now, am I being petty? Probably, from an individual perspective, but I get pissed off when big test taking companies take liberties assuming they know what happens in the classroom but caution everyone against making the same assumptions about them.

So, standardized test people, why don't we do this?

YOU stick to making your ever-changing, arbitrary tests and the subsequent prep materials from which you profit so richly from your constant "updating," and leave it to ME[2] to actually *educate* the children.

In the meantime, I'll consider it my job to educate YOU, the consumer (and thank you, very much, for consuming this book) as to the encroaching dangers of standardized testing, cookie cutter curriculums, and the massive corporate oligopolies associated with them that, by their nature, **do not care about you or your children.**

If it sounds like I say that a lot, it's because I *do*, because they *don't*.

I firmly believe that the sole purpose of this monochromatic monopoly of public education is to create compliant consumers; it sure as hell isn't interested in producing creative, well-read children who question authority and see the opportunity in adversity. Clearly, I am not alone in my beliefs; allow me to quote the erudite folks over at Gadflyonthewallblog from their intriguing piece *Standardized Testing Creates Active Markets*, as I believe they state, very

---

(2) I didn't want to take the liberty of speaking for all teachers, but if you (insert Peter Frampton voice) dooooooo DO! feeeeeeeel like I do, feel free to change my ME into US.

succinctly, exactly WHY these tests are given and HOW they led to the emergence of Common Core from the primordial ooze of profit driven indoctrination:

> The reason public schools give these tests is because the government forces them. The Elementary and Secondary Education Act (ESEA) requires that all students in grades 3-8 and once in high school take certain approved standardized assessments. Parents are allowed to refuse the tests for their children, but otherwise they have to take them.

> It wasn't always this way. When the act was first passed in 1965, it focused almost entirely on providing students with equitable resources. That all changed in 2001, with the passage of No Child Left Behind, a reauthorization of this original bill. And ever since, through every subsequent reauthorization and name change, the federal law governing K-12 schools has required the same standardized testing.

> The testing corporations don't have to prove their products. Those products are required by law.

> It's one of the largest captive markets in existence. That's some 50.4 million children forced to take standardized assessments. The largest such corporation, Pearson, boasts profits of $9 billion annually. It's largest competitor, CBT/ McGraw-Hill, makes $2 billion annually. Others include Education Testing Services and Riverside Publishing better known through its parent company Houghton Mifflin Harcourt.

> If many of these companies sound like book publishers, that's because they are or their parent companies are. And that's no coincidence. It's another way they bolster their own market.

Not only do many of these testing corporations make, provide and score standardized assessments, they make and provide the remedial resources used to help students pass.

So, if your students are having difficulty passing the state test, often the same company has a series of workbooks or a software package to help remediate them. It's a good business model. Cash in before kids take the test. Cash in when they take it. And if kids fail, cash in again to remediate them...

But that's not all. Once you have a system in place, things can become static. Once districts already have the books and resources to pass the tests, the testing corporation has less to sell them, the market stagnates and thus their profits go down or at least stop growing.

The solution once again is to create yet another captive market. That's why Common Core was created...[it] resulted in the need for districts to buy all new materials—new text books, new workbooks, new software, etc. It also required the states to order brand new standardized tests. So once again the testing industry cashed in at both ends.

(Stevenmsinger "Standardized Testing Creates Captive Markets" *Gadflyonthewallblog* 8 April, 2017 https://gadflyonthewallblog. wordpress.com/2017/04/08/standardized-testing-creates-captive-markets/)

I don't know that I could have said it any better; I particularly agree with the implication that students are now disincentivized to succeed (on these tests) because their success would stifle the vicious circle of fail, buy the remediation materials, change the test, fail again, buy the new remediation materials, change...

Infuriating, isn't it? Almost as infuriating as, say, an author not being able to answer questions *based on her own writing* as presented on a standardized test.

Yes, you read that correctly.

Sara Holbrook has written numerous books of poetry for children, teens and adults, as well as professional books for teachers. Sara is also a public speaker who visits schools and educator conferences worldwide, providing teacher and classroom workshops on writing and oral presentation skills. I think we can concur that Ms. Holbrook is a pretty intelligent and literate woman, so it may come as both a surprise and sweet, sweet vindication of my enmity of standardized testing when the author of the poem *A Real Case* COULDN'T ANSWER THE QUESTIONS on the 7th grade Texas State assessment test BASED ON HER OWN POEM!

I don't know if I can improve on the spectacular irony of this, so I'll just leave it at that.

Listen folks, any system that creates even the whisper of an opportunity to systematically facilitate failure is, in my opinion, evil, and any type of testing that bewilders the authors whose material is used in those tests is downright stupid.

Evil and stupid.

Which, coincidentally, leads us right down the gilded path to Hell that is Common Core.

COMMON CORE: ABANDON ALL HOPE YE WHO BELIEVE IN THIS

*"Knowledge is power; I can't complain about the system
if I don't know the system."*

—*Paige Hill*

I'm going to kick off this chapter, unequivocally one of the most important things I will ever write, with two quotes from men who are oft considered architects of our modern school system.

We will address these quotes again at the end of the chapter.

*"After a child has arrived at the legal age for attending school, whether
child of noble or peasant, the only two absolute grounds of exemption
from attendance are sickness and death...We who are engaged in
the sacred cause of education are entitled to look upon all parents as
having given hostages to our cause."*

—*Horace Mann ("Father" of Public Schooling 1796-1859)*

*"The children who know how to think for themselves spoil the
harmony of the collective society..."*

—*John Dewey (1859-1952)*

Hostages? To our **cause**?

Children **who think for themselves spoil the harmony**?

Only **sickness and death** will keep them away from school?

- Do those descriptions scare you?

- Does the idea of certain people using school to **control** and **manipulate** your children into little automatons that will do as they are told (**not** by **you**, but BY THE STATE) frighten you?
- And does the idea that the federal government and a small cadre of wealthy private interest groups could **control every facet** of your child's education (and possibly health?) using standards that are not only *unproven* but are also *developmentally inappropriate* terrify you?

Then be afraid, be very afraid.

I believe, with no exaggeration whatsoever, that Common Core is the single most destructive and counterproductive thing ever introduced into the American school system. If your kid is subjected to the Common Core, it permeates every. single. facet. of your child's education, with potentially crippling results, (and don't think you're escaping it if you send your kids to private or Charter schools either, because the architect of the Common Core designs the SATs, AP exams, and other admission tests now, too.) The aforementioned automaton, David Coleman, a man with NO BACKGROUND IN EDUCATION[1] said, and I quote: "Teachers will teach to the test. There is no force on this Earth strong enough to change that. There is no amount of hand waving, there is no amount of saying they teach to the standards[2] but not to the test...whatever."

Oh, fuck you David, you narcissistic insect; get over yourself.

Sorry, but the shady nature of how "The Core" was thrown onto our children and teachers, (there was no "vote" or "discussion" about this; it just appeared and everyone was expected to comply) and the arrogance with which its architects *brag* about that makes me hostile—so expect my language to be especially coarse, my opinions to be strong, and do not be surprised if the occasional (purely cathartic; I mean, I would never...) threat of violence creeps in.

---

(1) He was allegedly turned down when he applied for a High School teaching job in New York.
(2) We'll get to the dirty bomb that is "the standards" in a few minutes.

Note: If anyone is put off by the colorful language, I will actually include a short, bullet-style chapter following this one that you are welcome to pass on to other, more delicate readers, because EVERYBODY needs to know about this plague on the educational system.

Let's start with the ***incomprehensible*** idea that this <u>absolute transformation</u> of

WHAT your kids would learn,
HOW they would be taught it,
at WHAT SPEED they would be *allowed* to learn it,
and WHY you have no say in it,
was forced into your school with:

- No consultation of parents/guardians about it
- No State legislature vote on it
- No Teacher's Union discussion about it.

I could go on and on, but I'll ask you a simple question—how many of you really know what Common Core is? I'll ask again...how many of you *really understand* the force that **controls how your children are educated** (and, in my opinion, indoctrinated?) If you don't, that doesn't make you a bad person. You're busy working to pay for your kids and trying to raise them right; besides, the details have been deliberately kept from you. I am furious FOR you that this shit was kept all "Black Ops" FROM you.

My editors have suggested that I should quantify everything I tell you about Common Core, but I have to disagree with them on this point; whole books have been written and entire websites are dedicated to exposing the inadequacies and inconsistencies of Common Core, and some people make their living traveling state to state destroying the false claims of "the Core" with empirical evidence, so that's already been done by folks with more time on their hands than I have. Furthermore, that's not what I'm trying to do here; instead, I'm going to try to do what good teachers do and simplify something huge and complicated in a way in which you, the average citizen, can understand it.

Two disclaimers first: One, I am biased (I believe that is redundant at this point,) and two, you're not going to like what I'm about to teach you, but you NEED to know this.

Common Core is a simple term used to describe a set of *standards* (a LONG list of exactly what skills your kids should be taught) in Math and English,[3] that were created[4] by the National Governor's Association and the Council of Chief State School Officers.

Please do not be distracted by the term "School Officers;" the CCSSO is a non-partisan non-profit organization of public officials, and the National Governor's Association? Politicians. The truth of the matter is that the group of kids sitting in Friday detention at my school is probably bigger than the size of the group that wrote the bulk of the "educational standards" that currently govern public education, but those two groups DO have one thing in common: many of the members don't have any real educational background. According to historian of education, educational policy analyst, research professor, author, and all-around heroic defender of public education Diane Ravitch:

> Altogether, 24 people wrote the Common Core standards. None identified himself or herself as a classroom teacher, although a few had taught in the past (not the recent past). The largest contingent on the work groups were representatives of the testing industry.

Okay, so who are the members of this dirty double dozen that created the standards that currently drive public education in this country? Mercedes Schneider, 22 year public school teacher and education activist put her Ph.D. in applied statistics and research methods to the

---

(3) Yes, Science and History standards are coming, too. I can't WAIT to see what they do there; as George Orwell, eerily prophesized, "Who controls the past controls the future."

(4) and copyrighted

task and looked more closely at the 24 members of the two work groups to determine their past experience as educators; her results?

> My findings indicate that NGA and CCSSO had a clear, intentional bent toward CCSS work group members with assessment experience, not with teaching experience, and certainly not with current classroom teaching experience.

> In both CCSS work groups, the number of individuals with "ACT" and "College Board" designations outnumbered those with documented classroom teaching experience.

Both quotes courtesy of: Diane Ravitch "Mercedes Schneider: Who Are the 24 People Who Wrote the Common Core Standards?" April 28, 2014 *Dianeravitch.net* https://dianeravitch.net/2014/04/28/mercedes-schneider-who-are-the-24-people-who-wrote-the-common-core-standards/ accessed December 5, 2016

I think it's pretty obvious, given the small number, and general makeup, of the little coven that convened and created the standards, why Common Core is, at best, irrelevant and, at worst, developmentally inappropriate. If I may metaphor for a moment: the people that built the shark cage that your children have to go into don't understand engineering, have never been in the water, and wouldn't know the ass end of a shark from the business end if the latter bit them on their pretentious asses.

SHORT VERSION? The people who created Common Core were NOT educators.

I know what you're asking: Why in the holy hell would districts let a long, confusing, unproven and largely inappropriate homogenized system of "education" into their schools, ESPECIALLY when the 10th Amendment **expressly forbids** the federal government from meddling in state educational policies?

The answer is painfully simple:

$chool$ adopted Common Core becau$e they were given money for doing $o.

Where did the money come from? The [Bill] Gates foundation is a public trust, so check out where their money has gone and you'll get an idea who the biggest Common Core cheerleader is. I'll give you a hint—the pom-poms say Microsoft on them.[5] Along with big bucks Billy, your federal government,[6] a part of President Obama's *Race to the Top* program said *"if y'all want some of these 4.35 BILLION 'stimulus package' dollars, you best show us that you're doing what we want;"* and one of the easiest ways to prove that was to—you guessed it—bend over and take Common Core.

SHORT VERSION? Your school's "support" of Common Core was bought and paid for by the Federal Government, with a little help from wealthy private interest groups.

OK, so standards created by people who don't have educational backgrounds were forced on students, parents and educators that didn't get to look at them, and the tests that kids will be forced to take *based* on those standards are now replacing teacher created tests BECAUSE THE COMMON CORE TESTS ARE SO COMPLICATED[7] AND EVER-CHANGING THAT THEY TAKE UP ALL OF OUR CLASS TIME TRYING TO FIGURE THEM OUT AND TEACH TO THEM. Yes, you heard that correctly, teachers (you know, the ones who know your kids the best because, uh, **we spend all day with them**) are being **forced** to change the way we teach and test, so please don't blame us for the fact that your children's education is becoming increasingly irrelevant and one dimensional, because our jobs are on the line if we don't play ball.

Seriously, do you think WE wanted field trips, music, arts, reading of fiction, recess, physical education, creative projects, higher mathematical

---

(5) I'm sure it's just a coincidence that Gates drools over Common Core and that all of the tests associated with it are done on computers.

(6) And hey, we all know how much the Feds have your best interest in mind, right?

(7) Not rigorous, not academically challenging. Complicated. There's a Grand Canyon sized difference, folks.

instruction,[8] critical thinking, and anything even remotely spontaneous and enjoyable removed from your children's day? **Trust** me on this folks, we're as pissed as the kids are, and as pissed as their parents *should* be.

WE are interested in educating and evolving your child,

THEY are indoctrinating and evaluating your child.

SHORT VERSION? Your children's education is becoming homogenized because the Common Core standards, and the teacher accountability measures associated with it, were designed by people that don't understand kids in an attempt to measure two things (career and college "readiness") that can't *possibly* be simultaneously assessed efficiently.

"But wait, Step," you interrupt, "before we get into that—you seem to be implying that our children are being taught stuff that will be useless anywhere beyond High School—are you?"

Yes, yes I am.

"What do you mean by that?"

Glad you asked.

I know that many of you, whether you know anything about education or not, have heard the term STEM, right? Simply put, STEM is an acronym for the four specific disciplines—Science, Technology, Engineering and Mathematics—that are considered **absolutely vital** to the success of our future generations in this country. Again, you can do your own research here, but I'll let the folks *at sciencepioneers.org* speak more eloquently than I ever could about why the STEM fields are so important for our kids:

Let's consider how STEM affects what is closest and dearest to us—**our children.** STEM is their future—the technological age in which they live, their best career options, and their key to wise

---

(8) Want to know how badly Math instruction has been broken by Common Core? Go to the video the Case Against Common Core by Dr. Duke Pesta and just watch from 1:28 to 1:47:25. I promise you—in less than 20 minutes you will be educated and infuriated.

decisions. In 2009, the United States Department of Labor listed the ten most wanted employees. Eight of those employees were ones with degrees in the STEM fields: accounting, computer science, electrical engineering, mechanical engineering, information sciences and systems, computer engineering, civil engineering, and economics and finance. According to the U. S. Department of Commerce, STEM occupations are growing at 17%, while others are growing at 9.8%. Health care workers with associate degrees to doctors of medicine will average 20% more in life time earnings than peers with similar degrees in non-health care. A glance at 2010 starting salaries for engineers with $47,145 for civil engineers to $60,054 for chemical engineers is strong evidence that STEM related jobs can be financially rewarding careers for our children.

(Why STEM Education Is Important for Everyone)

OK, so we can agree that STEM is important, right? Good, then I'll make this short and sour. Jason Zimba, the lead writer of the Common Core Math Standards, said, and I quote, **[the Common Core] is "not only not for STEM but it's also not for selective colleges"** (a.k.a. the ones you actually want your kids to get into if they hope to work in one of these fields.)

Read that again.

Yes, you read that right. The lead writer of the Common Core Math Standards just told you it *wasn't* designed to help your kids get those "STEM related jobs [that] can be financially rewarding careers." If you don't believe me, (and I wouldn't blame you, because it's jaw droppingly ridiculous,) go to YouTube and watch *Jason Zimba interacts with Dr. Sandra Stotsky* and you can watch the entire exchange. A little over a minute of "you've-GOT-to-be-kidding-right?"

Sadly, I'm not kidding.

SHORT VERSION? STEM education is *universally* considered vital to our children, the future of our country, and our World.

But Common Core, in the words of one of its architects: "isn't for STEM."
You simply cannot make this shit up.

Actually, Common Core doesn't know *what* the heck it's "for." Despite the fact that it was rammed down your throat that Common Core was "better than what we already had" (a vague, bullshit lie that rode piggyback on all the "teachers aren't doing their job" rhetoric,) there is

no

fucking

evidence *whatsoever*

that Common Core is ANYthing except a giant experiment—and (news flash) YOUR kids are the test animals!—Billy Gates, champion pom-pom waver for CC, openly admitted in **2012** that *"it would be great if our education stuff worked, but that we won't know for probably a decade."*

A decade?!? This isn't upgrading the newest version of Windows, you colossal twat, this is the education of our children! In "a decade" whole goddamned **generations** of children could be lost if your "education stuff" doesn't (and it won't) work.

But Billy and the educational reformers (who, again, aren't educators and don't listen to educators,) don't give a shit about that. *Their* children are just fine, most likely receiving private educations unmolested by the Common Core,[9] but hey, it's ok for *your* children.

Here's another little news flash for you: In 2009 they were

---

(9) Bill Gates' three children all attended Lakeside School, an elite Seattle private school, feel free to do some research on it; but suffice it to say Mr. dropped-out-of-college himself didn't send HIS kids to a school where the curriculum is one-size-fits-all and I'll bet dollars to doughnuts that Jennifer, Rory and Phoebe weren't subjected to the battery of standardized tests that Mr. Gates wants YOUR kids subject to.

already writing the tests that would measure how well your children learned Common Core standards. BUT THE @?!&^%$# STANDARDS THEMSELVES HADN'T BEEN WRITTEN YET! If that seems ass backwards to you, congratulations, you have common **sense,** which, at this point, seems to be the antithesis of Common Core. So, the next time somebody tries to tell you that this was a tested, measured, proven system—call bullshit on them immediately.

SHORT VERSION? The Common Core is advertised as being "State led," "internationally benchmarked," "rigorous," "better than what we already had," and "generally praised." It is NONE of those things; it is an evolving *experiment* authored by people with almost no educational background who want to control your kids.

Oh, and they lied to you about it being universally passed, too. Flat out lied to you. I guess, like any team of supervillains,[10] these idiots believed that they were geniuses, and so they appointed a 30 person "validation committee" to approve the Common Core. Of course, they're supervillains, so they stacked the committee with non-educators, made them all sign a confidentiality agreement, and then pressured them to give the ol' "thumbs up," but…five out of thirty of the "validation committee" **(including, surprise surprise, the two preeminent educators on the committee)** refused to sign off on the Common Core EVEN THOUGH they were under enormous political pressure to sign.

Guess what happened to those five? They were given the legal paperwork version of what happens to political dissidents in dictatorships when they speak out against the government. They simply didn't exist anymore.

SHORT VERSION? Anyone that disagreed with Common Core was expunged from the record, and it was sold as having passed unanimously.

---

(10) Conniving C___s of Common Core, the "Legion of Doom" of education! (Insert bad guy music) Meanwhile, back at the lair of the Quadruple C Brigade…

I realize that this chapter is running long and that I am in danger of overwhelming you and thereby losing you. This often happens when I'm teaching something I'm really passionate about or something I KNOW the kids should understand. The evils of Common Core, it just so happens, are *both*. But I don't want to lose you, so I'll pull an old teaching trick out of my utility belt and finish with something true, but so *shocking*, that you'll actually WANT to know more. My students hate it (at first) when I do this, but love it (later) when they begrudgingly admit how much smarter they are.

Common Core is slowly, insidiously
replacing you with the State as the primary influence on your children:

- Students will not be allowed to "go ahead" if they happen to be really good in a subject; in fact, in some cases, they will allegedly be *punished* if you try to help your kid progress more quickly (not that you probably could, as math has been turned into something that doesn't even resemble the math we were taught as children; I'm sure some of you have already experienced this travesty of logic.)
- Students are allegedly, by demand of Common Core, being told they are WRONG for getting the correct answer *if the rest of the group agrees on a different answer,* **even if it is wrong.** Let that sink in; herd mentality as reinforced by compulsory education.
- Students have been given tablets with facial recognition software that SHUTS OFF when parents try to look at what they're studying.
- And I haven't even *started* on the fact that Common Core demands mostly non-fiction reading. With six corporations controlling 90% of the media in this country, I can't **imagine** why they would want your kid reading state manuals instead of *The Hunger Games* or *1984*. Can you?

Remember those quotes I shared with you at the beginning about *"parents giving hostages to our cause"* and *"children thinking for themselves ruining the harmony of the collective?"*

You paying attention now?

Still think this is just about reading and writing standards and "school stuff?"

Because I could go on and on and on and on, but if you're concerned about the future now, you'll probably go forth, learn more about this, and start fighting it. If you're too busy to actively fight against it, you can help by simply *not* fighting with the teachers that are trying to abolish it; most teachers are working their asses off to undermine this sinister bullshit, but we have to be careful in doing so,[11] for obvious reasons, so just work with us—I promise, we want what's best for your kid, too.

If this *doesn't* concern you, then you are far too anesthetized for me to help you; go forth in peace, but remember, you can't say you weren't warned.

Incidentally, as of the date I submitted this manuscript for publication, here in beautiful New Jersey, the eye of Sauron has reached forth from Mordor and doubled down on Common Core, PARCC, and other toxicity (that students, parents, and teachers actively and loudly protested against) by trying to make PARCC passing mandatory for graduation for the class of 2021 and beyond. *"Yeah, we know your kid is the valedictorian, earned a perfect score on the SAT, and got accepted to Stanford on scholarship, but she didn't pass the PARCC, so she's stayin!"*

I can't wait to see how this shakes out, but I'll be sure to keep you posted on this clusterfuckery most foul.

Oh, one final message for David douchebag Coleman.

I ***don't*** teach to the test, I ***never will***, and many of the really good teachers that I know don't teach to the test either—so I guess there is a "force on Earth powerful enough" to prove your invertebrate white bread ass wrong;

it's called "teachers' love of their students."

---

(11) Not me, obviously, I no longer worry about their petty repercussion. I call into evidence Exhibit A: This book. To quote Thomas Paine: "The world is my country, all mankind are my brethren, and to do good is my religion," and fuck anybody that has a problem with that.

41

So, sit on *that* and rotate,

asshole.

Some suggested viewing

I encourage you... No, I *beg* you to learn some more about this virus of stupidification and indoctrination that is Common Core. There are a ton of videos that you can check out to learn more, but here are some of my personal favorites, according to their running time.

Building the Machine: The Common Core Documentary (At just <u>under 40 minutes</u>, this is your CC 101 course. In the time it takes to watch 2 episodes of *Spongebob Squarepants,* you'll have a solid grasp of why Common Core is bad juju.) Of course, you'll have to purchase the DVD because—shocking—every time *Building the Machine* gets posted on YouTube, etc. it seems to magically disappear. That alone is reason to watch it, because people with enough power to keep this off of the internet <u>don't *want* you to</u>.

The Case Against Common Core (Actually *anything* by Dr. Duke Pesta is very good, but this talk, clocking in <u>a little over two hours</u>, might be the best overview on the evils of Common Core that I've ever seen. You'll see evidence of everything I talked about and then some; this is truly an eye-opening, life-changing watch.)

Reasons Why Common Core is Bad for Education—Fight Back (Don't sweat the religious overtones, instead, focus on the 9 simply and quickly (<u>about 8 minutes</u>) explained reasons why Common Core is that stuff in the fridge you can't identify and certainly shouldn't eat.)

Common Core: 101—5 Minute Breakdown with Dr. Duke Pesta (Doc Pesta again, but if you can only invest a few moments beyond having read this chapter in further educating yourself, this is a fast <u>5 minute</u> "highlight" of the lowlights of the shit that is Common Core.)

Gentle reader, before we dive back into my angry book raging against everything and everybody, let me talk directly to you for just a few seconds:

I *know* I asked a lot of you, asking you to stop reading to watch video clips, asking you to do further research on what I told you, then begging you to watch **more** stuff about Common Core, but please, PLEASE, if you can "binge watch" whole season(s) of your favorite show, you can invest a little time to learn about the machine that is slowly controlling our future generations, right??

I hope so.

Step

PG-rated Synopsis of the Common Core Chapter

- Your children's education was completely transformed with the adoption of Common Core, with ZERO consultation of parents/guardians about it, NO State legislature vote on it, and NO Teacher's Union discussion about it.

- The people who created Common Core were NOT educators.

- Your school's "support" of Common Core was bought and paid for by the Federal Government, with a little help from wealthy private interest groups.

- Your children's education is becoming "one-size-fits-all-nobody-can-go-ahead-useless-anywhere-beyond-High-School" because the Common Core standards are designed to keep it that way.

- Common Core does not facilitate STEM education, which is *universally* considered vital to our children, the future of our country, and our world.

- The Common Core is advertised as being "State led," "internationally benchmarked," "rigorous," "better than what we already had," and "generally praised." It is NONE of those things; it is an evolving *experiment* authored by people with almost no educational background who, the evidence indicates, want to control your kids.

- Anyone on the original "validation committee" that disagreed with Common Core was expunged from the record, and it was sold as having passed unanimously.

- There is ample evidence to indicate that Common Core is slowly, insidiously, replacing *you* with the *State* as the primary influence on your children; additionally, Common Core functions as a Trojan Horse for the federal government in ways you probably don't want to (but probably should) know about.

- Thanks to Common Core policies, students in CC schools will not be allowed to "go ahead" if they happen to be really good in a subject; in some cases, there will be punitive measures taken against kids that progress more quickly, or demonstrate alternatives to the way they are taught.

- Common Core strips children of an authentic educational experience that teaches them (among many other things,) critical thinking, compassion, and social skills; instead, students' "success" now hinges on how they perform on an endless battery of tests created by people who are politically and financially motivated.

OH WELL, AT LEAST I CAN SEND MY KIDS TO A CHARTER SCHOOL
(a.o.s.s.t.u.p.s.)

"Journalism is printing what someone else does not want to be printed. Everything else is public relations."

—George Orwell

The title of this chapter is a direct quote from a parent that wasn't happy with her children's grades. I had her son for English, and, apparently, the teacher to my immediate left[1] had her younger daughter for Science. Actually, the FULL quote was: *"Oh well, at least I can send my kids to a charter school; they know what they* [sic] *doing and how to teach all kinds of kids. Y'all just want things your way."* Even though that statement was:

A) 75% wrong
B) Irrelevant to why her kids' grades were bad[2]
C) Infuriating
D) **All of the above,** I chose to do what good teachers do; that is, I tried to educate Miss Guided regarding her misinformation about charter schools. *"I have to tell you, Ma'am, that's not correct at all; in fact, most charter schools..."*

---

(1) In the current parent-teacher conference format at my school, the teachers basically sit in alphabetical order at long cafeteria tables, shoulder to shoulder, about two feet from each other. Parents just find who they're looking for and stand in line like they're waiting to order lunch meat at the deli; obviously, this doesn't exactly facilitate private conversation...

(2) Might have had something to do with the fact that all three of her children (there was a younger brother still in Middle School) were in near constant trouble both in and out of school, but what do I know? I "just want things [my] way."

She cut me off, mid-sentence with, "Of course y'all don't like charter schools; you afraid of competition," and when I retracted my fangs and asked her, as politely as possible, why she was so pro-charter, she gave me the same lame ass answer that so many parents before her had given: "They give me a choice."

God, I love you fucking people; you're the same ones that love blowhard political figures and media constructed celebrities "because they tell it like it is." Actually, come to think of it, that's good—because if you like people that "tell it like it is,"

then you'll just *love* me.

You, the charter adherent squad, have been manipulated into thinking that your [often uneducated] opinion matters, so when you take sound bites and slogans—*"School Choice!"*—and wield them like some sort of imaginary weapon of profound truth, you're often proving yourself to be nothing more than the uninformed mouthpiece for some parasite with ulterior motives that isn't within a siriometer[3] of your children's best interest.

You're a photocopy of a photocopy of an outdated receipt; dull, faded, and largely irrelevant.

(Picture me now, palms up, big shit-eating grin on my face.) *Just tellin' it like it is, people!*

But back to our disgruntled and woefully uninformed parent. Yes, Miss Guided, *any* school beyond the one in which your kids are currently enrolled offers you a choice, but that shit filled dumpster around the corner with the dead guy's arm sticking out of it offers you a choice too; if you don't like the food that your cafeteria offers, you can saddle up to the dumpster and dig in. Just because something offers you a CHOICE, CHANGE, ALTERNATIVE or any other

innocuous term, it doesn't necessarily mean it's *better*, it just means it's **different.**

And yeah, I used the appallingly gross dumpster metaphor for a reason. If you knew 10% of the underhanded, undisclosed, unprofessional and, quite frankly, unbelievable shit that your beloved charter schools were guilty of, well, you *might* be singing a different song.

---

(3) Go ahead, look it up, I had to.

For example, if you were aware of how predatory some of the shady bastards that open and operate these places are, you wouldn't send your kids anywhere near them. Want an example of how widespread this corruption is? I thought you might, so here's one from the West Coast and one from the East Coast:

CALIFORNIA: Ah, the sun and the sand! The lying and the larceny!

> From 1999 until it went out of business in 2004, the California Charter Academy was the state's largest charter school operation, with more than 4,557 students in kindergarten through 12th grade. In 2004, the State of California Department of Education began looking into allegations of financial fraud at the charter chain. This led to criminal charges against the executives of one of their charter school operations after an audit found they had **misused at least $25.6 million** in public education money, including $2.6 million for personal expenses. The audit found that executives of the now-closed California Charter Academy used public funds to pay for personal boats, travel, health spa visits, Disney-related merchandise, and more. Two employees even paid their income taxes with $42,000 in school funds.[4]

Oh, there ae SO many more you could read about, but in the interest of fairness in this Tupac/Biggie rivalry of corruption, let's swing over to the Atlantic Ocean side and pay a visit to the City of Brotherly Love.

PENNSYLVANIA: Ah, the chutzpah and the cheesesteaks! The gall and the greed!

In September 2014, the Center for Popular Democracy, Integrity in Education, and ACTION United published a report that disclosed charter

---

(4) Weapons of Mass Deception, 3.3 Why Charter Schools
Are Fraud Factories https://weaponsofmassdeception.
org/3-charter-school-kid-prisons/3-3-why-charter-schools-are-fraud-factories

school officials in PA had **defrauded at least $30 million** intended for school children since 1997.

Examples of charter school fraud described in the report included:

- In 2007, one charter operator was caught <u>diverting</u> $2.6 million in school <u>funds to a church property he also operated</u>.
- In 2008, another charter school operator was caught spending millions in school funds <u>to bail out other non-profits associated with the school's parent corporation</u>.
- In 2009, a pair of charter school operators stole more than $900,000 from the school by using fraudulent invoices <u>for home improvement expenses</u>.
- In 2012, another charter school operator was sentenced to prison for stealing $522,000 <u>to prop up a failing restaurant</u>.
- In 2014, another charter school operator was indicted for diverting $8 million of school funds <u>to buy houses and an airplane</u>.

Again, thanks to

Weapons of Mass Deception, 3.3 Why Charter Schools Are Fraud Factories **https://weaponsofmassdeception.org/3-charter-school-kid-prisons/3-3-why-charter-schools-are-fraud-factories**

for the excruciating insight. And speaking of excruciating, the Governor of Ohio—the state widely agreed upon as the nation's LEADER in charter school corruption—John Kasich, tried a (thankfully failed) run at the Presidency.

To quote Joseph Conrad: "The horror! The horror!"

This was the guy, after all, that compared schools to pizza shops and said opening charter schools would "force the pizza shops that didn't give enough pepperoni" to change their ways. If one of my students had written that, I would have called immediately for both psychiatric and academic evaluations.

Unfortunately for Papa John, he wasn't the clown that the Republican party picked from their clown car full of ineptitude to represent the G.O.P. Thank you, people of America, for keeping this twat from being in charge of the entire *Nation's* school system! (Not that we did any better with Trump/DeVos debacle, but still…)

A nation full of kids unknowingly had a moment of inexplicable euphoria as they were spared a President that would have tried to run their educational system in a way that made them commensurate to Little Caesar's Hot and Ready pizza.

OK, so that was Whitey McWhitebread Kasich and his Ohio-no-you-DID'nt charter school conundrum, which, according to State audit, misspent public funds *nearly quadruple the amount **of any other agency** funded by the taxpayers.* Maybe things are better on the mean (and considerably more diverse) streets of my former home in Philly?

Uh, no.

The NAACP just passed a resolution at their national convention calling for a ban on privately managed charter schools, some of which reside in the City of Brotherly Love, wherein they accused charter schools of:

- Contributing to the INCREASED segregation of our public-school system.
- Suffering from weak oversight that wasted public funds and put students at risk, further eroding local control of public education.
- Practicing **predatory** *(isn't that the EXACT word I used back in 2015?)* lending practices that hurt both schools and communities.

Oh, sweet Lord of Vindication, where were you guys at the NAACP when Miss Guided (and the legions of subsequent parents that followed her) spouted their pro-charter prattle chit chat? Never mind, I'm just glad you helped lay the smack down on these predatory privatizing poop heads; and speaking of laying the smack down…

John Oliver, political satirist, writer, producer, television host, actor, voice actor, media critic, and stand-up comedian, absolutely

eviscerated **the charter schools-are-better myth during his August 22, 2016** *Last Week Tonight with John Oliver* **show.**

Seriously, YouTube that shit—*John Oliver destroys charter schools*—it's the sort of brilliant amalgam of informative, incendiary and hilarious that comes second nature to Oliver, and his impeccably researched examples of corruption make some of mine look pale in comparison.

I also take great pleasure in telling you that since John Oliver's brilliant and visceral segment on charter schools aired, (and was subsequently shared on social media like songs when Napster first started,) several emotionally sunburned charter advocates got their panties in a wad; none more so than the Center for Education Reform, who—and this is fantastic for *so* many reasons—announced a "Hey John Oliver, Back Off My Charter School!" video contest with a $100,000 prize, inviting charter school advocates to create a short, low-budget video about why they think their school deserved the cash prize. Because nothing says righteous anger like an exorbitant monetary carrot at the end of a self-serving stick.

I'll leave it to Alan Singer, Professor at Hofstra University and Historian, to take this chapter home with an erudite summary of the shoddy shenanigans that pervade many charter schools:

> Charter schools are contractors that receive taxpayer money to operate privately controlled schools that do not have the same rules and responsibilities as public schools. Investigations of charter school operations in Florida, Michigan, Ohio, North Carolina, and elsewhere have found numerous cases where charters used taxpayer money to procure school buildings, supplies, and equipment that they retained ownership of, even if the school closed. In most states, charter schools are exempt from most state and local laws, rules, regulations, and policies governing public and private schools, including those related to personnel and students.

Well put sir, well put indeed.

If you'd like to further educate/infuriate yourself about this dirty bomb of flagrant lies and financial laundering that is the charter school movement, may I recommend:

- Doug Martin's *Hoosier School Heist,* (2014) or
- The Center for Popular Democracy and Integrity in Education's report *Charter School Vulnerabilities to Waste, Fraud and Abuse* (2014)—which can be found at **https://integrityineducation. org/charter-fraud/**

These are just two of the stones of an ever-growing mountain of information about how charter schools are popping up, robbing people blind and, in the process, <u>compromising the education of tens of thousands of kids with virtually no federal or state oversight</u>; so**, feel free to jump online at any time and I *guarantee* you'll find something current to remind you that the privatization of your children's 'education' (at the expense of actually *educating* them) is alive and well.** Go ahead, jump on Twitter or Facebook or just Google "Charter Schools" under "News" and I all but guarantee the story will be negative in some way.

In the meantime, try to compose yourself when you hear "oh well, at least I can send my kids to a charter school," and other stupid shit that uninformed people say.

WHAT'S THE DIFFERENCE BETWEEN 75 and 32? (Hint: it's not 43)

"An investment in knowledge always pays the best interest."
— *Benjamin Franklin*

Woke up today in a great mood—second full day of summer vacation, my daughter Samantha has been promoted to manager at her summer job, my third child, Mason, graduates High School tomorrow night, my youngest, Frankie, is kicking ass at Boys State, and my stepson Brendan is flourishing. My wife is happy, (or as happy as she can be being married to me,) and a bunch of my students sent me emails with very kind words about my "impact" on them this year. If I could sing, I'd be belting out a few bars of *Walking on Sunshine*.

Leave it to Governor Chris Christie to shit on the pristine diaper of my day.

In the interest of complete transparency, I don't like Chris Christie. I find him to be a hypocritical misogynist who sycophantically panders to the wealthy (witness his corpulent concubine act during Donald Trump's Presidential run) while bullying (behind a wall of security of course) blue collar populations who question him in any way, and talking tough in sound bites designed to intimidate those with no immediate access *to* him. He is the prototypical "I'm better than you and you'll do what I say because I say so" politician. He is, pun fully intended, a "fat cat."[1]

According to the news brief assaulting me on Twitter, Facebook, several news channels and the local newspaper, GCC had just proposed

---

(1) A "fat cat," is described by the New York Times as a symbol of "a deeply corrupt campaign finance system riddled with loopholes…recipients of the 'perks of power' [who is] able to buy access, influence policy and even veto appointments."

a flat $6,599.00 per-pupil school aid system. Pitched as a means of property tax relief for many towns in the state, Christie's plan would boost the state aid distributed to many suburban and rural school districts, but it would cost kids from other, less privileged school districts. To simplify, he wants each student, regardless of where they live or what type of background they come from, to have equal, one-size-fits-all funding; this could, conceivably, financially cripple many of the state's urban districts that rely on the aid.

Witness the startling difference between what would happen to the kids in the district where I currently *live* (who would receive a 75% increase in per student spending,) and the kids in the district where I *teach* (who would receive a 32% decrease.)

Let me be blunt about this; I *live* in a district where stable parent families that prioritize education are the norm.

The district *where I teach*? Not even close.

I was fortunate that my father came over shortly after I read the articles describing our Governor's plan, and over several cups of coffee I got to hear his opinion, which, to be honest, is often synonymous with the general population. He thought it was a solid idea, and, rightfully so, he validated that opinion by citing numerous times where tons of money were dumped into "needy" districts only to be misappropriated or flat out stolen; he also articulated the age-old belief that if you continue to just give things to people, they never develop appreciation for what they are given, and you are left with unmotivated people with a sense of entitlement and zero work ethic.

While I generally agree with him that, in many cases, our government and "educational reformers" think that simply dumping money onto a problem will fix it (*No Child Left Behind*, anyone?) I thought that, in this case, he was painting with too broad a brush.

While I'm the first person to express my disdain about the over-enabling 'snowflakization' of our future generations, I am also quick to acknowledge that any time you try to employ a one-size-fits-all policy when your product is HUMAN in nature (education, health care, military operations, etc.) you are asking for trouble. Similarly, if you try to turn funding into a Hunger-Games-style competition (*Race to the Top*, anyone?) then you are being grossly unfair to kids from impoverished backgrounds who start "the race" behind the 8 ball.

If you see hypocrisy in my beliefs, I understand, and I am willing to sit with you, as I did with my Dad, and talk; however, my students are my kids, and, as such, I am pretty passionate about what gets done to them, and when what gets done to them involves a 33% cut in resources to assist them in the education that will shape their futures, I will call BS on that,

every

single

time.

PART II:
STEP WARS—
THE TEACHER STRIKES BACK

THE END OF THE YEAR GETS US STARTED

"I tried to be nice. I tried to live my life.
But everyone else is an asshole
I tried to forgive. I tried to live and let live.
But everyone else is an asshole."

—*Reel Big Fish*

If you'll continue forward in an orderly fashion, we're currently exiting the *y'all-need-to-beware-the-corporate-takeover-of-your-kids'-education* section of our tour. Watch your step, please, as we're now entering the narrative, *Step's-gonna-tell-you-some-stories-so-you-understand-some-of-what-teachers-go-through* portion of our journey. You might say that "part II" is a collection of tales designed to illustrate how the ever-changing notion of what is "best practice," along with the rancorous public sentiment regarding teachers, are the dragons that most [good] educators want to slay in pursuit of properly educating your children.

As such, things may get a little dangerous from time to time but hey, **all** of the really fun rides are somewhat scary, right? Please hold onto the handrails (or, at least, the book,) and, as always, feel free to go as fast or slow as you want to, and enjoy your travels through phase 2 of *Retribution: The Ride.*

It is June 15th, four days until the last day of school.

Kid has been in DANGER OF FAILING FOR THE YEAR since November. He knows this because it says "DANGER OF FAILING FOR THE YEAR" on four interim reports and three report cards that have been sent home, along with a tsunami of emails, texts, online grading portal reports, in-person meeting invitations, etc. etc. etc. etc. etc. et freakin' cetera until you want to scream.

Kid hasn't turned in shit since March. Nothing. Not a homework assignment, not a project, not a test, not a quiz, not an *in-class* assignment, etc. etc. etc. etc. etc. et freakin' cetera until you want to hurt somebody.

I called and emailed Mom. Nothing.

Counselor called and emailed Mom. Nothing.

Had the *vice principal* call and email Mom. Nothing.

Counselor finally leaves a message that…let's call him Iago…won't be graduating on time next year because he's failing my class (and three other classes, by the way) for the year.

Mom calls back five minutes later.

Miraculous.

I'll spare you the infuriating, soul-sucking, time-wasting back and forth and just summarize the entire verbal joust for you, ok?

Mom: "I'm *vaguely* aware that I'm teaching my son Iago to mess around and ignore the law, authority and proper social behavior in the hopes that some last-minute bitching and threatening will eradicate 7 ½ months of quantifiable apathy and, thusly, award him with something that he doesn't deserve. Furthermore, I *kinda* know that it would be grossly unfair to the legions of *other* kids you teach, **and** I *sorta* know that Iago has a FOUR in your class but needs a SEVENTY-FOUR to pass, **and** I *kinda, sorta* know that I'm asking you to defy contractual obligations and put your job at risk for a kid that *laughed at you* when you told him, back when snow was on the ground, that he had one last chance (over the Christmas break) to make up all of the work he owed, **but** we have a family vacation planned this summer and having Iago in summer school for your class (and three other classes) would be *très gênant,* so can he do a project or some extra credit to earn the points?"

The counselor, (and anybody else with a soul:) "You're kidding? Please tell us you're kidding? You're not kidding? Uh…no, ma'am, he cannot make up an *entire marking period's* worth of work for four classes in three days. Yes, we understand the inconvenience, but please try to understand: we hate seeing kids fail, but Iago was informed multiple times about his

questionable choices and failed to rectify the situation. Again, we're sorry, and we will be in touch regarding his summer school requirements."

Me: "No, and you should be ashamed for even asking. I care enough about your kid, as a citizen of the world, to be the 'bad guy' and teach him a lesson that, learned now, *might* save him some very painful, expensive, and possibly fatal lessons in the future. I tried to work with you when you requested that I 'stay in touch' a few months ago, but when you change your email address and fail to tell anybody, then change your phone number and, again, fail to notify me, then leave town for two weeks and (sensing a theme here, people?) fail to inform the school, what am I expected to do? Develop clairvoyance by convenience?

Can he do a *project* or some *extra credit* to earn the points? Jesus Christ on a cracker[1] where do they get these people?

Seriously, are you freakin' kidding? What kind of project earns 65 report card points and erases nine months of disrespect and disregard? If he offered to build me a vacation home and furnish it with supermodels carrying briefcases of hundred dollar bills I would still say "no" because nothing is worth compromising my integrity,[2] which is about all I have left in this shitstorm of a profession. Did I mention that you should be ashamed? Because you should. I did not fail your kid; he failed himself, and **you** didn't do anything but exacerbate that process."

Obviously, I'm paraphrasing. Clearly, I have no soul.

Mom confirmed this by strongly implying to the counselor that I was "out to get" her poor little Iago.

Gosh darn it, you got me!

I keep coming back to this place 24 years running for the sole

---

(1) A classic line which I oft borrow from my "work wife" and co-conspirator/ teacher Dee Flynn, who was taken from me when the powers-that-be recognized our combined awesomeness.

(2) Unless two of the aforementioned supermodels were Gal Gadot and Eva Green; in which case, my soul is forfeit, yet again, Lord Lucifer.

purpose of ruining kids' lives. Oh, and the money keeps me coming back, too. Nothing says financial security like a teacher's salary, after all.

It's all *my* fault.

I'm certainly not part of a failing SYSTEM, and poor wittle Iago is certainly not a product of a culture that the high higher ups (like the administrators that kowtow to these little shits) are creating in the name of anus protectus, and you, Mom, certainly are none to blame for being grossly negligent in the whole "enablement masquerading as advocacy" thing.

Sadly, I'm sure many of the teachers out there reading this can top that story for sheer audacity and pencil-snapping frustration.

Know that I feel your pain.

That's why I write these books.

Lao Tzu, master of the obvious, observed that "The journey of a thousand miles begins with a single step." So that little narrative gets the second, more anecdotal part, of our journey started. Please, walk with me as I strike back against injustice with a journey into the valley of righteous anger, through the dark forest of cynicism, and up Mount Reality.

WELCOME BACK: NO GOOD DEED GOES UNPUNISHED

"And I know what a scene you were learning in. Was there something
that made you come back again? And what could ever lead you...
Back here where we need you?"
—John Sebastian

Well, one year ends and another begins; sadly, it didn't take long for the book worthy material to start flowing in.

In fact, *school hasn't even started yet,* (it's a week until "opening day") but it seems I'm already taking up residency at base camp on Mount Bullshit.

A little background first, if you don't mind:

Four years ago, I was recruited to start, evolve, and be the English teacher for, an SAT prep program that would benefit our students in need. I, along with the Math teacher, would be paid based on student enrollment numbers, (that never happened) and the school was going to promote the program (and by "the school" I mean "the Math teacher and I.") Hey, 1600+ kids, hundreds of teachers/counselors/administrators, all promoting a ridiculous value (a little over a hundred bucks for over *16 **hours*** of SAT tutoring from two highly qualified teachers? Are ya kidding?! This is too good to be true!) Many similar programs charge *hundreds,* even *thousands*; this would sell like ice water in Hell.

Or so you would think.

The first year we promoted aggressively and had 24 kids for our first 8-week session. I don't remember their ages, genders or nationalities because, quite frankly, I didn't care. These were kids willing to give up time on Sunday nights to come back to the school they dreaded on

Monday morning to spend two hours learning how to beat the SAT, and that was good enough for me.

That *should* have been good enough for our then Superintendent; alas, once the program became successful—a program she had neither **knowledge of** nor **involvement with**—she demanded, "that it be available to a wide diversity of students" if it were to continue.[1]

'Twas about this time that the original architect of the aforementioned SAT program, let's call him William Soccer III, righteously angered by this edict, (which, in hindsight, implied that we DIDN'T offer our ludicrously bargain priced services to "a wide diversity of students") went back and checked his list. He checked it twice. He found out if we were naughty or nice...

Turns out we were, quite by accident I assure you, very nice. Our two years of tutoring had served a veritable United Nations of races, genders, socioeconomic statuses and (in at least two cases I know about) members of the LGBT community. Again, I didn't give a shit at the time; I just knew they were kids that wanted to learn, and that was good enough for me.

Again, that *should* have been good enough for our then Superintendent, but hey, nothing says natural diversity and academic progress like forced awareness and micromanagement. I'll say this in plain language: she wanted to see the list of kids that were going to be in the program, and then go over it to make sure the percentage of black and brown children suited her fancy. If it didn't, she was going to interview kids to find out WHY they hadn't applied, and interrogate us as to WHY we "hadn't promoted the program better to all demographics."[2]

By the way, neither Asian/Pacific Islander nor Native American nor White were included in that demographic according to Señorita Superintendent, so her definition of "all demographics" was a tad narrow. Somehow, word got around. (If you think you can keep things hidden from teenagers, particularly things that directly influence them,

---

(1) For more on this, consult The Bible of Shitty Leadership, under the chapter How to Foster Racism and Narrow-Mindedness When You Claim to Embrace Diversity and High Academic Standards.
(2) It should be noted that, after our first year, we didn't "promote" anything; word of mouth was all we needed.

think again,) and soon many of the students that really wanted to be part of the program were discouraged at the prospect of—and here I paraphrase a potential student that we lost to another [outside] tutoring program: *"a cool program being watered down by kids that really [didn't] want to be [there.]"*

Prophetic, really, as enrollment dropped to the point where we started having only one class per year instead of two, and eventually we (or rather, *I*, since I was the only one from day one still involved,) started having to pull kids from neighboring districts to fill one class.

But, as they say, every cloud has a silver lining. When enrollment started dropping, I tried (long before I started recruiting out-of-district kids) to promote the class again, "in-house." I started singing the praises of *super-inexpensive-yet-potentially-life-changing-if-their-scores-went-up-enough* SAT tutoring at parent teacher conferences, back to school nights and such. The level of resistance that greeted me would have been lesser if I had tried to walk my brother-in-law's porn collection into the Vatican:

"A hundred dollars? Don't you think that's kinda ridiculous?" (No, Mom whose kid has a $500 phone and several pairs of $100+ sneakers, I don't.)

"Does the book come with that fee, 'cause a hundred bucks is a lot of money" (Yes, it does, and no, it isn't, Mom whose kid makes more than that in a few hours selling weed.[3]

"Do you guarantee like, 200 points improvement or something?" (No Dad, we don't *guarantee* anything, but neither do those $800 to $1000 tutoring services.)

On and on it went, and we were slated to begin our 2014 class with only four students, so out of desperation, I started asking parents from a neighboring district if they were interested in getting their kids some SAT pre—

"Hell yes! When can she start?"

"That's $100 per class, right?"

"Can I get both my kids in?"

"I know what kinda money a few points on the SAT can equal;

---

(3) Fact. But I guess A) I'm not supposed to know that or B) you don't know that.[4]

(4) Either way, pathetic.

when do you start?" "Can you do privates with him [in addition to the regular class?]"

"Wait, it's only $100? And that includes the book?" and on and on and on.

Hmmmmm... I thought to myself, "Tis a tale of two cities, and city #2 seems to understand the value of investing in education." Then I thought to myself: "Self, the silver lining to this cloud has just peeked through..."

Fast forward to this week. We've gone through four Math tutors in four years, but I finally got the guy I wanted, and we have great ideas about how to evolve the program and make it really amazing; we're going to expand to ACT tutoring as well, and I think we can...(SPLASH)

That noise you just heard was a wave of bureaucratic bullshit putting out the fire of enthusiasm.

The Board of education mouthpiece, a young man who I love dearly but was firmly caught between a rock (me) and a hard place, (the current culture of our school,) was forced, in the name of job security, to respond to every one of our requests, aimed to expand and improve the tutoring program, with a resounding "no."

Every. Single. One.

Uh, that's not negotiation, folks, that's professional retardation bordering on hostile takeover. No good deed, it seems, goes unpunished. I shan't recount the full details of the Borg—McEnroe verbal repartee here, but if WE (the tutors) were the *defendants* of all things educational, realistic and pragmatic, (and we were, gentle reader, we were) then THEY (the Board) must've been the *prosecution*, right? Here are some of the prosecution's highlights:

- Apparently, everyone in our district is in Church from 8am to mid-afternoon on Sundays.
- Raising the price of a SIX WEEK tutoring class from $100 to $150 per kid (which included the $20 book, was considered "a little pricey.")[5]

---

(5) Just for a point of comparison, a certain "highly regarded" PR company offers SAT Classroom, an 18-hour course (the same length as ours) focusing on frequent test components and the essentials for around $600, at locations across the U.S., and more in-depth, 30-hour review courses are offered for around $1,000.

- Asking kids to be at tutoring by 10 A.M. the morning (for a test that is almost exclusively administered, in most cases, *at 8 A.M. in the morning*) "wasn't practical."
  And my personal favorite…
- We had no "quantifiable evidence" that our program warranted additional time/funding.

Yeah, ya got me there. Even though most of the kids that studied with us improved their scores (some dramatically enough to earn scholarships,) we did not, in fact, keep a ledger in anticipation of having to *prove* ourselves proficient. Must've been too busy thinking of ways to make the material more relevant and valuable to the actual sentient beings we were tutoring.

My partner, Mr. Banner, (think slightly less green version of the Hulk with mad math skills and a heart of gold,) and I agreed to disagree with the company's version of "negotiation" and wished them well.

EPILOGUE: A NEW HOPE!

At the time I submitted this book for publication (almost three years after the writing of this chapter,) Mr. Banner and I have run several eight-week SAT and ACT tutoring classes a year, and we're up to our ears in private tutoring gigs. Actually, listing the kids we've gotten into their colleges of choice and/or partial scholarships would be overkill, but here are just a few highlights for the purposes of validation:

- Antwan Dickerson needed 120 points to get a full ride to Clemson; we got him more than that. As of the writing of this chapter, he's currently at The University of Houston being trained by…wait for it…Leroy Burell and Carl Lewis (If you're counting, that's about a bajillion gold medals at the Olympics) and doing spectacularly well both academically, majoring in logistics technology and minoring in computer information systems, (you GO young man!) and, obviously, athletically (being trained by two gold medal Olympians to do the decathlon.)
- Got another local kid a 150-point increase that ultimately led to a

half scholarship at LaSalle University. That's a $200 investment that (along with his hard work and dedication to improving, of course,) ultimately saved his family around **Sixty thousand** dollars.

- Got a set of twins (Hi Katie and Mollie! You guys rock!) a combined $172,000—that's one hundred and six **TEE THOUsand** 'Murican greenbacks toward Loyola University Maryland, (sadly, given the cost of higher education, that still leaves them to pay over $200,000) but hey, if I told you that you could earn *five hundred and thirty-seven times the amount you invested, and it would be for a good cause,* **would you do it?**

- Last, but certainly not least, our new Superintendent got wind of our private success and is considering an actual SAT class elective that would allow the kids [where Mr. Banner and I teach] to benefit from our experience and improve *their* scores as well. Wow, administrative common sense, moving toward a shared purpose, that benefits the kids. That's a win-win, uh, win for everyone involved!

I could go on and on, but I'll spare you the time and simply, in good teacher fashion, bullet point the main ideas of this chapter for you:

- Investment in learning is always a good investment.
- One sided demands do not constitute negotiation.
- Don't say you're "all about the kids" when you really mean you're "all about your individual agenda." Oh, and…
- opportunity often lies within conflict; aka: "I paid the self-publication costs for this book with the tutoring money I made because *you* chased *me* into greener pastures."

Wow. The school year hasn't even *started* yet and **already** I am reminded of the bureaucratic bullshit, misguided parental prioritizing, and philosophical frustration that await me. Alas, such is the life of a teacher. Onward!

I RITE PURTY GOOD

*"Teaching might even be the greatest of the arts
since the medium is the human mind and spirit."*
—John Steinbeck

Actually, I think I write a *little* better than purty good, but opinions vary, and that isn't

the point of this little chapter any old way. Since we just touched on *demographic* diversity in the last chapter, I thought you might enjoy a little insight into the diversity in *ability* that teachers are often asked to deal with on a daily basis.

During the first week of the new year I asked the students in one of my 9th grade English classes to tell me, as succinctly as they could, how they rated their own writing skills. These were some of the responses I received **(along with some of my internal dialogue.)**

Please note: these are written <u>verbatim</u> as I received them, (although I wish you could have seen the actual handwriting) and *these kids are all in the same class.*

1. Feel like I write like a third grader I'm really bad at putting words onto paper but it's the opposite with my mouth
   That's actually a pretty spot-on assessment of most High School kids that have to write formally.

2. My writing skills are aight. Nah. I'm just kidding, they're really not haha. I would say my writings ok. but I wish I could use the big words and have smoother writing.
   "I wish I could use the big words..." Deep sigh from the depths of my weary soul.

3. I don't like to reed. I would describe my writing skills good

when i have something eesy to write about i'm not so good at essays about something but i can write good stories.
i can't wait to reed them.

4. I would describe my writing skills as ok , because it's not the best. (A.K.A) bad with spelling
Nope, not ok, THEY'RE not the best, A.K.A. bad with grammar, too.

5. My writing skills isn't that great but i will keep trying and never give up i will keep *trying until i 100% believe i'm done. U can believe that!!!!*
Save me the "I believe in myself" speech, Miss America, and master proofreading first.

6. I would describe my writing skills as average because I came from Vietnam and have to take ESL, thus my spelling, grammar and English is not very good, but I think I'm *improving*
This one was typed submitted using GoogleDocs, which is probably good, because only something as big as Google could handle the irony contained herein.

7. I would describe my writing skills as childish and sub-par. Through the use of a large vocabulary I make myself seem intelligent, when in reality I am just doing an extremely complicated Mad Lib in my essays. Also, I have atrocious spelling skills. Auto correct and the fear of grabbing a dictionary is honestly the only reason I'm typing this.
Do kids still DO Mad Libs? I hope so. And no, you do not have atrocious spelling or you wouldn't have been able to spell atrocious.

8. Given that I've been elected into the US Achievement Academy for my writing, I can safely say that my writing meets academic requirements to qualify as "good writing". We both know that

writing isn't simply about how much vocabulary you use or what format you're in though; it's about the expression of the writer through written language. I write like I speak, which is something that must be corrected for essays. However, I try to incorporate as much of my own personal style and attitude into my pieces as I can. I want to make it interesting and enjoyable for the reader just as much as I want to convey the information, and I'm lucky that I have the skills to accomplish this. What I'm trying to say here is that my writing is oftentimes very personal and unique to me, and I leave a *part of me in every piece I write*. **This person is in the same grade as the person that wrote #9**

9. My riting skills are good, but correk if I'm wrong.
   This person is in the same grade as the person that wrote #8

10. My writing skills I would have to say is at least desent?
   I'm sorry, good sir, but I must disagree with you.

Mmm-hmm. That's just 10 out of 36 Freshmen in "College prep" English class. The rest of the responses were similarly all over the place in terms of ability, and I, like any teacher, am expected to teach them **all** without frustrating anyone, boring anyone, losing anyone, or failing to stimulate anyone, etc. all while using the (insert corporation we paid to use their products) materials I'm told to use and with ever-increasing lack of autonomy.

Now, the parents that produced them, the counselors that put them in class together, and the administrators that evaluate me using the models forced on them by "educational reformers" that don't understand me would tell me that I: (insert snotty British accent and theatrical hand gesture) *"simply need to differentiate my instruction!"*

Riiiiiiight…just start this fire in the middle of this dangerously dry forest, while it's raining, but don't let the fire go out, don't burn down the forest, make sure you use the materials we gave you to start the fire, and make sure you document every step of the process, while keeping the fire going and contained, just in case we (the people "in charge,") ever decide we want to glance at that documentation. *

*Hint: We **won't** look at it, *unless* you screw up, in which case we'll use it to reprimand you OR unless we want to use your documentation to prove to someone higher up the food chain that ~~you~~, I mean *we* did our job.

Really? That's all I have to do? I just have to "differentiate my instruction?" Wow! Thank you. *Thank you* so much for that insight and oh-so pragmatic advice. Tell you what, while I'm doing THAT, **why don't you—**

This portion of Mr. Stepnowski's manuscript has been redacted in the interest of:

1. Protecting the reader (whom hereafter shall be referred to as "the consumer") from the most vulgar of suggestions
2. Ensuring that the consumer is spared from experiencing literature that would almost certainly force him/her to engender legal actions against the author (whom hereafter shall be referred to as "the author.")
3. Protecting "the author" from said aforementioned legal proceedings via his consumers, as he is already running toward poverty like a cellulite-challenged pre-adolescent (hereafter referred to as "fat kid") after an ice cream truck.

Sincerely,
The author's legal team.

and then write your grandma and the goat thank you letters for DOING it!

Now, where was I? Oh yeah, differentiated instruction. Come on, people, is there any way on God's green Earth I can teach each of these children at his/her appropriate pace with all of them in one room? Like most of the teachers I know, I agonize over trying to reach each and every kid on his/her own personal learning level, so when I tell you that this toxic mixture of "variable student product" and "impractical teacher micromanagement" is <u>setting teachers up to fail</u>, and <u>setting kids up to fail</u> as well—that is neither embellishment nor excuse making, I promise you.

"Nonsense!" croak the hordes of people that DON'T get evaluated or held accountable for this obvious bullshit, "just pull up your bootstraps, apply a little elbow grease, and you'll be on your way to making us happy, which is waaaaaaayy more important than, say, teaching kids."

Hmm...I've got a better idea. **Why don't you take those boots, and those straps, and—**

This portion of Mr. Stepnowski's manuscript has been redacted for reasons uniquely similar to the previously redacted text (which hereafter shall be referred to as "the shit we just omitted not two minutes ago.")

Angrily,
The author's legal team.

—and then, wipe the grease off of the aardvark's elbow, if you can FIND it, buddy!

Sorry, got carried away again. Where was I?

Right! I was discussing the subtle art of trying to teach 30 kids, who run the gamut from mid-3rd to 10th grade reading ability, and come from every conceivable background, (to say nothing of their dissimilar living situations,)

at the same time,

without losing anybody,

without boring anybody,

without frustrating anybody,

and do it all using the increasingly boring materials given to us so that your kids can pass the increasingly myopic testing that they have to pass to graduate because the millionaire testing corporations SAID SO.

No problem, I mean, it's not like they're independent organisms that might require someone to acknowledge their differences or anything. Mark Twain was eerily prescient when he said that **"teaching is like holding 35 corks underwater at once."** What he didn't know is that, in the modern era, we would be asked to do so in the ocean, with other people (who don't care about corks) trying to hold our arms.

Correk me if I'm wrong, but that's some bullshit.

THE ~~OAKLAND~~ ~~LOS ANGELES~~ ~~OAKLAND~~ LAS VEGAS RAIDERS OF EDUCATION

"Resistance to the organized mass can be effected only by the man who is as well organized in his individuality as the mass itself."
—Carl Jung

I love the Raiders. As the faded Polaroid evidence will verify, I've been a Raiders fan, from Oakland to Los Angeles, back to Oakland and now onto Sin City, since I was eight years old. Granted, it was easy to be a fan when they were the three-time Super Bowl champion silver and black, gangsta rap icon, bad boy Rrrrrraaaaay-duhs of the 70s and 80s;

Not so much so when they were the bottom dwelling "what are the playoffs?" laughingstock Raiders of the following two decades. Part of the problem for the decline in the team's dominance was a fracture in the continuity of the franchise. Let's face it, when you have a revolving door of managers, coaches, players and personnel, it's pretty hard to establish a consistently excellent product.

Which brings us to today's rant. I, along with my fellow teachers from the English department, found out today that our new Language Arts Supervisor has left for greener pastures. Can't blame her. More money, more autonomy, and a chance to impact a greater number of kids? Go for it. However, this is just one more instance of a revolving door of "leadership"[1] that has plagued our schools and MANY other schools across the country. Since I have been employed here, in thirteen years, we have gone through four Superintendents, four principals, nine

---

(1)   And by "leadership" I mean in title only—aka: those with administrative titles.

vice principals, three supervisors (in the English department *alone*,) countless board members, and a partridge in a pear tree.

Every one of them brought with them (booming theatrical voice, arms outstretched) "a new vision, a new system, a new curriculum, a new paradigm..."

or whatever you want to call the educational plan that they were promoting (along with all the new costs, materials, software, books, discipline and evaluation methods that come along with those 'visions.')

In short, we, the teachers, are continually asked to reinvent our goals /curriculum /teaching styles /methods of assessment every other year. Let me repeat that, in paraphrase, because it's kind of important:

We were being asked to change the goals for our living, breathing, soon-to-be-applying-for-college-or-going-into-the-world-of-employment kids *about every other year.*

That shit doesn't work for a professional football team, and it sure as hell doesn't work when you're preparing a generation of kids that are going to be running and influencing this country.

So whaddya do?

Just teach, baby.

Confession time: I haven't followed the aforementioned musical chairs approach to education. I saw the writing on the wall during my teaching infancy and decided that I would follow my own conscience and subscribe to a sort of educational version of the Hippocratic Oath.

According to a modern translation of the oath, doctors pledge that they:

> Will apply, for the benefit of the sick, all measures which are required...will remember that there is art to medicine as well as science, and that warmth, sympathy, and understanding may outweigh the surgeon's knife or the chemist's drug, [and]...will not be ashamed to say "I know not," nor will I fail to call in my colleagues when the skills of another are needed for a patient's recovery.[2]

---

(2) "Bioethics." Hippocratic Oath, Modern Version. John Hopkins Sheridian Libraries & University Museums, n.d. Web. 13 Oct. 2015.

That's pretty close to the teaching code I chose to live by some quarter of a century ago: **I'll do everything I can for my kids, remember that loving them takes precedent over following the curriculum, and, if someone else is better qualified to get the job done, I'll defer to them. In short, neither my ego nor the "vision du jour" takes precedent over my kids getting the best education available**.

If it makes you feel any better, I *know* that a lot of teachers, nationwide, share a similar approach to teaching your children, although I speak only for myself when I say that I haven't, and won't, let the changing winds of educational policy dictate how I teach your kids.

If we're going all in with the football analogy, I'm the coach, and your kids are my players; thus, they are my priority. To me, they are more than "the product on the field," and I care a lot more about their health, and their growth as people, than I do about their "performance" as measured by "the owners."[3]

Hey folks, I might play for the Raiders of education, but that doesn't mean that I won't play every game like it's the Super Bowl.

---

[3] Sadly, calling the people who are controlling education in this country "owners" is getting disturbingly close to the truth.

SAME OLD SONG AND DANCE

"What you allow is what will continue."

—Anon

I'll let you be the judge.

I feel like I've told a version of this story in every book I've written, but damn if it doesn't come up again and again. Because of my unapologetic approach, I've been accused of everything from misogyny to racism, and called everything from a bastard to the Antichrist himself (true story, 1993; I'll tell you about it over a beer someday.)

While I am, if my parents' lineage is to be trusted, neither of the above, I don't give such imputations much thought because they're the ammunition of idiots. Specifically, idiots that don't want to address the actual issue at hand, *whatever* it may be and *however* it may, inevitably, prove them to be insufficient in some manner. And just like "the wicked flee when no man pursueth," (Proverbs 28:1) so does the honest man not giveth a shit when armchair educators (usually in the form of parents that are a wee bit embarrassed of their offspring's behavior) accuseth him of fabricated fecal matter.

But I digress, I was telling you about this month's version of my story, and you were going to decide if I was a supersexypsychoSatanwithasideofsadism or whatever they're accusing me of this month.

Hey teachers! I'll give you the outline; tell me if you've heard this one before:

I. Student turns in work sporadically at best.

II. When the work is turned in, it's sloppy, incomplete, late, fails to follow directions, etc. Largely because of this, student is in danger of failing your class; you, trying to help the kid, check with other teachers, only to find out that...

III. student is failing multiple subjects (and this, upon investigation, is not a new phenomenon.) In addition, the student in question has a laundry list of disciplinary infractions; nonetheless...

IV. you give the student chance after chance after chance to get his/her shit together and demonstrate some degree of contrition and/or effort so you can justify possibly passing a kid that continually demonstrates academic and social ability several years deficient of their current "rank." Kid ignores you with impressive consistency; has been taught that somebody will invariably bail them out no matter what. Meanwhile...

V. calls, Emails, report cards, interim reports, etc. have yielded no return contact from home, so...

VI. you have no choice but to be honest with the kid and tell him/her that passing for the year is looking about as likely as Sean Hannity voting Democrat.

VII. After a short conversation that looks, from the outside, like Einstein trying to explain the theory of relativity to a rock, (because the kid still has no idea (?!?) why he/she is failing) student runs home and "paraphrases" your conversation in such a way as to make it sound like: (fill in the blanks with your own experience)
You called them 'retarded'
because you are a racist asshole
that doesn't like him/her, and
even though they "do their work,"
you still told them they're failing for the year and called them 'retarded.'

VIII. And so, (surprise surprise) the legal guardian now wants a meeting, which will take place during **your** prep time, thereby costing you valuable time used to prepare lessons for the kids that DO care, so you can deal with a disgruntled, hyper-enabled kid you've been trying to help for months, and an absentee, delusional parent just because it happens to suddenly be convenient for *them*. [1]

That sound about right?

Yep, I know.

So, the student and parent that inspired this particular anecdotal record fit all of the aforementioned criteria and then some. Do NOT, gentle reader, let that distract you from your assignment! YOU are to be the judge in this war in Heaven 'twixt this poor misguided angel and his mother of mercy and me, Mr. Meanie McMorningstar. [2]

PART I—COTTONBALLS and CODDLING

My student, let's call him Cottonballs Mayweather, was failing my class. I spoke to him several times in private, offered him supplementary assignments that I created just for him (centered around his interests,) and finally—just prior to Phase VI—gave him an ultimatum that, in order to pass for the year, EVERY assignment from there on in had to be **done, on time, complete,** and **typed or Emailed** (unless there was an extenuating circumstance.) I gave the same speech to two other female students that were in similar deep water.

His next assignment was a late, sloppily handwritten mess that was carelessly torn out of a spiral notebook and showed no attempt whatsoever to follow the directions for the assignment.

The other two students? One turned in a beautiful, thoughtful assignment; one submitted nothing. I called all three of them into the hallway and thanked the first girl—let's call her Cassandra Contrition—for the effort, but warned her that failure to sustain it would put her

---

(1) Largely because they think they have something to yell at you about, as opposed to having to face their own inadequacies.

(2) OK, so that was intentionally leading the witness via biblical blasphemy disguised as humor. I'm sorry.

"right back in the hole." She smiled, nodded, and went back into the room.

I told the second girl, Alyssa Von D (to whom I had spoken several times privately, trying to help her out and get to the bottom of her apathy) that she had sent a very clear message by submitting nothing after my warning. She forced a "tough girl" laugh and said "[she didn't] care" "Yes," I replied, *that's the message I got, and now I no longer feel compelled to care either."* She stared at me, stone faced, and when asked if she had anything else to add, continued to smile at Cottonballs, ignoring me and saying nothing.

Cottonballs' response, when I held his work in front of him, was to exhale loudly and roll his eyes and suggest that "At least I did somethin', and you should be happy with that."

I told him that I have an 11-year-old stepson with special needs (true) that would *never* be allowed to turn in work that looked that that (true.) I also told him that his work was a Grand Canyon away from 11th grade College Prep quality, (very true) and that while some teachers might be ok with that, I wasn't one of them. (true x infinity.)

Apparently, when I left, Alyssa Von D found her voice and told Cottonballs, and I quote: "Damn, Step called you retarded," and Mr. Mayweather took that information home to Mommy, who (after multiple unfruitful attempts to reach out to her) suddenly wanted a meeting.

I know I speak for teachers everywhere when I say how much we love this.

- You've had three interim reports,
- two report cards,
- an online parent portal with comments updated in real time,
- two parent teacher conference opportunities,
- and a back to school night.
- Your kid has been in detention,
- in-school suspension,
- and suspended *out of school* for a variety of offenses that would have gotten him thrown out of any college or business in the "real world,"

and only NOW,

after one teacher *allegedly* hurt your easily folded origami offspring's feelings,

do you demand we drop everything and meet with you?

Yes, we love that.

I tried, for years, to be compassionate to parents like this, only to be stabbed in the back and thrown under the bus by spineless administrators, and then attacked by parents and their obligatory representation,[3] who inevitably interpreted my compassion as weakness.

Boy, were they surprised, and offended, and *defeated* when I was finished with them.[4]

Now I just, unabashedly, treat these people the way they *think* they can treat others.

Example: Counselor (in this case Ms. Yellyfush,) calls parent, (in this case Ms. Imputen,) on speakerphone to accommodate (euphemism for bend over for) her request for an *immediate* meeting.

Counselor: "I have Ms. Imputen on the line."

Me: *"Who?"*

Counselor: "Ms. Imputen."

Me: *"Who?"*

---

(3) Because hey, you can't really talk about a kid you don't raise without a lawyer in the room, right?

(4) Here's a simple rule to live by: Don't fuck with people that are smarter then you, who also happen to have nuclear-grade legal representation, ESPECIALLY when your entire argument is based on the conjecture of a kid that doesn't know what conjecture means and MY rebuttal is based on extensive documentation.[5]

(5) I'm a writer, you nitwits; I write down EVERYthing.

Counselor: (nervously) "Ms. Imputen, Cottonballs Mayweather's mother."

Me: *"Oh, nice to finally meet you…"*

Ms. Imputen: "I don't know if you're going to…"

Me: (interrupting her, intentionally, with enough sweetness and venom to give you a cavity and kill you at the same time) *"Because I tried to reach you so many times, in so many different ways; I'm glad we can finally hook up."*

Ms. Imputen: "I'm coming in on Monday and…"

Me: *"No, that won't work, I have prior obligations all day Monday,* (true) *and Tuesday,* (true) *and besides,* (looking directly at the by-now-you've-noticed irrelevant counselor) *as **you** know, we're contractually obligated to have at least two working days to prepare for these meetings, so set something up with Ms. Yellyfush any time after Wednesday morning. I look forward to talking to you, and I'm **sure** Cottonballs' other teachers will want in on this, too."*[6]

Counselor AND Ms. Imputen: "Well if we could just…"

Me: *"And now if you'll excuse me, I really have to go. You know how it is, 120 kids that all want my attention, gotta go; looking forward to seeing you next week."*

And I'm off faster than a cheap prom dress. I've already wasted too much time on people that obviously don't give a shit about this kid's education, let them sort out the particulars and I'll be there when surgery is scheduled with my scalpel of truth.

---

(6)   They did. Oh yes, they did.

PART II—THE TRUTH IS THAT THE TRUTH HURTS

THAT FRIDAY MORNING: Surgery scheduled for 9:45 a.m.

Not Wednesday afternoon or even Thursday morning?

Interesting. I guess Cottonballs' current situation wasn't *that* urgent, after all.

I said that I would meet with Ms. Imputen *after some of the other teachers met with her* because:

1. I had a feeling she would be late. She was. Been there, done that: parents of misbehaved kids often try this power play, trying to give off the impression that they're too busy to be punctual. Screw you, I'm busy too, and I don't wait around for anyone, let alone someone who is inconveniencing me because they finally started pretending to act concerned about their kid's education.

2. I've been doing this long enough to know that Ms. Absentee Parent was going to try to shoot the messenger, so I felt bad for the teachers scheduled to speak before me. My plan was to enter, eviscerate, refute her accusations, and leave the leftovers for any teachers (un)fortunate enough to be scheduled after me.

Folks, if that sounds harsh, remember that, back on page one of this chapter, I asked you to be the judge. *I only ask that you read on before passing judgment one way or the other.*

And just so you know, I didn't START like this 24 years ago, but years of getting my heart broken, back stabbed, and dignity discarded (by the people who are supposed to support me) have thickened my skin and sharpened my fangs. But, as I may have mentioned before, I shake my rattle LOUDLY before I bite.

Which brings us back to Ms. Imputen, Cottonballs, Ms. Yellyfush and your favorite pseudo author. I entered the fray with the cool confidence of someone that had his facts straight, observations well documented, and case airtight. Yellyfush looked like a ship caught between the Scylla and

Charybdis[7] and Momma Imputen looked like she'd eaten a bad oyster and had a sneaking suspicion that she was about to eat an even bigger one.

I will recount the meeting in edited fashion so as not to bore you:

Ms. Imputen: "Alright, what bad news you gotta tell me?"

Big Bad Oyster: *"I don't have any news, beyond what we already discussed, I just have grades and facts, which I'll present, give you a copy to look over, and then I'll answer any questions you may have."* (I presented, gave, and waited.)

Ms. Imputen: "You said he didn't turn in some assignments…"

Cotttonballs (suddenly becoming circumspect): "What work didn't I do?"

Me (annoyed): *"What do you mean, what work didn't you do? I spelled out every assignment you didn't do at the time you didn't do them, and I just went over them with your Mom AND gave her a printout of them, but thank you for proving my point that your lack of attention is a bigger overall problem than one or two assignments."*

Cotttonballs: "See, you act all disrespectful…" (And Mom actually *nodded,* like she AGREED with him!)

Me (deadpan, and staring right at Cottonballs): *"Pointing out that you didn't do work is disrespectful? I'll just let that sit there for a minute.* (Now looking directly at Mom) *Ridiculous, right?* (Back to Cottonballs) *You've got a 36 in my class, but your other grades for the second marking period report card are 63, 35, 43…"*

Cottonballs: "That ain't got nothing to do…"

---

(7) Mythology reference—the monster and whirlpool that Odysseus had to sail between on the way home; often used as a metaphor for an unwinnable situation.[8]

(8) If you knew that, thank your English teacher, or whoever promoted literacy in your life.

Me (ignoring him): *"…41, 90 (in gym) and a 42, so are all those teachers disrespecting you, too?"*

Cottonballs: …

Me: *"No answer, right? I thought so. But I will tell you what is disrespectful, accusing someone of calling you retarded for constructively criticizing your work."*

Ms. Imputen: "Yes, I was going to bring that up, I find it…"

At this point, another teacher, Mr. Barg, who happened to be within earshot, felt compelled to interject on my behalf, letting mother of the year know that I am VERY publicly outspoken (both in speech and in print) against the use of the word retarded as a derogatory adjective.

Duly chastised and put in her place, **especially** after hearing the details of the actual alleged name calling, Ms. Imputen allowed me to nail the dismount.

Me: *"Now that we've established that MY points and concerns are based on facts, figures, and quantifiable evidence from myself and a host of other teachers, and that Cottonballs' arguments are based on miscommunication, lack of paying attention and/or outright lies, what would you like me to do for your son, moving forward, to facilitate his success?"*

Ms. Imputen: "Can he make up the work he missed?"[9]

Me: *"No, that would be an insult to the kids that actually DID the work on time and properly."*

Ms. Imputen: "Can he come to you for extra help?"

---

(9) Parents, please do not ask if your kid can make up all the work he/she chose to ignore all year. Try not doing your job for the next two months, then ask your boss if you can just "make it all up" now that it's convenient for you. Good luck with that.

Me (staring directly at 'Balls, who was either high [again] or almost asleep): *"Does he WANT to come for extra help?"*

Cottonballs: "Aight, I guess so."

Me: (Thinking to myself: "He sounds thrilled.") *"Fine, he can schedule help with me, and would you like me to keep you updated on his progress?"*

I got Mom's cell phone number, Mayweather remained, for the most part, conscious, other teachers filed in to assist in the surgery, and I was off to ponder how long it would take before Cottonballs shit all over the concerted efforts of all of the people trying to help him.

PART III—YOU CAN'T SPELL MANIPULATE WITHOUT I-M-P-U-T-E-N

Alyssa Von D, the charming young lady who would be out of school for 6-8 day stretches and return with new tattoos, she of the inflammatory "Damn, Step called you retarded" miscommunication, has dropped out of school. Apparently her second pregnancy would be complicated by pending possession-with-intent-to-distribute charges. Shocking, I know.

Meanwhile, Cottonballs is now up to—I shit you not—***sixty-one*** disciplinary referrals. I only point this out because Mom sent me an email that could only be described as confrontational regarding a 30/100 that Cottonballs 'earned' on a recent paper. OK, the email could have been described as confrontational AND grammatically deficient, but I didn't want to be petty, so I didn't say that.

She implied (even though I provided ridiculously specific rubrics, examples, sample papers, everything short of artificial intelligence to *do* the paper FOR him,) that his grade was an indication that: "prehaps [sic] you may not have done a most affective [sic] job in teaching him how to write the paper that he had to write."

(Yes, I printed that <u>exactly</u> as it was sent to me.)

So let me get this straight: 61 write ups, 9 detentions, 8 in-school suspensions, 6 out-of-school suspensions, his report card for the 3rd marking period reads 36, 63, 35, 43, 41, 90, and 42, he's in danger of failing 4 of those 7 classes for the YEAR, and he has come to school, at least twice, high as a kite, and *I'm* not doing *MY* job?

Well, you got part of that accusation right, lady;

someone isn't doing their job.

But, in the immortal words of David Hackworth: "If you find yourself in a fair fight, you didn't plan your mission properly." So, I sent home (as I told her I would) a copy of the paper with extensive notation all over it, along with the rubric with, again, extensive notation written all over it, and (I know—this was excessive—but worth it) a copy of the SAMPLE PAPER I gave the students, so she would know, with surgically acute precision, exactly why her little Cottonball got [an admittedly generous] 30 out of 100 on the paper he wrote that he had to write.

No response.

At all.

Ever.

And Cottonballs asked me if I could stay after school because he didn't understand the directions for a lyrics project that, I swear on the heads of my children, a fifth grader could understand.[10] I was so thunderstruck that I HAD to ask: "*did you give your Mom the envelope I sent home?*"

He smiled and said "Yeah."

"*And did she say anything?*"

"She said I should ask you to stay after school every day for you to help me."

"That's not going to happen, Cottonballs; one, anything we're doing now that it's almost May is review of things we've gone over multiple times all year. Two, one-on-one time out of my schedule to cover "new" material is called tutoring, and that's not what is warranted here."

---

(10) That is neither exaggeration nor conjecture, I stole the directions, verbatim, from one of my stepson's 5th grade class projects.

(Another fully baked smile) "So you sayin' you won't stay after school if I need help?"

*"No, that's what you **want** me to say. Or to be more specific, what your Mommy coached you to try to get me to say, but you're just two people in a long, LONG line of people that have tried to twist the truth so they could blame me for being responsible for their own shortcomings."*

"So you sayin'…"

*"I'm not done speaking yet, but I can tell that all of these words are too much for you, so just try to remember this part when you go in the hall and whip out your cell phone and call Mom to tell her it didn't work. Tell her that I will be here, every morning, from 6:15 to 6:45 **AM,** and every **FRIDAY** after school, if you need help."*

(No more smile, surprise surprise) "So if I come after school…"

At this point I almost lost it. *"It didn't work, Cottonballs, ok? It. Didn't. Work. And the fact that you don't get that explains why you're failing most of your classes. You're dismissed, I have prep work to do for my next class."*

"Y'all teachers are supposed to…"

*"Report you every time you come to class smelling like weed. Yes, we are. And I will, every time, from now on, **including today**."*

"What that got to do…"

"You're dismissed. And the next time you ask for time out of my schedule, at least have something ORIGINAL to say, instead of just being a puppet for somebody that's trying to get the one person that actually tried to help you in trouble."

Even though these events are some months behind me, I still get angry as I recall them; this is the type of shit that makes good teachers want to get out of the profession. To be honest, it's the second most disheartening thing about this job: trying to help kids become independent, autonomous, accountable beings for 8 hours a day, 5 days a week, *knowing* that many of the people influencing them for the *other* 128 hours of the week are fighting you every step of the way.

PART IV—WHAT GOES UP…

I was excited. I thought maybe my harsh reality pep talk turned things around with Cottonballs (sometimes that *does* happen with students) because he made it a point of getting to class on time for a few days, actually participated in the class discussion a few times, (little victories, people, little victories…) and turned in a fairly decent (albeit still containing errors that should've been corrected months ago) paper.[11] Then the warning signs started:

DAY ONE: *"Cotton, wake up, dude."*

       "I'm aight…" (Falls back to sleep)

A FEW DAYS LATER: *"Where is the written part of your assignment?"*

       "See, what had happened was…"

A FEW DAYS AFTER THAT: *"Where's Mayweather?"*

       (Destiny Acidosis) *"He's in in-school suspension."*

       "For?"

       (Destiny, along with a chorus of other students) *"Dumb shit!"*

DUMB SHIT: [dum shit] *noun.*

1. **Any act(s) perpetrated by an individual that could be universally agreed upon as beneath proper civilized behavior.**

---

(11) Sorry about the over-parentheses-ed paragraph; such are the drawbacks of having multiple voices in one's head.[12]

(12) The medication works, I just stop taking it when I write; you see how I'm willing to suffer for my readers?

2. The standard behavior of what we will politely call "at-risk" adolescents.

And what, you may ask, was *this* particular stick that Cottonballs added to his ever-growing[13] Wicker Man of dumbshittery?

Allow me to paraphrase from the actual disciplinary referral as it was posted:

[Cottonballs] Mayweather came to class 15 minutes late wearing a non-uniform hoodie and carrying a Burger King bag full of food. I told him he could not have that in class and he laughed at me. I asked him to get rid of it and he laughed at me again and started eating. I sent him to the office and he refused to go, so I called for an NTA[14] and he left before someone came. He came back 15 minutes later without a pass, sat down as the bell rang and left abruptly.

Charming.

I've been through this movie enough times to know when the Wicker Man is getting ready to burn, so I sent, in the name of proactive due diligence, yet another Email to Ms. Imputen letting her know, in unmistakable detail, exactly where our self-destructive mutual acquaintance stood, grade-wise. Shortly thereafter, I received an email from (Ms. Imputen's Email address) containing the written portion of Cottonballs' latest assignment, along with an explanation that they had been out of town for a wedding,[15] I sent the following email in return:

Ms. Imputen,

I hope this Email finds you well. Thanks for the assignment. I am not sure if you got my last

---

(13) As of the time of this writing, sixty-three disciplinary referrals. No additional comment needed.
(14) Non-teaching assistant.
(15) A three day, mid-week, hiatus from which he returned with a brand new, and pretty substantial, forearm tattoo.

91

extensive Email regarding Cottonballs' grade, so I reattached it below. The written part of this particular project didn't help matters much, and he still has to present (75% of the grade) but he was absent from Tuesday to Thursday—and he's in ISS today—so please let him know that he'll do the presentation portion of the project on Tuesday; enjoy your Memorial Day holiday.—Step

(Copied from May 12th Email.)

Ms. Imputen,

I'm in the process of alerting parents whose children are in danger of failing for the year and I wanted to give you a real-time update on Cottonballs. Obviously, from our two face-to-face meetings, texts, interim reports, report cards, GENESIS comments, etc. you know that your son has been up and down, grade-wise all year. Lately I've had to tell him to wake up in class and, despite the fact that he comes for help occasionally, it is usually not for assistance but merely for me to repeat what he failed to 'get' because he wasn't listening in class.

The hard numbers are as such: [His] current grade is a 45 and he needs an 88 to pass for the year. (The 45, to be completely honest, is generous on my part because, as all of my students know, during the 4th marking period, late work = 0 in my class and I have graded [his] late work, albeit taking points off for the lateness.)

We have 20 full days left and less than half of those will afford opportunities for grades, so I STRONGLY recommend he turn in the logical fallacy [extra credit] bingo assignment and get every remaining assignment in <u>on time</u> or he will be going into the final exam (which, I have been telling the students for a month now, is a monster writing assignment) needing, numerically, more than a perfect grade to pass.—Step

I expected an incendiary response.
I sharpened my fangs.
I prepared an erudite, albeit surgical retort.
I could not have been more wrong.

Hi Mr. Stepnowski,

Thank you for the update.

I will let Cottonballs know that he needs to be ready for Tuesday. I appreciate all of your efforts to help [him,] but at this point [he] needs to take responsibility for his actions or lack thereof. We all have gone above and beyond to help Cottonballs be successful. He's a smarter kid than he lets on, and I think he's totally capable of doing the work. I am at a loss as to why he insists on taking the difficult road. I hope he takes these last few weeks seriously.

Enjoy your Holiday as well,
Pseudonym Imputen

Damn.

Now I'm sad.

For real.

All I can do is shake my head, exhale, and move on; I grow tired of this same old song and dance, which always seems to end with me silently commiserating with a parent that is losing their child to a swirling vortex of bad decisions and peer pressure.

Normally I am brutally outspoken as to *why* these things happen, but now is not the time for that; now is the time to hold out—against what my past experiences have taught me—hope that C.M. will get his shit together in time to salvage the year and, in the process, get his Mom out of the doldrums that have taken ahold of her.

PART V—MUST COME DOWN.

Monday—Cottonballs cut my class, an act I took personally (and I told him so) because in my 24 years of teaching, literally, thousands of kids, I have had thirteen total cuts, and most of those came from two kids: one of whom was a self-destructive young man who—surprise

surprise—is currently having his daily itinerary designed by a Pennsylvania correctional facility, the other being a young lady that we'll discuss in a later chapter.

Tuesday—Mr. Mayweather was absent.

Wednesday—I was out getting a colonoscopy, which was OK because my other pain in the ass was in in-school suspension because of the cut and a few other disciplinary infractions performed *during* the cut.

Thursday—No Cottonballs in sight, because…

Friday—Cottonballs Mayweather, arrested on possession with intent to distribute.

The "difficult road?"

No.

The easy road, a well lubricated water slide right down the classroom to prison pipeline that has been working with ruthless efficiency for decades in this country.

And just like that, chapter over.
And you are left unfulfilled, as we teachers often are.

JEUSUS—0,
JERSEY DEVIL—1

"Just as every cop is a criminal,
and all the sinners saints,
as heads is tails just call me Lucifer,
'cause I'm in need of some restraint"
—*Mick Jagger & Keith Richards*

After I, or a student, parent, co-worker, counselor, "educational reformer,"[1] administrator, or anyone else for that matter, engage in some epic screwupery, I am fond of observing: "Sometimes this shit writes itself!"[2] Such was the case with this particular chapter.

I had just finished reading several of the cantos (chapters) from Dante's *Inferno* with four of my classes. The kids actually liked it; I think I weaved enough of the contemporary zeitgeist in with the 14th century epic poem to keep it relevant and exciting.[3] Come on, what teenager doesn't love the concept of a Dungeons and Dragons topography of perfectly executed punishment spread out among mythological beasties and a landscape that would make any video game designer proud? A chance to hate on the haters and describe it in epic detail; awesome, right? Right.

---

(1) When speaking of said 'reformers,' I must defer to Garrison Keller, who brilliantly observed that "When you wage war on…public schools, you're attacking the mortar that holds the community together. You're not a conservative, you're a vandal."

(2) The irony—and possible accuracy—of referring to my own writing as shit is not lost on me.

(3) Mind you, Dante Alighieri needs about as much help making his work exciting and relevant from me as I need help from gorillas on how to fling shit. SEE PREVIOUS FOOTNOTE.

Wrong. Well, not totally wrong, because it wasn't the teenager that had a problem with it.[4]

I gave my students a project to design their own "9 levels of Hell," and put whomever they wanted in there, but, in keeping with the theme of 'perfect justice,' their explanations of the crimes (and their subsequent punishments,) had to be precise and eloquent, even if they were twisted in nature, (and I certainly hoped they *were*.)

For the sake of supreme clarity, here are the instructions that were given, along with the rubrics (which I won't waste precious pages showing you; assume they were more specific than your weird neighbor's "safe word" when he goes to the bondage club.)

HERE ARE THE INSTRUCTIONS THAT WERE GIVEN TO EACH KID

Survey of Lit & Comp GT/CP   Step's Class   The *Inferno* Project

In *The Divine Comedy*, Dante takes the reader on a journey through Hell. For this project, you will create your own version of Hell, loosely based on what we read in *The Inferno*.

You must include a *guide* (and a picture OF that guide, and an explanation as to WHY you chose him/her; fictional characters are fine, provided the explanation is appropriate.)

> ➢ Your Hell must contain, as Dante's does, nine sections.
> ➢ You must include a different vice/sin for each section <u>and</u> *what you feel is an appropriate punishment* for the people in that section and, in keeping with the theme of the poem, focus on making your punishments 'perfectly fit' the crime.
> ➢ You must include ***an example*** in each section (a specific person or type of person (profession?) that belongs there.)

---

(4) Teachers out there—you probably already know where this is going and can finish the chapter in your heads, having dealt with similar shite yo damn self, so feel free to move on to the next chapter (or, stick around for some of that cheeky linguistic assault and battery I know y'all love.)

➤ Reminder, this is a contemporary interpretation of a 14th century poem, so you need not include any religious affiliations, nor are you constrained by the ideals of the time (unless you WANT to, or want to be.) Have fun with it—I gave you **funny** and **serious** examples; so you know what's possible.

➤ Check your rubrics and/or go to our Google Classroom for SPECIFIC information and examples of what I'm looking for.

Your project must be **visual.**

➤ You may make a poster, a PowerPoint, a Prezi, etc., in which **all** nine sections of your Hell must be represented.

➤ Some of you are techno-geniuses, so this is a chance for you to flex your muscles and wow the crowd (and your archaic teacher) with some killer visuals.

➤ BONUS POINTS for "stunning" visuals

You MUST include a **written explanation** for each level

➤ One short paragraph per section and one paragraph explaining your choice of guide—10 paragraphs in all—will suffice.

➤ You must explain why you find each particular vice/sin so vile and why you feel that those who commit this vice/sin must be punished.

➤ You must justify why their punishment fits the crime.

➤ BONUS POINTS for thoroughly detailed/thought provoking explanations

You may present, **for up to an additional 50 BONUS POINTS**, your project to the class.

➤ You may **not** simply read your written explanation; you know me, I **rarely** offer extra credit, so if I do—you're going to have to EARN it with some solid public speaking. (See extra credit rubric.)

> ➤ WHY is the vice/sin a problem to you, the world, society, etc.?
> ➤ HOW do your punishments "fit" the crimes?
> ➤ WHY did you choose the visual images in your presentation?
>   Assignments are due, and presentations will begin on
>   _____.

Pretty standard, right? I showed the students some prior kids' work, and made a few funny "Step's Hell" slides myself so they had a variety of visual examples to work with, and I gave them two full days in class[5] to get started on the project, and an additional four days at home to finish it, along with the plethora of bonus point opportunities you read about.

Generous, right? Giving my cherubs a chance to start their final marking periods off with all of those easy points. I mean, you could say I was downright *angelic*.

Fallen angelic, according to one disgruntled mother. Alas, this would not be the first time I was put in the company of the man downstairs, and it probably won't be the last, but this one—for purposes of unique entertainment—took the Devil's food cake.[6]

On the day the project was due, N'Aybuld Johnson, 9th grader, tried (**while** I'm getting class started, taking attendance and prioritizing volunteers to present their projects) to hand me an envelope with N'AYBULD written on it. *"Why are you giving this to me?"* I inquired, *"it has YOUR name on it."*

She just shrugged, smirked, and held out the envelope, which I ignored until she mustered enough effort to mumble "it's from my Mom." The rest of the kids, annoyed by her blatant disregard for, uh, EVERYthing else going on in the class, seemed ok with me taking the envelope and remarking that *"she might want to put MY name on the envelope next time, then, yes?"*

Another shrug, and an eye roll. One can only wonder why N'Aybuld has a "D" average across the board and is currently failing my class for the *year*.

---

(5) Thank you, Tara "TG Punk" Gillespie, for securing the laptop carts for me two days before Spring Break—you're a goddess.

(6) Or Angel food cake, whatever gets your flag up the pole.

The letter started with three words in blue ink

My Mom Said

Followed by, I kid you not, a letter (in different handwriting and black ink) that explained why

"I will not be doing the "dante Inferno" [sic] project because it goes against my religion." (NOTE: it's not *your* project Mom, but whatever, I know what you mean.)

First off, please understand that no matter how accurately I reproduce this letter, I can't do the *appearance* of it justice: A piece and a half (yes, the second sheet was torn unevenly in half) of handwritten (complete with cross outs, scribbles, and words crammed into the margins) rambling.

I know I have made several references already to my stepson Brendan, and how [despite his clinically diagnosed "learning issues,"] I don't allow him to turn in half-assed, sloppy work; so, just for confirmation purposes, I'll call him in.

"Hey Bren!"

"Yeah?"

"What would happen if you tried turning this in as your homework?"

"One of your students—wait, did **you** tear the second paper in half?"

"Just answer the question, Bren."

"You'd kill me."[7]

"Thank you. You can go."

_____

(7) The boy speaks metaphorically, I have yet to kill any of my offspring for any of their improprieties, big or small.[8]

(8) Yet.

"One of your students turned that in?"

"No, a parent did."

(shocked look) "A GROWN UP did that?"

(Admittedly devilish smile) *"That's what I thought. Thank you. You can go."*

Furthermore, the letter was—well, let me just give you a little taste. Here are the three opening [run on] sentences, reproduced, verbatim, to the hastily written letter:

" I willnot be doing the "dante Inferno" [sic] project because it goes against my religion." Jehovah set the standards for us to stay away from the unclean things (2 Corinthians) 6:17)[9] "Therefore, get out from among them and seperate [sic] yourselves, says Jehovah, and quit touching the unclean thing and I willtake you in." I want to have an approved relationship with the God of the Bible Jehovah, and I am doing so I am trying to follow in Jeusus Christ [sic] footsteps..."

And on and on for another page and a half (and a half!) with no mention whatsoever of me, N'aybuld, the project instructions, OR her sister Humilde', who was in my class (at the 12th grade level), and also had to do the project. The letter ended, predictably, to be honest, with

"So therefore I willnot participate in any part of the Inferno projectt." [sic]

Yeah, Mom, believe it or not, I managed—in between the hastily written Catechism lesson—to figure that out.[10] I guess you missed that whole thing about **NOT NEEDING "[to] include any religious**

---

(9)   I didn't verify if this was correct or not, because I didn't care; mad props for the parenthetical citation though!

(10) Before you pick up YOUR black or blue pen and write me a hate letter telling me I'm a judgmental prick who mocks people for less than stellar literacy and/or their religious beliefs, let me save you some time.
  1.   Fuck you, I don't care what you think, and
  2.   I am not mocking her writing ability, simply questioning the righteousness of someone that would judge ME (remember, you didn't get the whole letter) and yet represent themselves as a guardian in such a manner; finally
  3.   I'm not anti ANY religion, provided its followers don't have the narcissistic audacity to tell me what is "right" or "wrong."

affiliations...unless you WANT to" in the directions.

And, just for the record, I thought Jehovah's witnesses respected the choices that others made in religious matters. "So then, each of us will render an account for himself to God"[11] sound about right?[12]

Alas, I guess I won't be one of the 144,000.

And your daughter N'Aybuld won't be getting out of doing SOMEthing to earn the points she will so desperately need to pass *this* marking period, despite her blatant (blasphemous) attempt to wield YOUR religious beliefs to get out of doing HER work. You see, Humilde' was very forthcoming about the fact that neither she, nor N'Aybuld were offended, or in any way opposed to, the project. That being said, I will never fault a child for honoring her mother's wishes, as N'aybuld was doing; I only question when that acquiescence disguises a deeper motivation. After all, "lying lips are an abomination to the Lord, but those who deal truthfully are his delight." (Proverbs 12:22)

So, I took the liberty of responding, in kind with, what I thought was a firm but fair riposte:

Ms. Johnson,

I will certainly accommodate your personal feelings regarding the Dante's Inferno project; however, telling me that you and your daughter wouldn't be participating <u>on the day the project was due</u> (versus 6 days ago when it was assigned) leaves us with minimal time to arrange a suitable replacement, as N'Aybuld must do <u>something</u> to earn the 200+ points the project could have earned her.

Perhaps she can just modify the assignment and describe 9 potential rewards in heaven, with a specific description of the rewards each soul is afforded for his/her good deeds on Earth? If you'd prefer to avoid any religious subject matter at all, you'll have to let me know quickly so I can arrange a suitable replacement project that N'aybuld can do by Wednesday. (That will give her the 6 days provided to the other students, and get the grade in by the established deadline.)

N'Aybuld's current grade—not counting this project, or lack

---

(11) Romans 14:12 (12)

(12) News Flash: I've read your book, and all similar texts, more than a few times.

*thereof—is a 50, which, combined with her 52 (2nd marking period) and 62 (1st marking period) puts her in **serious** jeopardy of failing this particular class for the year, so time is of the essence. Please, help me to help your daughter by offering an acceptable alternative to the project as quickly as possible. Thank you.*

—Mr. Step

I gave that letter to N'Aybuld at the end of class (Wednesday) with specific instructions to give it to Mom so we could come up with a mutual solution, and informed her (for about the 666th time) about her current academic situation.

Wednesday night? No Email, no text, no call—nada.

Thursday—rien.

Friday—nichts.

"No response to my letter from Mom, huh?"

N'aybuld smiled that teenage girl smile; you know, the one that announces the naïveté of a kid that is painfully unaware how obvious they are.

"Because you never gave her the letter."

N'aybuld frowned that teenage girl frown; you know, the one that announces the shock of a kid that can't figure out how you KNOW that (because they're painfully unaware how obvious they are.)

*"Because you didn't **start** the project until the **night before** it was due, which is why your mother didn't contact me until two days ago. Then she heard you complaining, loudly, about how 'hard' the project was and then she asked you about it, and when she expressed her offense, you played along, although we BOTH know you don't share Mom's faith and dedication, because you thought it would get you out of doing the project."*

N'aybuld's eyes got progressively wider, as I got progressively closer until, by the end, I was about 12 inches from her face and she looked, for all the world, like a concerned PowerPuff girl caught with her hand in the catechism cookie jar.

I continued: *"But you forget, I teach your sister Humilde', and* **she** *was almost halfway done her project a few days ago, so she had to be—what?—just about wrapping up when you pulled your stunt, which probably pissed big sis off just enough to* (and I will confess to having enunciated the next five words for dramatic effect) *Call. You. On. Your. Bullshit*[13] *right in front of Mom, which probably led to a near fistfight between you two while Mom was off in the next room writing her letter to me. That sound about right?"*[14]

As if the forces of nature wanted to show me that I was justified, the bell rang JUST as I finished.

Me: Cat that ate the canary smile.

N'aybuld: Canary in a coalmine.

Monday—không có gì.[15]

So now it was time to get proactive and prove my fortune telling skills yet again:

"Still no reply from Mom?" (Deep breath from N'Aybuld, complete with a look that would freeze beer.) *"Interesting. You know Humilde' emailed me Friday night asking for anything she could do to make up the grade, right?"*

---

(13) Don't even act like you didn't read that slowly for dramatic effect.

(14) Not exactly, but DAMN close, as verified later in the day by Humilde', who laughed at how close I was in my prognostication of the actual events that went down at casa de Johnson.

(15) Having exhausted my usual Spanish, French and German, I consulted one of my Vietnamese students for the word for "nothing." I cannot verify whether this is correct or not, but she's a great kid, so I'm going to go to publication with tin tưởng in my heart.

"That's her; that ain't me."

"Very true, that's why I requested a parent teacher conference. Mom's coming in tomorrow, so she's finally going to see those grades you've been trying to keep from her. Mom's not much for computers, right? So, she really has no idea how you're doing in here, (more enunciation for dramatic effect) Or. Every. Other. Class."[16]

TRUTH: I never requested the parent-teacher conference, Humilde' already informed me that Mom wouldn't come, and that after she was informed (BY Humilde') about the reality of the situation on all sides, Ms. Johnson said, simply but eloquently, "That's on N'aybuld."

True dat, Momma J.

"Seriously," I continued, *"'cause I have to ask—did you really think you could just keep your mother in the dark until you had to be driven to Summer school five days a week? Or did you plan on trying to hide that, too? Seriously, N'aybuld, how the heck did you think this was going to end? Or did you just not think at all?"*

Nothing. Nada, rien, nichts, không có gì, *nic nie*[17] from our young canary in the coal mine. I know, you're thinking: "Wow...really?"
Really.
Well, you'll be happy to know that Humilde' turned in a stellar presentation on a short 2015 article by Anya Kamenetz called *How Schools Are Handling an 'Overparenting' Crisis*[18] and went on to do very well for the 3rd marking period.
And N'aybuld?
Apparently, she saves up all of her talking for the minute she leaves

---

(16) It's hard to shock me, after everything I've seen in my teaching career, but I'm still dumbfounded when teenagers believe that, if they just ostrich their heads in the ground and act like (insert dilemma) doesn't exist, that they can keep it hidden forever with no eventual accountability.
(17) Polish—just showing off now. That's for you, Babci!
(18) Yes, absolutely intentional; I am nothing if not a master of irony.

class, as it was reported to me by more than a few of my fallen angels that, according to the crestfallen canary, "it's a good thing Mr. Step give Hell projects 'cause he the devil."

Pleased to meet you,

glad you guessed my name.

Epilogue
The Devil is in the Lil' Durk Details

As happens so often in this job, many of our little leopards spend an inordinate amount of time trying to change their spots, only to walk into a clearing, totally exposing themselves to predators.

And I, my friends, would be remiss if I failed to tell you about our little leopard's lapse in logic regarding lyrics that she loved that led to laughter and sweet, sweet vindication.

After yet another incident when N'aybuld, tried (unsuccessfully, Humilde' was on to her now and threatened to go to her counselor) to get out of another homework assignment "because it offend[ed] [her] religiousness,"[19] little Miss get-right-with-God and the rest of her classmates had to do the Lyrics Project, a Mr. Step original that students look forward to all year.[20] They have to choose a song, based entirely on the lyrical content, that they love. One paragraph on what they think the artist is trying to say and another paragraph or two on why the song resonates with them. They start playing the song and, as I play DJ and fade it out, they present their responses to the class.

Easy peezy lemon squeezy; a fun and high interest project to start ringing the year to a close. I always offer the kids who are struggling a chance to go first, second or third for bonus points.

N'aybuld had to be almost forced to go next to last (insert eyes looking skyward in frustration emoji.)

But oh...sweet mother of redress, was it worth the wait.

I will assume, gentle reader, for purposes of not casting aspersions, that you are not familiar with the vocal stylings of one "Lil' Durk," 23-year-old rapper from Chicago. Allow me, then, to quote extensively

(19) Yes, she used the word religiousness.
(20) Got a whole chapter dedicated to this one comin' up.

from N'aybuld's favorite song, *My Beyonce (featuring Dej Loaf)*, which spoke to her because, and I painstakingly quote N'aybuld correctly here: "I got a boy and I know he might be doin' me dirty but I'ma do whatever I got to do to hold onto him."

Trippin' on that drank, but I know she worth it
Independent baby, I know she workin'
Adriana Sevan dranks, 20 bottles, urgent
I know it can be better but nobody's perfect
We flirted for a minute, DeJ, that's my baby
I ain't trippin', I'm like Henny, yeah I'm in her kidneys
She like to play her songs to the way I'm hittin' it
Turn around like, "Damn Durk I like the way you hittin' it"

I hit it from the front, I like the back too
She say, "Lay down so I can ride you"
I know that she feinding
She scratchin' my back, I like how she screamin'
I fuck her and leave her, she feinding
Shawty my Beyoncé[21]

Call me crazy, but I do not think Jesus, Jehovah, Jay-Z or any other deity starting with "J" would approve of these shenanigans; and I'm pretty sure Ms. Johnson's head would explode if I informed her as to just how far little N'aybuld had strayed from that "approved relationship with the God of the Bible Jehovah."

Does it make me immature that I smiled like the Cheshire Cat on nitrous oxide while this presentation was going on? So be it.

Of course, to drop this 10-megaton bomb of inappropriateness and gratuitous sexuality on poor Ms. Johnson (who had, just last week, apologized, via Humilde', for N'aybuld's behavior) would be just mean spirited, and N'aybuld **did**—according to the letter of the law—satisfy all of the requirements of the project, so I gave her the appropriate grade, which no doubt perked up the Johnson household for a few days.[22]

---

(21) Lyrics by Lil Durk. From the album 300 Days and 300 nights.
(22) Suck on THAT, people that think I'm just a big Blue Meanie!

I did, however, call Humilde' into the hall three periods later when her 12th grade class arrived. She's a pretty sharp cookie, so she knew *exactly* what I wanted to talk about: "I know. I know, Step. N'aybuld's song…that's nasty, right? You shoulda heard the FIRST song she was gonna do. (Winces) I was like 'N'aybuld you can't play that mess in school. That's disgusting. Nigga this and nigga that and all that nasty sex stuff.' But (sighs) Nay made her own bed and now she's gotta lay in it."

Hard to argue with that, so we laughed and went back into the room to begin another round of lyrics project presentations; as we were going in Humilde' actually said: "You should put this in your new book, Step. It's crazy." I agreed (obviously) but pointed out that *"you know I'm gonna come across like the bad guy though, right?"*

The first presenter of the day was Victoria Thorisdottir.

Her song?

Runnin' With the Devil by Van Halen.

I took that as a sign.

A 2 FOR NO DESK = 1 FINGER FOR LADY MACBETH

"Leadership can't be fabricated.
If it is fabricated and rehearsed,
you can't fool the guys in the locker room."
—*Junior Seau*

Let's jump right into another sad but unfortunately true anecdote from the anals[1] of (oh, let's call it) MacDuff High School:

TEACHER EVALUATIONS. A term that conjures the same sort of warm, fuzzy feelings as other two-word colloquialisms: inconvenient truth, root canal, premature ejaculation, and human centipede, just to name a few. Actually, those terms are serendipitously appropriate, because teacher evaluations are usually preceded by teacher *observations*, which are usually inconvenient, invasive, too short to satisfy anyone, and usually involve unpleasantry of the highest level.

Let me tell you a tale. *(Feel free to insert a crusty pirate voice to this anecdote for additional flavor.)* A tale of woe, heaped upon an innocent lad[2] what had his furniture pilfered and was subsequently forced to walk the plank.

Seriously, I got punished because someone *stole a chair* from my room during a period *when I wasn't in there*. But that's just the **start** of the epic screw job here, folks, trust me.

One of my administrators, Lady Macbeth, wanted to come in and observe my class. At a time of her choosing, although I would certainly

---

(1) Yes, I KNOW it is spelled annals, and that it means historical records, but since this story is about an asshole or two, I thought you'd appreciate the cheap pun.
(2) OK, maybe not innocent, but certainly righteous.

be consulted about whether there were any cool lessons on the horizon I would *like* her to see. She would come in, sit for an entire period, perhaps engage with the students and myself. Later, we would get together, discuss the things she liked about the class, and then we could engage in some spirited dialogue about how I could improve as an instructor. After signing the obligatory paperwork that accompanies such mandatory unpleasantries, we would agree to meet at a later time. Maybe Lady Macbeth would even come and visit again to observe whether I had improved in those fields we had *mutually agreed* were areas of need.

HaHAhaHAhahAHaHa! Yeah, that's how it's *supposed* to work.

SSShhhh…if you're vewy vewy quiet, you'll hear the sound of tens of thousands of teachers laughing that sour, decidedly un-funny laugh.

Instead, it went something like this:

Lady Macbeth told me she was coming in to my 4th period class on a Wednesday in April to observe a Socratic seminar (think organized debate/discussion) we were going to have about—mother of all ironies—the state of education in America.

Lady Macbeth didn't show; she was busy.

No worries, one comes to expect these things. See you tomorrow? Sure. Same time? Sure.

Again, Lady Macbeth didn't show; she got "caught up with pressing business."

Deep breath. How about next week? We'll be working on a follow-up, but nonetheless relevant, non-fiction article that I just found about the cram schools in China; the students will be writing papers that correspond with their SGO[3] goals. How does that sound? Great.

L to the McB didn't show. To be fair, PARCC[4] testing had just begun, so the entire administrative team were running around like

---

(3) SGO = Student Growth Objective, which = long-term academic goals for groups of students set by teachers in consultation with their supervisors. At least, that's what they're supposed to be. Be vewy, vewy quiet…hear that?

(4)) PARCC—*Partnership for Assessment of Readiness for College and Careers*. Quite simply, one of the most apocalyptic clusterfucks to ever be forced upon the student population of this country,[5] but you already know that if you've read up to this point.

hyper-caffeinated Chihuahuas on fire.

Fast forward about ten days; the fallout from the PARCCocalypse was still lingering around MacDuff High School like the smoldering ruins of Tokyo, post-Godzilla visit. Your humble author and his co-teacher, Ms. Lionheart, had had[6] our class cut in half during most of that time to allow for testing, so we were just coming back together, as a class. The students were righteously and severely pissed; they were also nearly anesthetized from two weeks of time wasted in stiflingly hot rooms staring at computer screens and waiting for poorly performing technology to cooperate.

Lady Macbeth texted me: "Can we do tomorrow? I can come in tomorrow for a few minutes." Only now, as I type this, do I realize there is no "Are you fucking kidding, motherfucker?" emoji.

So I typed "Sure" instead.

This, folks, is called "playing ball."

I informed the students that we would be getting observed tomorrow—their responses were epic, but profanity-laden, and there is simply no room for such salty language here—and Ms. Lionheart and I stayed after school to review what we were going to do to salvage the educational week following the PARCC testing (aka-Gojira-meets-Tokyo tour.)

The good news? **We're kick ass teachers and our students love and/or respect us because they know we bust our asses for them,** so things would still go smoothly and the kids would still learn something valuable.

None of which, apparently, meant three witches' worth of shit to Lady Macbeth.

To accommodate her, I did my "pre-conference," literally, minutes before walking into the class. The pre-conference is *supposed* to be where we go over what the administrator is going to see, how it coincides within the context of the current lesson, etc. so the observer in question has something resembling a clue about what he/she is about

---

(5) "The opinions of Mr. Stepnowski are his alone, and do not reflect the opinions of any place wherein he is currently employed."—Love and kisses, His legal team.

(6) Yes, it's grammatically correct. Look it up.

to observe. Again, in my experience, this almost never happens, and this was no exception.[7] We finished a hasty *"hey you DO realize this is only the second time we've been together in almost two weeks, so observe accordingly, ok?"* and I left as the bell rang to start 4th period with Lady M following shortly behind.

She stayed for about 15 (of the 45) minutes, looked at her laptop for most of that time, didn't speak to one student (although one student felt compelled to say something to *her*,) and called me into her office over two weeks later[8] to review my performance.

If you're a teacher, you know the drill; if not, I'm sure our evaluations are similar to whatever methods they use to evaluate you at your job: they change often, they discourage actual interaction between you and your "evaluator," and they offer a cookie-cutter drop down menu of wordy, irrelevant, legalspeak bullshit that does nothing to professionally evaluate, engage, or evolve you. How could it? If I pop my head in Lady Macbeth's office for 15 minutes and she's eating lunch and watching platypus porn, I don't assume that's what she does all year, and I certainly don't assume that adequately reflects her yearlong grind.

No such luck the other way because, to quote the old saying, "shit rolls *downhill.*"[9]

It got a little heated between me and Lady MC to the B, so I'll just give you the juicy parts. Most of these things are done on a 1—4 scale. In this case: Non-efficient, Partially Efficient, blah blah blah. Seriously, anybody reading this knows 4 means you're awesome, 3 means you're good, 2 means you need work, 1 means you suck, so why disguise it?.[11]

---

(7) More on the whole dog and pony show that is "teacher observation" in a later chapter, I promise.

(8) She must have been busy trying to get that damned spot out.

(9) Oh, and by the way, our lovely "$chool reformer$" and the corrupt politician$ that $upport them want to tie teacher evaluation$ to their $alary and JOB $ECURITY.[10]

(10) How very convenient...an arbitrary method to use as "proof" that teachers "aren't doing their jobs properly" (as if one of these fucktards would even know what that looks like.) That might be just we need to grease the wheels for the privatization movement, dontcha think?

(11) If you ever get a chance to read my 2nd book SC.R.E.W.E.D., An Educational Fairytale please check out pages 146—148 to see how this grading insanity has trickled down to the elementary level.

In twenty-four years of teaching, I've endured about 60 of these things, and I've never received anything below a 3.

Lady Macbeth gave me four 2s.

Four 2s.

Let's get ready to rumble.

Let me state for the record that **one** of the "2s" may have, according to a strict literal interpretation of the drop down menu criteria, actually been justified, because I did carry most of the conversation during the whopping 15 minutes my fair Lady spent in the room, largely because, *again*, this was our second day together as a class after two weeks of bullshit testing and I spent the FIRST day listening to my crass constituency complain about how the last two weeks were bullshit... and testing...and bullshit...and testing...and bullshit.

So ya got me there, Lady Macbeth.

Well played, you spectacularly non-empathetic, gloriously out of touch bitch.

The OTHER 2s were so obviously manufactured (mandated?) "knock those teachers down a peg" nut shots that they almost don't warrant discussion.

Almost, except for the one I received *because there weren't enough desks in the room*.

Here's the scenario: I hadn't **been** in the room for two periods, and you'll remember, she squeezed the ol' pre-conference in right up to the bell, so I didn't have time to, nor did I expect to have to, *count the fucking desks* in my room.

Started teaching, everybody's paying attention; one student who, (and this is well known,) cuts almost every class except mine, comes in a few minutes late (with a pass,) and knows not to disturb me in mid-speech. So, he looks around, grabs a chair, pulls up next to another student's desk, and starts reading along with the article we're covering; he even asks a question (this is a big deal for him) during the lesson. I should mention that, in addition to cutting more than an ADHD scherenschnitte artist, the aforementioned "deskly challenged" lad is *allegedly* minoring in pharmaceutical distribution and aggravated assault, so the fact that he CAME to class, OVERCAME the obvious distraction[12] and got down to WORK should have earned nothing short of a major street named after me.[13]

But Noooooooooooooooooooooo...

INTERMISSION: Those of you out there not in the teaching profession? I hear you, my astute readers. You're thinking: "This dude is spending a lot of my valuable reading time bitching about some 2 on some evaluation and a stupid desk." And right you would be(!) were this not symbolic of a more insidious "bigger picture" that threatens to chase the few remaining dedicated teachers out of your children's classrooms.

But it is, so with your permission, I'll continue.

Now, where was I? Ah, yes...

But Noooooooooooooooooooooo. Instead, I was told that I was partially effective in the keeping of my room.

Me. The guy who came, (after finding out he was being moved, literally, two doors down the hallway,) during the Summer, in 100-degree weather, on my own time, to clean up, hump out, and/or move around filing cabinets, teachers' desks and other furniture/ accoutrement that were just dumped unceremoniously into my new home.[14]

Me, the guy who, literally, fixed the [one salvageable] teacher's desk and podium with my own tools, *before* arranging, and re-arranging, and RE-rearranging the room for maximum available space *before* decorating it with posters and bulletin board material.

Me, the neat freak idiot that cleans up even after the other teachers I share the room with let their little cherubs destroy it and steal my shit.

Oh, and just so ya know, FOUR teachers share that room with me. Know how many didn't do diddly dick in the "maintenance of the classroom environment?"

---

(12) Anyone who has ever read an IEP or taught/lived with a student of this nature knows that ANY small deviation from the norm is usually grounds for a shit storm of classroom disruption.

(13) OK, maybe an alley, in a small neighborhood, in a non-major metropolitan area.

(14) Fact. Documented. I'm mildly OCD so I show up every summer and get my shit together, no matter what it takes, so I can sleep the week before school starts.

Three. So, by my math…

4—3 = 1, which is the number of fingers I have for the Lady Macbeth.

Needless to say, our *post* conference ended with two words. (Yes, *those* two words; not kidding, I was that pissed.) The fact that those words went largely unchallenged, and the fact that I still have a job, autonomy, and—if you can believe it—the respect of Lady Macbeth, lets me know, in some small Shakespearean tragedy way, that she *knew*, by trying to screw me with an unfair evaluation, she was the equivalent of the police officer that pulls over the minivan going one mile over the speed limit because it's *safer* than pulling over the sedan with the blacked-out windows doing 60 in a 25-mph zone.

It ain't illegal, but it sure ain't right.

Alas, "Life's but a walking shadow, a poor player that struts and frets his hour upon the stage and then is heard no more: it is a tale told by an idiot, full of sound and fury, signifying nothing" *(V. v. 2381—2384).*

And speaking of a tale told by an idiot, on to the next chapter!

A STRANGE REQUEST THAT TURNED OUT TO BE A NOT-SO-STRANGE REQUEST THAT TURNED INTO A FRIGHTENING REVELATION

"Well, I went to the doctor.
I said, 'I'm feeling kind of rough'
'Let me break it to you, son, Your shit's fucked up.'
I said, 'my shit's fucked up?
Well, I don't see how.'
He said, 'The shit that used to work—It won't work now.'"
—Warren Zevon

How's *that* for a chapter title? Bit wordy, right? I know, but it fits. In my 3rd book, *Teaching Sucks; But We Love It*, I had a chapter entitled *You're Killing Me (quite literally,)* and the message contained therein has not, I regret to say, become irrelevant some five years later.

I have been enjoying a standing blood pressure of 200/110 for about a month now. I know this only because my wife is a doctor and, as such, just happens to have a blood pressure cuff and stethoscope handy, as well as nearly unlimited access to me.

"Yes, hon, I know that's bad. Yes, dear, I know that when I was powerlifting my BP was probably in the 'near spontaneous death' range. Yes, my love, I will go to the doctor's, and yes, I will even consider taking... TAKE! I meant TAKE! medicine if you think it is in my best

115

*interest. Other than that, I don't know WTF to tell you, darling. I don't smoke, don't do drugs, I work out religiously, eat generally healthily and all that jazz, but we do have four teenagers, your parents live with us, and, oh yeah, **I teach High School**, so that nuclear-grade plutonium stress level ain't going anywhere in any fucking hurry, my precious flower."*

*"No, I'm not getting an attitude[1] ...yes, I'll check in with the school nurse if I feel like ...NO, I was NOT rolling my eyes...[2] yes, I understand the severity of this, and yes, I'm aware, but are YOU aware that this **conversation** is raising my blood pressure?!?"[3]*

So, after an unusually refreshing Sunday night slumber[4] I was up and out by the usual 6 A.M. to make Monday my bitch and teach the daylights out of some teenagers, willing or unwilling. Strangely, as of nearly 1 P.M., my plan was working flawlessly—the lessons were flowing like pristine spring water and the kids were drinking it like thirsty forest animals.[6] So how surprised was I when, around 1:30 P.M., during my prep period, as I sat in the library editing and grading papers at an unusually leisurely pace, I suddenly felt like John Travolta slammed me in the heart with a needle full of adrenaline?[7]

I went into the nurse's office and, bless her heart, she smiled and asked what she could do for me; no easy feat to be charming after a day of what the normal school nurse endures, I can tell you. I told her I had a strange request, and wondered if she could take—

"Your blood pressure? Sure, sit down right here," she replied, as if I'd asked her to borrow her stapler, picking a blood pressure cuff that was conspicuously **right there.**

---

(1) Yes, I was.

(2) Yes, I was.

(3) Yes, I was going to sleep alone that night; shoulda never used the old question mark/exclamation point/question mark combo...

(4) Very unusual, ask any teacher; the anxieties of the week ahead very often seize teachers around late afternoon on Sunday, thus heightening their awareness and anxiety.[5]

(5) While this adds to the je ne sais quoi of watching The Walking Dead, it sucks for facilitating restful sleep.

(6) OK, so that was a bit of overindulgent metaphoring...

(7) Pulp Fiction allusion. The part of Uma Thurman was, in this case, unfortunately, being played by me.

The surprise on my face must have been easily identifiable, and she and her assistant chuckled "that's a very normal request here, right?" Her assistant nodded and confirmed that several people A DAY came in to make sure they weren't in (her words) "the danger zone."

Several people *a day*? I wondered. There has *got* to be something behind that cardiac conga line.

Could it be the profession itself?

I took to personal interviews, emails, and social media to do some informal research into whether a jokingly titled chapter from a former publication turned out to be prophetic. The responses I received and the information I obtained after just a few weeks of casually looking into this were frightening enough that I am actually considering a later publication project delving into the adverse physiological effects that the contemporary teaching profession is having on people.

After less than *one week,* and a veritable tsunami of messages, Tweets, Facebook posts, private messages, verbal conversations, emails and two handwritten letters, I had to cut my search for information off after I exceeded, by my written calculations, almost TWO HUNDRED TEACHERS and a handful of medical personnel, none of whom—in keeping with my promise—will I mention by name here.

Consistently, across the board, I was regaled with repeated stories of severe anxiety issues, insomnia, migraines, panic attacks, high blood pressure and heart issues, MOST of which were being suffered by otherwise *healthy* people with *no* family history of any of the aforementioned afflictions. Many of these people told me their symptoms did not manifest until they were in the profession for several years and—here is where it gets interesting—many of the folks that got out of the profession reported *significant diminishing/complete disappearance of the symptoms after getting out of teaching.* While I know this is far from O-fish-ul research, I did speak to two different cardiovascular specialists who both told me, quite offhandedly, that they "treated an inordinate number of teachers [as per their usual patient ratio] for valve issues related to long term stress."

OK, *that* got my attention quick, fast, and in a hurry.

I won't belabor the point here, but I think it's worth exploring the idea that many, many teachers are getting busted up doing this job.

A caveat I feel compelled to add here: **I was raised firmly, and efficiently, in such a way that I feel open and unapologetic disdain for what I will politely refer to as the mitigation of our culture. We are becoming physically soft creatures of alleged entitlement that lack both emotional resilience and intellectual stamina, but that is not what we're talking about here. This isn't a "woe is me, my job is SO hard I can't take the pressure" problem; this is a very real adverse physical manifestation created by an ever-intensifying workplace problem, which is then compounded by the fact that the ones doing the suffering are, with sickeningly frequency, *vilified* more for having their symptoms than they are recognized for *enduring* them.**

Think of it, when a professional athlete—who makes millions and millions of dollars in salary and endorsements—is seen as "leaving it all on the field/ice/court/whatever," they are seen as praiseworthy heroes of modern society. Why then are teachers, who, let's face it, get paid shit in proportion to the responsibilities they are asked to shoulder, not given similar regard for, quite literally, giving their hearts to their jobs?

I'll leave you all to ponder and argue that one. As for me, I've got an appointment tomorrow about that "Optimus Prime-sized possibility for a heart attack" blood pressure issue.

Please know that I don't cast aspersions at anyone for my BP issues, if it's part of the job, so be it;

you sign the contact you deal with the side effects.

HowEVer, I would appreciate it if you, at least, acknowledged the effort (and the subsequent ailments that come about as a result) that I demonstrate in the pursuit of your child's education by keeping your uninformed nose out of my ass while I'm *engaged* in said pursuit.

Which, as you may have guessed, leads us to the next chapter…

I AM IGNORING MY OWN CHILDREN *BECAUSE OF MY DEDICATION TO YOURS*

*"You begin saving the world by saving one person at a time;
all else is grandiose romanticism or politics."*
—*Charles Bukowski*

I hate myself for it, but there it is; I've done it before, and, god damn it, I'll probably do it again, and I'll hate myself again. This particular instance—and there have been, with not even the slightest exaggeration, **a hundred** (maybe more?) in my 25 years of teaching—began with my stepson Brendan. He had a monthly current events project due the next day; you know, find an article, answer the questions on this template, yada yada yada. Fortunately [for him] I am able to access a website that allows me to modify the Lexile score of the article, (that's the reading level of the vocabulary in the story to you non-English teachers), another nice perk of having an English teacher for a 'dad.'

> **DISCLAIMER:** Or so *I think*; trust me when I tell you that my kids could come up with an interminable list of CONS to the alleged PROS of having English-teacher-author-guy as the pater familias. They quickly forget the comfort of being able to say *"Hey Dad, can you summarize Hamlet in, like 5 minutes, AND give me a good idea for a research paper based on one of the themes?"* the minute you proofread one of their homework assignments and eviscerate it like the bear did to Leo in *The Revenant*.

119

But, again, I digress…Bren, typical 12-year-old testing the waters, chose to wait until the last minute to address the article I gave him, along with the disclaimer that "I thought he could handle a more challenging piece, *two weeks ago*," and tried to half-ass a lazy, sloppily written, plagiarized response.

Key word: tried.

Uncle Frank (I'm still Uncle Frank, we have legal custody of Bren but never formally adopted him) has deadlines for ALL of his children's work on his desk calendar, (and the instructions printed out and carefully stored underneath it.)

I threatened him with bodily dismemberment, homelessness and several combinations of the two, all of which were overreactions stemming from the fact that he interrupted me during…wait for it… correcting paragraphs that my students had written that day. And we were only *working* on *paragraphs* because the *essays* I tried to give my 11th grade "College Prep" students resulted in such an unspeakable Pequod-meets-the-White-Whale failure to follow directions, inability to meet deadlines, and lame-ass excuses that I—in rare form—chose to lose the battle to win the war and retreated to an easier assignment in the hopes of building up the **work ethic** and **accountability** that, for all intents and purposes, nobody seems to have taught these kids during their 17 years on the big blue marble.

So, temporarily enraged at having been removed from my outrage, I printed out an easier article, along with another template, chucked them at Bren, and told him that he was—and I'm paraphrasing now—going to do nothing until THIS version of his project was finished, correctly, and typed, awaiting my approval.

Did I address the fact that I might have overshot his reading ability with the "more challenging piece"? No. Did I take a few minutes and explain why, exactly, I was disappointed and offer a few suggestions as to how to avoid a similar issue in the future? Nope. Did I… alright let's just say I didn't do *any* of the things an enlightened human being should have done, because I *simply haaaaaaaad* to get back to the hot off the presses shitty paragraphs that I, for some reason, feel compelled to return in a timely fashion to the ungrateful little pricks that couldn't hit a deadline I gave them if I tied a Meteor BVRAAM missile to their asses and shot them at it.

Don't let my silver-tongued snarkiness and/or verbose venom fool you folks, I'm disgusted at myself. Just rereading this makes me want to (as I have every time I talk about similar occurrences in my other books) call up my three living offspring and ask them to forgive me for putting other people's children ahead of my own. They would laugh. They'd tell me some shit about "that's what makes me a good teacher" and "that's why my students love me" and a bunch of other stuff that would make me feel even lower than the whale shit I already feel like.

NOTE TO SELF #1: Funny how forgiveness you don't deserve hurts more than anger when it comes from those you truly love.

NOTE TO SELF #2: Must explore what is, in fact, lower than whale shit. Flounder poop? Manta Ray diarrhea?[1]

Doesn't matter, the bottom line is that <u>I, like legions of teachers across this nation, ignore my own children's educational needs because of my dedication to the needs of YOUR children</u>. Maybe it's because I know I'll always be available to my own kids (although email and mobile technology has pretty much made me available 24/7 to *your* kids too.) Maybe it's because I am trying to fix more than just academic issues with your kids (I already hammered home punctuality, accountability, and resilience to my offspring, from **birth**,) or maybe it's just because I feel compelled to prioritize your children over my own because I'm getting *paid* to teach your kids, (which is, I realize as I sit and type this, the lamest excuse the English language could muster up;) whatever the reason, you should know that this is a reality. A reality that you would do well to acknowledge before you bitch and moan about the individual attention you *don't* think

---

(1) There I go again, trying to be funny to distract you (myself?) from how embarrassed I am for being a tool. It is an acknowledged character flaw.

lovely little Laura or your darling Denzel is getting from me. In fact, let's address that. **Consider this, for purposes of catharsis, a formal response to any parent/guardian (and, for that matter, administrator or counselor that enable said guardians) that verbalizes their lack of satisfaction with the lack of "individualized attention" that they perceive I'm giving their legal progeny**:

1. I'm your child's teacher, not his/her tutor. My tutoring clients pay dearly for their immediate access to me so, if you're interested in your kid's education, you'll need to reach out to me a little more than the once or twice a year (usually associated with a bad grade) that you normally do. That being said…

2. I make myself available [for individual help/reinforcement/etc.] to your kid as much as I do to my own children;[2] **however,** your kid "doesn't want to come that early," or "doesn't want to miss lunch," or "doesn't want to stay after school," or "can't miss one day of practice," or "can't stay on a Friday!" Listen, I'M doing YOUR child a favor, so he/she will attempt to work around *my* availability, and if that doesn't work for you, then neither you nor your child is as serious about improving as you collectively claim that you are.

But hey—let's try to be preemptive about this and attempt to avoid unpleasantries.

3. *Before* you bitch about what you perceive is a lack of effort on my part to accommodate and assist your child, you'd better do YOUR homework with more consistency and punctuality than your kid does, because, every year, I defuse a substantial number of angry parents with a long, meticulously detailed report of what their child *hasn't* done leading up to this meeting.

NOTE TO STUDENTS: Before YOU have Mom or Dad or whomever come up to "take care of me," you should note my placid countenance

---

(2) And in some cases, in keeping with the theme of this chapter, more available.

You *think* you know what's going to happen in that meeting; I <u>know</u> what's going to happen.

You should also be aware of the First Law of Thermodynamics and how it relates to your life. *"Energy can be changed from one form to another, but it cannot be created or destroyed. The total amount of energy and matter in the Universe remains constant, merely changing from one form to another."* That means that all that anger you built up in your parents has to GO *some*where once I've shown them, in painful detail, that it shouldn't be aimed at *me*.

I wonder where it will go? Enjoy that car ride home, sweetheart.

Now, this may sound unnecessarily confrontational to those of you outside the teaching profession (or to those of you lucky enough to be in districts where these problems don't exist,[3]) but I assure you that, for most of us, our tendency toward preemptive strike is the default response to careers spent getting attacked for "not doing our jobs" when, in fact, we are doing 25 to 200% more than what we are *contractually obligated* to do. (This is why I increasingly refer to the teaching profession as **"parenting with a paycheck."**) And on the subject of parenting, I have—as I mentioned earlier—neglected, shortchanged, or given less than my best to the flesh of my flesh, blood of my blood, simply because I was exhausted from giving my best to *your* children all day (and sometimes all night.)

Please do not misunderstand me, I don't begrudge the latter commitment, and I don't think any good teacher does; we *want* to go above and beyond to help your children, (we have to live in this world together, after all, and a rising tide lifts all ships) but that desire to exceed expectations can become a bitter pill *when you catch yourself becoming annoyed that your youngest son is trying to talk to you:*

Frankie, my youngest, will often just plop down near me to talk about everything from what he's studying in school, (AP Physics, *way* over my head, but I'll listen,) to his latest workout (he's a health nut.) We'll shoot the shit about everything from his latest obsession (currently black holes,) to our favorite TV show (Samurai Jack.) Unfortunately, I am

---

(3) Apparently, these teaching jobs DO exist; know that I am profoundly jealous of any of you that work in these la-la lands of academia.

ashamed to say that there have been more than a few occasions where my son,

my youngest *son*,

politely excused himself and left, mid-conversation, because my body language must have exuded agitation at not being able to finish editing the paper written, late, by the kid who will ignore most of my suggestions until he's failing for the year and then ask me why.

If that hurt when you *read* it,
try to imagine how it felt to *write* it.

But it doesn't end there. No sir—my daughter is currently in her 4th year in college, and, in between bitching about what an oppressive dictator I am, she brags to her friends about what a great writer I am, and how I can, when editing a paper, turn chicken shit into chicken salad like nobody you've ever seen. So, imagine her feelings when, two or three times a year, she'll send me a paper (usually a group collaboration) asking me to look it over for continuity, clarity, grammatical correctness and such, only to receive some sort of exasperated response from a douchebag[4] that is *fried* from having edited and returned 120 papers over the last few days.[5] Two months ago, she sent me a paper on eco-friendly alternatives to fossil fuels (important stuff, right?) that she and her collaborators were very excited about having completed. They had worked into the wee hours of the morning to make it perfect, and just wanted ol' Mr. Step to polish the gem with a little editing. I did, in fact, edit the (already very good, and very interesting) paper, but not before I sent Sam a lengthy[6] email explaining how busy I was, and you can't just throw this stuff on me at the last-minute blah blah blah…The damned email probably took me as much time to fire off as the actual editing process of the paper, and yet all it did was manage to alienate me from my daughter, make her friends uncomfortable, and give voice—for

---

(4) That would be me.
(5) Even though that IS your JOB, and she IS your DAUGHTER…douchebag.
(6) And, upon re-reading, angry sounding…

what it was worth[7]—to my frustration. I was only frustrated, and tired, because I had, in very real life, spent every night until well past midnight collaborating with my students on Google Drive to ensure that they all had solid papers that they could use as templates going into their final exam (which would be a similar type of paper.) The fact that, because of *that*, I lashed out at a group of eager young minds, (one of whom is my oldest living child and only daughter) makes me cringe with self-loathing and should, at the very least, elicit a little bit of empathy from you. I, and many of my peers in the field, really are short changing our actual sons and daughters because we are exhausted from having given 100% of my efforts to ensure the success of yours.

Listen folks, despite the popular rhetoric, teachers DON'T "get done at 3:00" and we most certainly DON'T get "weekends 'off;" we're spending a whopping amount of our "free time" cultivating an intellectual relationship with your kids or repairing the unattended personal relationship with our own that, sometimes, is a byproduct of our dedication to our craft.

I have rushed a special needs child, whom I swore to protect, educate, and raise as my own, through an assignment because I thought I needed to get back to working on grading homework for my students, I have made my youngest son feel unimportant because I felt compelled to get back to online collaboration with my students, I made my daughter and her friends feel inadequate for asking for my help because I was tired from giving my all to my students,

and I have made myself a liar, the thing I despise the most, to my oldest living son, because I wanted to be punctual for my students.

Mason has always been pretty self-sufficient, from the time he was a little guy, tying his little work boots and helping with household projects, so when he asks for help, it's rare enough to warrant my full attention, especially when it involves his future.

But no. *"Not right now Mas, I'm trying to get this stupid Google Classroom thing to work so I can list it on my domain 4, and then when I get observed I can validate that…"*

And when I looked up, Mason was gone.

---

(7) Nothing. It was worth nothing.

Gone. The way he'll be gone in a few months; off to Thomas Jefferson University to pursue his degree and build his future.

Gone, with memories of his family, including the one where his dad rattled off a string of nonsense about how he had to fix some disposable new technology so he could "prove" to some soon to be replaced administrator (who doesn't give a rat's ass about him) that he is "doing his job" because hey, just killing yourself and compromising your job as a parent to be everything to your students doesn't prove anything these days, because it isn't quanti-fucking-fiable.

Gone.

I couldn't let that happen, (luckily, THIS time, I caught myself) so I went into the other room and sat down next to Mas. I tried to rekindle the conversation, but he was (with just a touch of righteous indignation) placating me with "it's ok, get your work done" and "it's not really that important," until he saw the tears.

We Stepnowskis pride ourselves on suffering in silence, so when Mas saw me crying he knew a nerve had been struck. I went to him, put my hand on his face, and asked that he forgive me for being a liar. *"I always said that I would drop everything if you ever needed me, and I am so sorry that I allowed work to take precedent over that. Please, **please** let me rectify that?"*

He let me,

this time.

I feel empty inside after recounting just these few instances of how I defaulted on my parental promises because I was dedicated to keeping my word to my students and my job, so you'll forgive me if I just end this chapter here,

knowing that I'll probably do it again.

"YOU'RE A FAT FUCK IN A BULLSHIT CLASS!"

*"I'm not concerned with your liking or disliking me...
All I ask is that you treat me as a human being."*
—Jackie Robinson

That chapter title, ladies and gentlemen, is a direct quote from a student, aimed at a teacher. I think we can all agree that this, on the surface, tastes bad enough, but let us dig a little deeper into the flaky layers of the baklava of bullshit.

The student in question currently has enough disciplinary write ups to sink an aircraft carrier, for everything ranging from insubordination to dress code violations, from being in an unassigned area to threatening students. He's received more detentions and in-school suspensions than I had time to list, and he's been suspended OUT of school 5 times and counting.

SIDE NOTE: After reading up to this point, you're probably wondering how kids with all of these discipline issues get to stay in our school? *Yeah, we wonder that, too.*

Oh, and he's currently failing three of seven subjects and *barely* passing two of the others; no surprise, he was in summer school last year. (Rolling my eyes) He's killing it in gym and cooking class, though.

But hey, here he is, in class with *your* kids. Oh, did I mention that *one* of those out of school suspensions only happened because:

- The kid, (let's call him Jeshua Jerkoffia,) cursed out his teacher because the gentleman had the audacity to ask him to remove his non-uniform hoodie (a recurring problem, as evidenced by his TWENTY-THREE other uniform violation write ups.)
- Little Jeshie was **sent back to class 5 minutes later** after being told he could "just keep the hoodie on his arm."

127

- (And you think YOU get disrespected by management at YOUR job?)
- The "fat fuck" teacher in question (who happens to be battling prostate cancer,)
- that teaches the "bullshit class" (Financial Literacy,)[1]
- brought this lack of disciplinary response to the attention of 'others,' whereupon
- J.J. got one day out of school (essentially a long weekend) and was right back in "bullshit" Financial Literacy without so much as an apology or a reprimand.

But hey, here he is, back in class with *your* kids.

Sad. Pathetic, if we must be honest, that *that* is what teaching so often comes to: flagrant disrespect from the ones you're trying to help, defensible only through the most primitive of means (*if* available) because THEY are enabled by "guardians" trying to be their friends instead of their role models, and YOU are left to the dogs by those appointed [and paid considerably better than you] to protect (or at least *respect*) you.

Welcome to the world of the contemporary teacher in America.

I don't hesitate to tell you that Jeshua Jerkoffia "graduated"[2] since I originally wrote this chapter. I ran into him at his place of work when I was dropping off clothes just prior to the Christmas holiday. The young 'man' who cursed out his teacher in the latter chapter, refused to even make eye contact with me when I saw him working at the local Goodwill.

Mr. "I—make—more-money-than-y'all-so-fuck-school" apparently ran afoul of his, ahem, 'pharmaceutical benefactor' and was now trying to support his three-month-old son[3] on the $7.55 an hour he made as a retail sales associate.[4]

Karma, it seems, is a bitch with a long memory.

---

(1) On a personal note, I honestly don't know of a more pertinent, practical class that it taught in High School; I know I wish I had been taught financial literacy the easy way before I learned it the hard way.

(2) AKA "was allowed to complete 'non-credit status' bullshit assignments" combined with some mathematical voodoo cooked up just to get him out of the building.

(3) Because the father of the girl hunted him down after Jeshua tried to deny paternity. What a sweetheart.

(4) I know because I asked his manager. I then gave her $50 to give to J.J. for the explicit reason of making sure his son had a decent Christmas. I want, desperately, to believe that money went where it was supposed to go.

CRY HAVOC, AND LET SLIP THE DOGS OF...WHAT? WE'RE FRIENDS NOW?

"...ranging for revenge,
With Ate by his side come hot from hell,
Shall in these confines with a monarch's voice
Cry "Havoc!" and let slip the dogs of war."
—William Shakespeare

A few chapters ago, I was pretty definitive in my disdain for Lady Macbeth (she of the bullshit teacher evaluation from last year.) So, as you might imagine, I was ready to prick her thumbs (and any other body part that got in my sights) when we met for *this* year's post-observation conference:

- I was armed to the teeth with relevant paperwork validating that I checked all the bullshit boxes on the bullshit evaluation drop down menu.
- My pre and post observation notes were so thorough that an OCD Velociraptor couldn't have found a weak spot in them.
- My Domain Four artifacts (the stuff I need to prove that I am a "professional and good teacher")[1] were on point.
- And I had the trump card sitting in my pocket; you see, Lady M was ***four months late*** getting around to this conference. (Yes, you read that correctly, I was observed in the pre-Christmas chill of mid-December and I was finally getting called to hear about

---

(1) I can't even go into the level of malarkey here; just more time ACTUALLY BEING a good teacher put on hold to prove to people who are scared to come into my classroom that I AM a good teacher.

her recommendations for what I could improve as the tulips bloomed in late April.)

- I had contacted my union reps and prepared them for future legal proceedings. In short, I was ready to cry havoc and let slip the dogs of motherfucking war on her ass.
- I was **not** prepared for what actually happened.

The day before the conference my wife, the always astute, and often brilliant Dr. Dawn, sensed that kind of agitation I used to get prior to my fights[2] and inquired as to why, so I told her the whole story and—true to form—she shot my whole plan to Hell with about seven words.

"Why don't you try being nice?"

OK six words, but, to be fair, there's a contraction in there.

After a lengthy and occasionally heated discussion that more than occasionally sounded like a metaphor for our marriage, Dawn psychotherapeutically slapped me into thinking that, just perhaps, Lady Macbeth might be on the defensive as well. Having been recently thrust into a higher spot on the food chain (and subsequently micromanaged) by the acting director, my nemesis might WANT to (cue the Public Enemy music) "do the right thing," but—thanks to the toxic environment created by the powers-that-be—may *also* be home preparing for war.

Maybe Lady Macbeth wanted (marriage metaphor alert) to just hug it out, but was waiting for me to take the high road and switch from assault mode to agreement mode?

Ooooh, I hate it when my wife is probably right.

OK...olive branch first, sound and fury if that doesn't work. Let's see how this goes. The time arrived, Lady Macbeth didn't cancel, and I arrived promptly 5 minutes early. I imagined both of us stockpiling snowballs behind our makeshift forts in anticipation of the coming assault.

---

(2) Kickboxing, MMA, Toughman competitions...a whole litany of misguided, purely physical stuff I used to do to attempt to overcome my massive inferiority complex. (3)

(3) Didn't work, you can't punch, kick or grapple your way to enlightenment, THAT shit requires some self-examination of the ol' noodle. (4)

(4) Which still hasn't worked. I mean, have you been reading? Seriously.

Again, I was spectacularly, irrevocably wrong.

Something happened when we sat down and the Lady started actually *talking to* me.

NOT staring at a laptop while talking *about* me. (The last principal.)

NOT talking *at* me while rushing through an obviously rehearsed but completely irrelevant monologue. (The one prior to the last principal.)

NOT *interrupting* a mutually beneficial conversation with non-sequiturs that were both blatantly forced and corporate in nature: "What pedagogical approach does that employ?" or "What district standards do you think that lesson adhered to?" (BOTH of the aforementioned principals.)

No, Dirty Harry and Crazy Lady just started the meeting by talking, real talking, with eye contact and everything. As a self-professed man of words, that loosened something in me, and it was I, this time, that did the interrupting: *"Ms. Macbeth, before we go any further, can I ask you a question?"*

"Sure," she replied with just the slightest pinch of apprehension.

*"All checkboxes and 'evaluation frameworks' and all that aside, do you know—let me rephrase that—do you **believe** that I am a good teacher?"*

"Well…"

*"And so we're not vague here, by **good** I mean, specifically, one of the hardest working people in this building, who obviously cares about his students as though they were his own children?"*

She smiled, nodded, collected her thoughts and replied with an impressive jambalaya of measured professionalism, ("Let's take a look at all of the things I used to form my impression of you") painfully neutral commentary, ("everything you're expected to turn in as 'quantifiable proof that you do your job according to the stipulations of your contract' is extremely proficient,") and personal vindication, ("I'm human, and everything outside of all the boxes I personally have to check to protect MY job tells me that you are one of the people I never have to worry about.")

"Thank you. Do you understand why that's important to me? You guys are coming from a world of dehumanized checklists and

pedagogical practice and data collection,[5] but I'm coming from a world of flesh and blood and tears and ink. There is common ground, but if we're starting the whole thing with you not KNOWING what I am, then we're trying to build a house on shifting sand. Also—and please let me finish—if I know YOU care, then I'll take all the constructive criticism you have to dish out, and honestly work to improve because I'll respect your opinion enough to consider it as I work."

"Are you saying you don't respect all of your administrator's opinions?" A smile, and a palpable sense of mischief. "Don't answer that; I started reading your books, and I already know the answer."

Full of surprises was Lady Macbeth, (and it was probably for the best for *both* of us that she didn't get me started on answering her question.)

40 minutes and change later, I signed off on another round of observation paperwork, and left with a profound sense of exactly what was missing in the contemporary educational landscape, and what, in its absence, continued to widen the chasm between educational staff and the educational "leaders" that are supposed to assist, and advocate for them.

COMMUNICATION.
FACE TO FACE, HEART TO HEART,
HUMAN ENGAGEMENT.

Yeah, there were still some Danielson frame working[6] and minutiae

---

(5) I know this, sadly, to be a fact; my M.Ed. is in educational administration, and my studies during that time convinced me, beyond a shadow of a doubt, that I did NOT want to become an administrator, specifically because, based on the way public schools are run these days, you almost have to, (as an administrator,) stick it to your teaching staff. Sorry, but I'm one of those guys that can't go from being a soldier to a guy that sits in an office and sends soldiers to die. I've been in the trenches too long to become a paper pushing, status quo maintaining office dweller; my life is in the trenches, up close and involved with the kids

(6) THE DANIELSON FRAMEWORK: An elaborate (and, in my experience, convoluted, irrelevant) system of teacher evaluation created by Charlotte Danielson, "an internationally-recognized expert in the area of teacher effectiveness" (whatever the fuck THAT is) that the New York Times called "mostly a weapon to harass teachers and force them to follow dubious scripted lessons" (7). More on this later, I promise.

pondering, but you ain't gonna find common ground without a little bit of compromise, and I was already thrilled that the whole meeting hadn't ended in blood and fire, so...

The sad part about this whole thing (which I can rationally reflect upon now that my tail hath stopped rattling and my fangs hath retracted) is, I suspect, having read between the lines of her comments and reactions during our conversation, that Lady Macbeth and those of her ilk are being pressured to objectify their staff and, in many specific cases, bust teachers' balls in an attempt to demoralize us[8] and reduce the whole profession to an expendable, faceless series of cogs that could easily be replaced by, in the best case, inexperienced neophytes that will do whatever they're told to do (i.e. tell your kids WHAT to think based on someone else's corporate agenda?) or, in a worst-case scenario, machines.

Think I'm paranoid?

Do some research.

In the meantime, if you're working in education, in any capacity, TALK to each other, get to KNOW each other and try, as best you can, to suppress your egos and *get things done in the best interest of our kids*.

Everything else is a story, told by a moron, full of noise and anger.

(That's Shakespearean paraphrase, kiddies!)[9]

And speaking, superfluously, of Shakespeare and tales told by morons, on to the next chapter!

---

(7) A framework WHICH, by the way, Ms. Danielson said was never meant to be a system of evaluation.

(8) You need go no further than our current Governor here in the Garden State, Chris Christie, to see an example of how teacher bashing and corporate cock sucking reigns at the top of the food chain. Go back to your private beach, you corpulent Hellspawn, the only thing you do consistently well is lower your approval rating among New Jersey residents.

(9) Students! (and well-read people!) Did you catch that? You did? Jello with extra whipped cream for the smarty pants people!

ROMEO (h no, it's state testing time) and JULI(we can't get to the important stuff y)ET

> *"Sometimes, the most brilliant and intelligent minds do not shine in standardized tests because they do not have standardized minds."*
> —Diane Ravitch

High stakes, standardized testing is kind of like the guy at your table who, after wiping his nose, puts his fingers all over the last three buffalo wings, the ones with all the sauce on them, the ones you *really* wanted, only to decide that he doesn't really want them. More simply put, all this testing ruins the important stuff, the good stuff, the *I-see-a-need-and-I-require-time to-address-this-properly-so-my-students-get-a-quality-education* stuff. The people that design these tests don't care about your kids' actual learning any more than Mr. Nastyfingers really wanted those wings, but, much like he of the despoiling digits, these pillars of arbitrary irrelevance ruin the party for everyone.

'Step," you say, "we **get** it, dude. Standardized tests are bad, you're just beating a dead horse now." *"Yes,"* I politely retort, *"and dystopian novels and films have been dropped on your heads in record numbers since H.G. Wells wrote The Time Machine in 1895,* **but y'all clearly haven't fully processed, and acted upon, those warnings yet,** *have you? So I'ma gonna keep driving my point home, ok?"*

Case in point, the way New Jersey PARCC testing nuked the way I wanted to teach Romeo and Juliet this year. Clearly, Pearson, the London-based international publishing and education goliath, and little old me, are star cross'd lovers* doomed to end in profit[1] and publication.[2]

Allow me to elaborate, as simply as I can. Last week was the English/Language Arts section of the PARCC, so this week some of my students had to take the Mathematics section. I say *some* because some of my 9th graders are in Algebra and some are in Geometry, so different kids will be testing at different periods of the day and, provided that the computers and servers all work,[3] they'll only be out of my class for 3-4 days.

Oh, did I mention that we're on a block semester schedule, where each class only lasts half a scholastic year, and that I only have *thirteen days* left with these particular students before we part for the year? Because we are, and we do.[4] So, (deep breath) I'm going to have to **teach** a Shakespearean play with *some* degree of proficiency, **give** some sort of "Hey!-here's-proof-they-understand-this" benchmark ON the play, **grade** and **record** the aforementioned benchmark, and **say** "Parting is such sweet sorrow!" *

in thirteen days,

with several students missing,

in different classes,

over the course of HALF of those days.[5]

Now, that would be hard enough 'twere I teaching youth that were

---

(1) For them.

(2) For me, as in this book you're holding.

(3) Not gonna happen, but hope continues to spring eternal.

(4) Trust me, I could write an entire chapter on how many of our students will now graduate after four years of High School with only two [broken up] years of English, or how Gifted and Advanced Placement classes have been cut into half year classes, that leave a 4-5-month gap before AP TESTING, but brevity, in this case, is the soul of wit. *

(5) Normal, "everything goes right" testing takes three days, but there's make up testing for kids that were absent, didn't finish, got kicked out for threatening to hit someone with a laptop, etc.

reading on level and able to tackle Shakespeare (even the adapted text) with semi-speed and semi-understanding, but, in the case of teaching my little cherubs, it's best to go "wisely and slow; [because] they stumble that run fast." *

What kind of children are you teaching that can't knock out a five act play in two weeks? Well, since you asked:

The kind of kids that have to be reminded, *every day*, how to pronounce Montague (MONT-AH-GYOO!) even after they've heard it about 100 times so far.

- The kind of kids that laugh and get off task for about five minutes every time they catch one of Big Willy's sexual innuendos.[6]
- The kind that flinch visibly and exclaim audibly "oh my god" when they turn the page and realize that someone has to read more than half a page of dialogue at one time. God forbid!
- The kind of kids that have to be reminded (even if the last time they read was a minute ago) that we're reading the text on the RIGHT side of the book.[7]
- The kind of kids that ask you—*after* you've finished reading *Act III* together, gone over the details of the play in class, and showed them the cinematic version of what you've read so far—"*Wait! So is Juliet a Moontacue or a Capalet?*"
- The kind of kids whose eyes glaze over and whose heads start to nod even during the most dynamic reading of the most exciting/sexual/violent/funny scenes in the play, but the minute they're given a few minutes to themselves, immediately spring to life with loud, animated conversations about "how Tanisha is crazy for liking Devante because he's playing her," or "how 'fire' that video of Eric and Ronald fighting in the cafeteria today was," or "how this person on that reality show is soooooo craaaazzzzy..."

(6) Thank goodness, they only usually catch every fifth or sixth one.
(7) For those of you unfamiliar, The SparksNotes company (may their gardens forever be free of cobras) produced an entire series of NO FEAR Shakespeare books that feature the original text on the left side and a contemporary (and much more accessible) translation on the right side.

I could go on, believe me I could, (and I'm guessing that a veritable plethora of English teachers out there could add pages to this list,) but "that which we call a dope by any other name would sound just as lazy." *

So, to review, these are the kids to whom I'm supposed to teach the finer points of Shakespeare while being interrupted by the "Oh $o Important $tate Te$ting."

Yeah? Let's see *you* do it! In fact, "I **defy** you stars!" * to show me somebody that can teach ANYthing meaningful properly when you're up against a deadline, some of your class times are cut (from 90 to 45 minutes,) while others are extended (from 90 minutes to nearly two hours,) a different group of kids shows up every day, and you have to create a one-size-fits-all assessment for what you taught.

Send your reasonable solutions to *The Fans of the Author Frank Stepnowski on Facebook*. I'm all ears.

But before I "lend [you my] ears," * let me tell you, with specificity, what I mean when I say that I want to teach my kids PROPERLY:

- I'd like to be able to stop when my kids don't know a word and explain to them a variety of meanings for that word, and maybe come up with some kind of mnemonic tricks so they can expand their vocabularies.
- When we reach the part about Romeo and Juliet's suicides, and one or more of my kids bring up the fact that they considered (or tried) suicide, or a loved one did the same, (and this ALWAYS happens,) I'd like to have more time to discuss this openly and informatively; I could possibly bring in a guest speaker to help discuss a very sensitive subject.
- I'd like to have my kids write something to show that they really *understood* the themes of the play, take time to teach my kids what a proper thesis statement is, have them submit theirs, and then sit down and go over how they could (if they need to) improve theirs so they could start writing with clarity and purpose.
- I'd like to debunk the myth that iambic pentameter is some

cryptic thing, to teach my kids about how sonnets work and how the same rhyme schemes are used by some of their favorite rappers and musicians, maybe expose them to the Hip Hop Shakespeare Company.

- <u>I'd like to</u> actually ACT OUT the play (or at least parts of it) onstage, and I know the Speech and Drama teachers would totally be down with this.
- <u>I'd love to</u> show them documentaries like Shakespeare Behind Bars and/or have them read books like *Romeo and/or Juliet*: Choosable Path Adventure books that involve interactive (and often hilarious) student interaction with the story

You get the point. Teachers would prefer to have some breathing room to make reading interesting and relevant to our already literature allergic kids, and to take the time to address problems organically as they arise.

Unfortunately, there are some people HEAVILY invested in those computerized, standardized, your-kids-will-soon-be-anesthetized tests, and your kids will take them whenever they're scheduled because those people said so. <u>You'll know when the tests are going on; your kids will complain loudly and often about them or, at the very least, they'll come home and tell you no learning is going on</u><u>; **I guarantee it.**</u>

Despite the immovable object that is the NJ PARCC, (our own little slice of Hell here in the Garden State,) I bob and weave and counter punch the crap out of the ever-changing schedule, the rotating attendance, and the frustration and exhaustion that drum into the ears of my kids during testing like Queen Mab* run rampant.

I'll keep loving my kids and trying to teach them Romeo and Juliet, (and any other book/lesson that gets thrown in the centrifuge and tossed down a set of uneven stairs by testing interruptions) in a way that is fun, interesting, and informative.

Alas, if "under love's heavy burden do I sink," * I can think of no better way to go.

NOTE: I hope you enjoyed all of the gratuitous Shakespeare references*
throughout the chapter. I thought they added a little sweet seasoning to
an otherwise sour chapter.

ON PROFANITY and PROFUNDITY

"What I'm saying might be profane, but it's also profound."
—Richard Pryor

Last night I had the great pleasure of recording with my educational aide-de-camp Andy Vasily for his *Run Your Life* podcast. Andy is currently in Nanjing, China. I was speaking from the decidedly less exotic (albeit significantly less polluted) New Jersey, and our cross continental let's-just-shoot-the-shit-and-see-what-happens session was, at turns, enlightening and inspiring.

One of the things that I am, inevitably, asked about in any interview/ broadcast/ writer's workshop/ etc. is the copious use (and variety) of profanity in my first two books. I should offer the caveat that the overwhelming majority of people that have read the aforementioned books loved them, and you should understand that if you walk the hallowed halls of any urban (or suburban, don't kid yourself,) middle or high school in this country, you'll get a free lesson in the kind of vocabulary that won't be on this month's SAT. Simply put, I didn't invent profanity, nor do I eschew it (as you've no doubt discerned having read *this* particular tome up to this point.)

"So why bring it up then, Step?" you ask, with perfectly reasonable inquisition.

"Because," I reciprocate, *"of the hypocrisy inherent in the verbiage of those who would condemn me, or my peers, for indulging in the occasional vulgarism."*

You see, I've been told enough times that, as a teacher, *especially* an **English** teacher, I should "know better" and be able to "find better words" to express myself.

(In my best Jeremy Irons voice) *Oh DO shut the fuck up, please.*

Know better than what? Where do you live?

Cee-Lo Green charted number TWO on the Billboard Top 100 with a song called *Fuck You*. At the peak of its popularity, the mommy porn monster *Fifty Shades of Grey* was being sold at a rate of one book **every second** somewhere in the world,[1] the charmingly titled *The Subtle Art of Not Giving a F*ck*[2] is currently a best seller, and even the bazillion selling phenom that is Adele[3] drops f-bombs on the stage of every stadium she continually sells out and awards show that she subsequently dominates.

I DO know better; I know well enough to know that, particularly in the world of teaching, you need to be **authentic** or your students will write you off quicker than a cheetah with a rocket up its ass.

Now, about that whole "you're an English teacher so you should be able to find better words to express yourself" bullshit.

Listen folks, I'm an omnivorous reader, I've been published in a myriad of forms, and I've been teaching language and literature for the better part of a quarter century. So, if we must be forthright here, my active vocabulary, compared to these self-proclaimed profanity police wankers, probably looks like China's standing army versus the Oregon militia. However, I understand that there are no "better" words because there are no "bad" words; only the context in which they are used, and the person using them determines the substandard nature, or lack thereof, of the text in question.

So, if I were to say—for example—that I wasn't interested in what a bunch of self-righteous, monosyllabic twats who probably don't understand a lot of the words in this chapter think about my cursing, SOME people would find that ironic and cheeky, while others would surely find it distasteful and offensive.

Context, people… it's a motherfucker.

---

(1) EVERY SECOND?!? Dear Lord…E.L. James, I worship at your [no doubt leather bound] feet; I'm happy to sell a book a month., to my family, at a DISCOUNT.

(2) A former student purchased it for me (I have the best students!) and I thoroughly enjoyed it; well done, Mark Manson!

(3) Anybody who knows me knows that I have been a diehard member of the Adele adoration club since 19 dropped some nine years ago, largely because—in addition to her whopping talent—she keeps it real, particularly in conversation; hence, the occasional potty mouth.

So, when Andy and I waxed poetic about the books and the educational endeavors that were the genesis of those stories, we laughed at the similarity of our shared experiences, and rolled our eyes at the collective consciousness that would condemn how we engaged and enthralled our students. There will always be those who frown upon the words and/or methods I use to keep my students *literally* running to my class, but, to quote the fictional Colonel Jessep:

> I have neither the time nor the inclination to explain myself to [a person] who rises and sleeps under the blanket of the very [engagement] that I provide, and then questions the manner in which I provide it. I would rather you just said thank you, and went on your way, Otherwise, I suggest you [get your ass in a classroom or, at the very least, teach your own children.]
>
> Either way, I don't give a *damn* what you think.[4]

That being said, let's talk a little about the hypocrisy of you expecting me, because I'm a teacher, to somehow be "better" than everyone else…

---

(4) Obviously, I edited the famous monologue from A Few Good Men for my educational purposes, but, in terms of the matter at hand, I simply couldn't have said it better myself.

ON HAUGHTINESS and HYPOCRISY

"By the sword you did your work, and by the sword you die."
—*Aeschylus*

"You're a teacher, so…"
Yeah, let me stop you right there.
Unless you have done anything close to what I've done in the classroom, **you're not <u>qualified</u> to finish that statement.**

If you'd like to tell me that, as a concerned guardian, you'd like to see me work on *x* or *y* with your child, I'm all ears and legitimately thrilled that you are taking an active hand in your child's education (because you, sir or madam, are an endangered species.)

But very few of you do that; most of you want to tell me what [you think] I have to do "as a teacher." In the interest of fun, fourth wall irony, legitimate instruction, and gratuitous self-promotion, let me quote—well, *myself*—from my last book, *Teaching Sucks; But We Love It*:

Many people feel so enabled to criticize teachers; [these same] folks get their homes repaired multiple times, but they don't automatically think they could be construction workers, plumbers, etc. People and their family members undergo surgeries and visit hospitals, but they don't instantly assume they could be doctors… yet, because they went to school, or have children in school, legions of people feel like they know what it is to be a teacher. They're wrong; and the evidence is in both the children they send us, and the fact that they stand idle, ignorant to so many "educational" decisions being made about our children that could irreversibly damage future generations. (Stepnowski)

Sorry for that moment of self-indulgence, but that's how I feel, *(and **NOW** I have a convenient excerpt that I can use to teach block quotation, bracket and ellipsis usage to my actual students!)*

To continue on that theme, I'm always amazed at how:

A. certain some people are that *they* know what *my* job entails,
B. hypocritical some people are about the social standards *I'm* supposed to uphold, and
C. defensive those same people get when I ask to be treated equally to the OTHER professions to which I am, for purposes of their arguments, compared.

Let's address point "A" shall we?

Yes, let's talk briefly about the people, who have never worked in any facet of the educational field, who are sure they know what my job "as a teacher" entails.

You don't.

Moving on to point "B," the hypocrites who don't live by the same standards they are so adamant about *me* upholding.

Example: You're offended that I curse in my books and, occasionally, in class?

Really? Interesting, because your daughter has a Miley Cyrus (the "new" Miley) backpack, your son draws Five Finger Death Punch logos on his notebooks, your daughter has a Juvenille ringtone, and your son walks into class rapping Lil John's *Real Nigga Roll Call*, and you think the occasional curse word in the context of a heartfelt conversation, a lesson or in a BOOK THEY ARE READING is going to hurt them?

Grow up.

Incidentally, those are all *actual* stories of parents whose kids were doing less than stellar in my class, (because they didn't turn in work, didn't study, plagiarized, etc.,) but rather than take *any* accountability for that, the parents thought they would "lean" on me a little by bringing up that I cursed occasionally in class. I don't respond well to that weak shit, so I pointed out the aforementioned things, along with a few other "eye opening" issues and—in every case except the Miley Cyrus girl—*had to explain to the parents exactly what their children were watching/listening to, who they were hanging with, etc.* (Way to be on top of your kids, folks.) Imagine Ms. Brownstone's surprise when she went home and pulled up the Lil' John song on her son's iPhone and got treated to 330 curse words in a FOUR MINUTE SONG.[1]

I don't want to belabor the point, so I'll simply ask, on behalf of teachers everywhere, that you practice what you preach [to me.] I probably know many of your kids as well or better than you do, as I'm around them for at least half of their waking hours,[2] and I am well aware of what offends/hurts them, and I actually *do* care and do my best to avoid those things, so the benefit of the doubt would be a well-earned courtesy, agreed?

And on that note…

Let us address point C, those sensitive folks who get defensive when I ask to simply be treated with the same courtesy that you would extend to any other professional.

Listen, I understand that you are passionate about anyone that impacts your child; what decent guardian wouldn't be? However, I highly doubt that you would try to micromanage a pediatrician trying to fix your child's broken arm, or question the intentions of the dentist working to repair your child's tooth decay, or harass the accountant working to secure your child's financial future; I don't even think most of you would pressure the trainer you hired to make little Manny and Fiona faster and stronger for (insert sport of choice.)

---

(1) Impressive, no doubt, (but I think the sheer artistry was lost on her at the moment.)
(2) And we BOTH know they spend a lot of those other hours staring at screens, not at you.

So why, in the name of all that is holy, would you micromanage, doubt, harass, or negatively pressure the teacher working to improve your child's INTELLECT and CHARACTER?

I guess if we made the same amount of *money* as those professionals…

All venomous sarcasm aside, I have seen (and been told about) too many incidents like this to count. I have a few suggestions as to why this may be the case:

1. First, and I hate to sound like a broken record, with the increasing awareness about Common Core, the issues associated with it, and the incessant testing that it promotes, I can hardly blame you for thinking that the agenda of most schools might not be in keeping with your kids' best interest. (Again, refer to the Common Core chapter for a definitive answer on <u>where I</u>, and <u>legions of other educators</u>, <u>stand on CC</u>.)

2. Secondly, the unfortunate fact that—despite massive evidence to the contrary—you feel, for one reason or another, that you understand the subtleties, intricacies, and intellectual demands of the teaching profession. I guess I have to throw some of the blame on the media for that one; not exactly a pro-teacher climate in this country right now (which is part of the reason I wrote this book.) Also, you'll ALWAYS have some form of *Grey's Anatomy* or *Law and Order*-type shows on television, and there are whole CHANNELS dedicated to money matters and sports, but not a whole lotta "Teacher TV" except the occasional breaking news story that some twisted fuck in North Carolina had sex with his or her students.[3] The ESPYs are on television tonight, but there won't be an EDUCATYs anytime soon, I can guarantee you that.

3. Finally, and again I'll sound repetitive here, the teacher-parent-client relationship is more susceptible than any other profession

---

(3) Or you get articles like *How Many Kids Are Sexually Abused by Their Teachers? Probably millions*. Courtesy of Slate.com. Thanks, guys; nothing like implicating an entire profession regarding the most heinous crime imaginable. I'm looking forward to your articles on journalistic irresponsibility, malpractice, fraud, corruption and general malfeasance in other professions.

I can think of (with the glaring exception of law enforcement) to the racial, social, and socioeconomic divisions that plague our society. If you had to count the number of times, in my two and a half decades of teaching, I've been told—to my *face*—a version of *"no rich white man is gonna tell my kid what to do"* you would run out of fingers and have to take off at least one shoe to keep counting. This, of course, is probably the tip of the iceberg of how many people *thought* it but were kind enough to give me the benefit of the doubt before actually *announcing* it. My response to such blatant distrust is now what it always was and always will be:

Rich? Guess again.

White? Yep, last I checked.

And I'm not *telling* your kid what to do, (unless you count asking them to follow the basic principles of civility and respect that make up most of civilized society;) I'm trying to *teach* him the subject material. So, you're 1 for 3 right out of the box.

Oh, and **you don't know *shit* about me**, **personally**, so keep your assumptions to yourself.

Unless you'd be Ok with me replying *"That's OK, I'm not really interested in teaching the thug offspring of a poor minority woman anyway."*

Oh wait, that **offends** you?

Well, we both know that it **should** because it's appallingly judgmental (and racist,) and any sensible person would be insulted; but if you think you can be the person in my #3 reason and still be offended by my *hypothetical* response, well, the fourth word in this chapter title is, after all, HYPOCRISY.

Lest you think I'm over sensitive to the encroaching wolf of teacher bashing hidden in the sheep-like guise of "child concern," you need look no further than the case of Marianne Kennedy.

I've lost count of how many articles I've read over the last three years about "exceptional," "well-loved," "model of leadership" compassionate teachers being removed from their positions because of parents/guardians that have overreacted, (usually thanks to the prodding of ambulance-chasing legal parasites,) to common sense situations in an attempt to purge their own anxieties and inadequacies. The most recent example is Marianne Kennedy, a 20+ year veteran teacher described as "a model teacher: caring, devoted, personally invested in children." Her own principal referred to her as the "heart and soul," of the Willard Elementary School in Kensington, near my old stomping ground of Fishtown, Philadelphia (NOT an easy place to teach.) But that didn't stop the aunt of a troubled boy "with a history of emotional trouble" who "had kicked [another teacher] and tried to punch him" from calling the Department of Human Services on Kennedy, who had been called in to calm the boy down and prevent him from hurting himself.

The aunt's refrain? "The school failed him."

One, that sounds like lawyer talk to me, not aunt concerned with her nephew's well-being talk.

Two, the *school* failed him?

Really? Anybody *else* fail him, perhaps?

Of course not. Not in this day and age, when personal accountability, (or, at the very least,) self-awareness and honesty among "guardians" are in short supply. These days, it's:

- "Here, raise our kids for us, but don't take any liberties."
- "Discipline our kids for us, but don't cross any lines."
- "Teach our kids, but within these parameters; and don't fail, ever, even if you obviously love and respect our kids, because, hey, *that's your job.*"

Really? **What's YOUR job?**

Marianne Kennedy's co-worker summed it up best when she

observed: "If this[4] has happened to Marianne, who's done nothing but good for anyone, what's going to happen the next time a parent is unhappy?...It's scary."

You're damn right it is.

...and for more musings on the anemic wielding of the race card and limp dick waving of political correctness, curl up in your favorite reading spot, fasten your seatbelts, and get ready for the next chapter.

ABC
A Beatific Conclusion

Normally, having to go back into a massive WORD document and move **everything** around just to incorporate a few lines of suddenly relevant information make me angrier than The Hulk in a hornet's nest.

However, I am thrilled (and a little bit surprised, to be honest) to tell you that, prior to this book going to publication, Marianne Kennedy's charges were, after a thorough investigation, expunged, and she was cleared to return to work. Her principal, her peers, and her supporter and students were overjoyed.

As for Marianne: "I just want to be there with the kids again," she said. "I'm ready to go back tomorrow."

No surprise there.

---

(4) Labeled a child abuser, put out of the school since September, barred from contact with children, considered by the School Reform Commission for termination, etc.

YOU'RE RACIST.
YOU'RE WRONG.

"When 'I' is replaced with 'We', even the illness becomes wellness."
— Malcolm X

It's an ugly subject, and it's bound to inflame passions and court controversy, which is why so many people (particularly white people, parTICularly white teachers) are reluctant to discuss it.

I'm not most teachers.

As a 25-year veteran of classrooms that have traditionally been populated by inner city kids of every shape, size, sexuality, and sanity level, I've seen, experienced, and been subjected to racism from all sides, and yes, I've been called racist on more than a few occasions.

I don't sweat the accusations, because they almost never come from the kids. However, I have seen over the years an increase in the propensity for my Black and Hispanic students to label EVERYthing as racist, even (and sometimes especially) situations that they don't fully understand. It's a disturbing trend that plays right into the hands of the "divide and conquer" mentality that has been working with time-tested efficiency since Philip of Macedonia [allegedly] gave voice to it.

While I will certainly comment on, joke about,[1] or elaborate upon miscellaneous incidents that may have involved race in some capacity, this chapter is intended to be a frank discussion about something that is increasingly tearing apart the fabric of our classrooms, which, to be honest, are microcosms of our society at large.

This pains me deeply because I believe our children hold the key[2]

---

(1) Yes, I can joke about it; you can do that when you're self-aware, accountable, practice transparency, and are willing to learn. You disagree? Great, that's what makes democracy wonderful. Go read another book.

(2) I almost typed "I believe the children are our future," but all I could hear in my head was my sons' Whitney Houston impersonations (they're actually eerily good) and I thought the laughter this early was unbefitting the serious nature of this chapter.

to fixing this colossal imbroglio we've left for them, but that will never happen unless we help dissolve the fault lines that are calcifying between us, and *that* is never going to happen until we can embrace frank, yet empathetic discussions, particularly in our classrooms, about the factors that facilitate our widening divisions. I can tell you personally that every time something potentially incendiary (particularly if it involves racial tensions) happens in our country, my email and social media inboxes are bombarded with a variety of messages all proclaiming some variation of: *"I wish I was still in your class because I know we'd be talking about this and you would be honest with us."*

So let's start with that, and allow it to be a segue into the three anecdotes that follow.

I think it's appalling that I could get in trouble for doing the one thing that my students have consistently BEGGED me to do—***talk*** to them about the issues that influence their lives. Discussing sex, politics, religion, family issues, money issues, educational policy (You know, the stuff that REALLY affects the lives and futures of our kids?) is widely considered bad juju by the tone-deaf suits. Better that the kids learn the Pythagorean theorem or why Moby Dick is a metaphor. Listen, I get it— if the teacher/professor is TELLING the kids WHAT to think, or openly ridiculing them for their (or their parents') beliefs, that is obviously unprofessional, and those people should be vilified and unemployed, but I'm here to tell you, folks, that only truly shitty teachers and parents, (yes, I said it) want unequivocal **compliance** and blind **obedience**; the good ones want your/our kids to question *everything* and to be better than the previous generation in every conceivable way. That way, they can fix this society *we* fractured and dumped on them.

That being said, the "That's racist" rant will continue to ring out in classrooms with increasing frequency, and now that the people who occupy the highest echelons of government seem to perpetuate their employment by unceremoniously dividing their constituency, I fear that the winds of racial insensitivity will get even more intense. And while the racial recrimination will often be the righteous rage of the disenfranchised, there will, undoubtedly, also be times that it will hold no weight and, in fact, do more damage than good.

151

By way of example, let me regale you with three very recent and very real anecdotes wherein your humble author was: implied to be racist, flat out accused of being racist, and accused, albeit subtly, of "not being black enough."[3] All by people that I went above and beyond to help. Alas, no good deed goes unpunished, no rest for the wicked, and all that. And so, without further ado, a few lessons on how crying ~~witchcraft arbitrarily in 1692~~ racism irresponsibly in the modern era can be downright counterproductive.

Meine erste Anekdote

Philomena Fragile's mom didn't like me from day one;[4] largely, in hindsight, because I was white[5]. It should be noted, before we begin, that Philomena did not meet the criteria to be in this particular Gifted and Talented class, but Mom pressured her middle shool teacher and badgered the powers-that-be to get her into said class. No worries, that happens a lot more than you would think, but certain things most certainly do NOT happen regularly, for example:

- A parent who texts and Emails you (attaching every administrator from the Supervisor to the Superintendent) *2-3 times a week* asking you to explain every comment and quantify every grade, even when there were specific directions, detailed rubrics, and extensive commentary made readily available through a *variety* of previously provided sources.
- A parent who then demands 'in person' meetings with you, Philomena's counselor, any remaining administrator, (more on that in a minute,) Ms. Glassmaker's[6] legal counsel, etc. for the sole purpose of going over—now for the 4th time—all of the material covered in the previous, exhaustively covered, texts and emails.

---

(3) Yes, you read that correctly; and yes, before you Google my picture, I am 100% Eminem white.

(4) That's cool, more often than not, I don't like me either.

(5) Now that shit ain't cool, but what are you gonna do? Cest la vie mon ami'

(6) Mom's last name was different than Philomena's; a pretty common occurrence. Sorry for the confusion; I should have told you that earlier.

- A parent who brings, to those meetings, multiple transcripts [sometimes accurate, more often than not incorrect] **of my classroom discourse** (Was Philomena instructed to copy this stuff down?) with the intention of *having me quantify every word* that she found "questionable!"

A parent who, after being told by most of the exhausted and, quite frankly, annoyed educational staff that she simply couldn't monopolize any more of their time with continued (and, as yet, unfounded) implications of "questionable teacher behavior," went to the Board of Education with *implications* (never *accusations*, of course, because that would require a set of balls and some self-awareness) that the administrators were blindly supporting me.

Administrators... blindly supporting *me*, Mr.-perpetual-thorn-in-their-sides? Riiiiight. Her behavior was, in a word, harassment.[7] But I just rolled with it. Some of my "questionable behavior" involved showing Mom a copy of one of Philomena's assignments (the original went mysteriously missing) involving *verbatim* plagiarism of a poem. I was accused of "badgering" her daughter FOR POINTING OUT THAT SHE BLATANTLY PLAGIARIZED. It was also *implied* (never *accused*) that I may have "doctored" the original.[8]

I started taking perverse enjoyment in watching Ms. Glassmaker reveal her true colors as she got more desperate to prove that Mean ol' Mr. Step was targeting her black daughter who, I may have mentioned, NEVER QUALIFIED, BASED ON A CLEAR, CONCISE, BOARD APPROVED SET OF STANDARDS, TO BE IN THE CLASS IN THE FIRST PLACE. The upbraiding continued in earnest until signs of Ms. Glassmaker's real agenda started to reveal themselves in between the cracks of her mission of mammoth micromanagement. Earlier on, she told an administrator—Mr. Atlas—that she was "disappointed" because

---

(7) Actually, in legal terms, several words: (a) Employees shall not be subjected to harassment, inappropriate behavior or interference by a parent or any other person in the performance of the employee's duties... (b) Inappropriate behavior includes chronic and continuous badgering, as well as verbal abuse. Verbal abuse includes abusive language...insults, threats, profanity and upbraiding.

(8) Actually laughed out loud at that particular implication; I mean, I had to, right?

she "thought he would be a sympathetic ear" (aka: black) and then promptly refused a meeting with a counselor because "she had already heard from two *men*," (me and Mr. Atlas.)

Well now...

Let's just say that a blind man could see that there were issues here that went far beyond the sacred walls of my classroom. Meanwhile, I started to see a change in Philly herself, and not a pleasant one. Her classmates saw it, too, and they didn't like it.

Apparently, they were familiar with this cycle of maternal malpractice, having witnessed it in the middle school, but they never saw Philomena *herself* "buy in." A few of the members of the class let me know, in private conversations and emails, that Philomena Fragile was making comments about my "obvious bias" and "racist tendencies," to which my other students, bless their hearts, responded in well-articulated, but nonetheless defensive [of me] verbiage. Mother Bear, however, had gone into hiding, but the texts, emails and digital onslaught increased to a pace that tested the limitations of a variety of Apple products.

I figured it was time to address the African elephant in the room, and I was going to do it the only way things of this nature should be done—face to face.

It was two days until parent-teacher conferences, so I would take care of Ms. Glassmaker then, but I was conferencing, privately, with each student in the class (regarding their most recent essays,) so this was a perfect opportunity to just talk, openly and honestly, with Philomena. After we concluded our conference and I helped her understand the issues with her paper, of which, to be honest, there were only a few,[9] I asked her—as I did every other kid—how she was liking the class, did she feel that she was improving? etc. Then I told her that I had something more serious to ask her.

She knew what I was going to ask.

We spoke for a few minutes, and I think she came away both relieved and rededicated. In my case, I was relieved that a young woman did

---

(9) The truly tragic part of this whole exhausting anecdote was that Philomena was, despite all of this, learning a lot and working her way toward performing at a truly "advanced placement" level.

not inherently believe that I was "out to get her," nor did she consider me, by any stretch of the definition, a bigot. I believe her words were something to the effect of "an equal opportunity prick," which, I confess, made me laugh out loud. (Hey, there are certainly times when that description is spot-on accurate, so if the shoe fits...) I was also rededicated to confronting the person that was making my life, which included the teaching of her daughter, excruciatingly cumbersome because she convinced herself to think I was a racist.

The plagiarism incident was followed by a quiz that Philomena *admitted* to not studying for—she earned a 55—because she had flugelhorn practice[10] and it ran late. I told her that EVERYone in that class was involved in various extracurricular activities; therefore, no excuses—you failed. Mom accused me (by email, of course) of "crushing her daughter's dreams" by repeatedly "SETTING HER UP TO FAIL." (Yes, that was typed in ALL CAPS). [11]

I responded, in print, that I "look[ed] forward to finally seeing [her] in person[12] at parent teacher conferences." Yes, the "finally" was intentional. Fuck her. She was compromising *her own child's education* because her vindictive protectiveness was unintentionally softening her daughter against potentially growth-inducing constructive criticism, and the gloves were off.

Glassmaker came with an "associate"[13] to parent teacher conferences, offered no handshake or "hello" despite my extended hand and greeting, and led off with "You know, I just started liking you, Mr. Step and..."

"I went and told the truth again?"

I've been told, by my lovely, borderline omnipotent wife, that when I'm angry, it "radiates" out of me. It's a character flaw, I guess, but at least I'm authentic. I'm guessing Glassmaker and her 'associate' felt the

---

(10) No, she doesn't really play the flugelhorn, you knuckleheads; but she was at SOME kind of practice and I think the word flugelhorn is funny. (11)

(11) Apologies to any and all flugelhorn aficionados nationwide; I'm sure it's a kick ass instrument.

(12) All of our previous 'contact' was, as you made have discerned, NOT done as such.

(13) Cowardly but not unanticipated.

radiation because their posture changed, and Glassmaker's tone was a little less haughty when she continued:

"Well, now 'the truth' (she made air quotes when she said this) is open to interpretation."

"No, it's not. The truth is the truth. Quantifiable facts are, by their nature, incontrovertible. Plagiarism is, in fact, provable. A three-year public record of academic mediocrity is indisputable, and (pause, lean in) harassment, by definition, is truth, provided the person being harassed is a fastidious record keeper."

At this point, the 'associate's' body language strongly indicated that she felt that she may have backed the wrong horse in this race, and the teachers on either side of me (we sit nearly shoulder to shoulder at cafeteria tables for parent-teacher conferences) stopped what they were doing to listen to where this was going.

Somewhat undaunted, (you gotta hand it to her, folks) Mom pressed on. In fact, she doubled down: "Well, I don't know about all that mess, but I do know that Philomena will be doing better in your class…"

"She's already doing better…"

"…because I got her a tutor, and she is an amazing teacher, so Philomena's grade will no doubt improve." She smiled like she won something. Sad.

"Where did you find this amazing teacher? If you don't mind me asking."

Another self-satisfied smile. "She just graduated from _____ college with…"

*"So, she hasn't actually **taught** yet."*

Smile gone. "… with a degree in African American Women's studies."

"And there we have it. She's black, and she's a woman, so, without the benefit of ANY teaching experience, you think this woman will be

a (air quotes) *'great teacher'* based on nothing more than the fact that *she looks like your daughter. If that was what you were looking for, why didn't YOU just homeschool her?"*

(Indignantly) "Because I am not qualified."

"And yet you continually feel qualified to question any teacher that doesn't hand Philomena good grades?" (I felt an instant wave of sorrow for Philomena, so I reached out, one last time, on her behalf:) *"Do you honestly feel like this is helping your daughter, Ms. Glassmaker?"*

Her 'associate' knew the right answer, as did anyone in earshot, as did I, as did [I believe,] Ms. Glassmaker.

Unwilling to compromise, however, she offered her final shot. "You are an arrogant ass, Mr. Step. I'll see you around."

"And I'll see you in court."

She almost shit herself right there, but it stopped her in her tracks, which was all I wanted; no way this conversation ended without closure of some sort.

"Arrogant? Guilty. Ass? Sometimes. But, unlike you, I'm not a racist, and the 'truth' (**extremely** exaggerated air quotes) *doesn't change according to your ability to accept it."*

She was seething now. She moved in close, apparently unconcerned that anyone else could hear her (which was good, because somebody must have informed Mr. Atlas that a fight was brewing and so he had entered the cafeteria and made his way toward us within earshot.) "I don't like you Mr. Stepnowski, I never have, but I want the best possible education for my daughter, period."

"I know; you've had multiple chances to take Philly out of my class. Mr. Atlas (I gestured behind her) *offered twice, almost begged you the second time to stop the tidal wave of emails, but you didn't move her. Because, despite the fact that I'm a man, and a white man at that, you know I'm the best English teacher for your daughter."*

Noticing Mr. "not a sympathetic ear" Atlas behind her, the conspicuous evacuation of her "associate" (whose name I never got,) and the line of parents behind her, clearly pissed at having to wait so long to see me, Ms. Glassmaker walked out of my life. Good riddance.

Philomena, it should be noted, finished the year, and is doing well in her English class *this* year, although I warned her teacher (white male) about what was on his horizon. To date, no incessant intervention from Ms. G and her iBigotry onslaught yet.

So, parents of all Crayola colors and beyond, let me implore you. If there is a clear case of bias or racist behavior, of course you should pursue that like a rabid dog after a mailman that smells like beef, but if your problem comes from a place of personal bias—don't do that shit to your kids or their teachers; it isn't cool, and it hurts teachers' abilities to do what we want to do most of all—teach your kid.

Eine andere sorry Geschichte (a.k.a. Kangaroo Court)

Parent #2 didn't beat around the bush; he came right out and called me a racist, but only after...well, let's just say there are some stunning parallels to the previous story here, despite the fact that **this** one took place almost exactly one year prior. (I guess I should thank Ms. Glassmaker for making me remember this and go looking for my old notes.) See that, my comrades in comprehension! Every storm cloud has a potentially silver lining! Please pay particular attention to how this unfortunate autobiographical anecdote *ended* because, as many teachers will tell you, this has become a pathetic, albeit recurring theme in the life of the contemporary teacher.

There I was, ready to start my endless summer of sleeping, sun worshipping, drinking skinny margaritas and enjoying social media;[14] alas, I had a student in my GT[15] class this year, let's call him Joey because he was a mischievous male kangaroo,[16] that was "struggling.

Joey should not have been in a GT class.[17] Low ASK scores, below average IQ, consistently mediocre grades in English throughout Marsupial middle school, and stunningly lukewarm reports from his former teachers and kangaroo classmates regarding his in-class performance. What Joey

---

(14) Please, again, if you truly think that teachers have summers "off," come a little closer so the Easter bunny and I can stab you in the neck with a unicorn horn.

(15) GT = Gifted & Talented. Every school has their own name for these classes; basically, often a none-too-subtle euphemism for the [alleged] "smart kids."

(16) Well I thought it was funny.

(17) Every kid is smart at something, that's no feel-good bullshit, it's the truth; in this case, we usually mean the ACADEMICALLY INCLINED kids actively seeking to excel in post-secondary education.

did have—and every teacher reading this knows what's coming—was a hyper-enabling, teacher-bashing, conveniently delusional parent, let's call him Buck,[18] with plenty of free time to harass the school and everyone in it several times a week regarding every perceived threat to the surely predestined meteoric rise of his little Joey. Joseph, for his part, was a great kid: polite, pleasant, and punctual (at least about getting to class on time;) in fact, he was often early, and he and I would talk about whatever he wanted to talk about, which usually involved refurbishing old cars and/or vampire stories. The one thing he wasn't so good with was turning in work, and by 'wasn't so good with' I mean Joey failed to turn in 80% of ALL of the assignments for the YEAR.

It should go without saying that Joey was failing for the year.

ASIDE:[19]

Before I go any further, let me say this as clearly as possible (with the firm intention of printing this out later on heavy card stock and paper cutting problematic parents in the forehead with it.)

- As *warm-and-fuzzy-infomercial* as it sounds, every kid really is a genius at *something*, and…
- …our boy Joey was an amazing technician when it came to anything automotive (and vampiric, to be honest, but not much money in that unless you're a Twilight-y wanker, which he wasn't.) Sadly…
- …we only measure an increasingly small handful of skills in our antiquated school system, so kids like Joey wind up feeling disenfranchised to the point where they—oh, I don't know— stop turning in shit in an attempt to commit academic seppuku. HE was totally cool with the fact that "GT English [wasn't his] thing."

---

(18) Adult male kangaroos are referred to as Buck, Jack, or Boomer (Who knew?)

(19) A term used in drama and theater, asides are useful for giving the audience special information about the other characters onstage or the action of the plot, in this case, my boy Joey, the automotive savant brown male kangaroo.

Alas, Big Daddy Buck didn't share Joey's sense of reality.

I'll spare you the elongated story, but here are the quick details:

OCTOBER: Assignments start not coming in; phone calls to "casa de kangaroo" go unanswered.

NOVEMBER: I contact Joey's counselor who, after repeated calls, finally gets a response from papa and mama marsupial.

DECEMBER: A meeting is set up, which the 'roos cancel until after the holidays.

JANUARY—MARCH: Enough emails, texts, and phone calls to sink the Titanic (again,) resulting in a face-to-face powwow with Buck and the enablers[20] that resulted in the agreement that Joey would bring home weekly progress reports so the K clan could know what he was doing/ not doing[21] in my class (and the other classes he was failing.)

SOMETIME AROUND MARCH 14th: Joey stops giving the progress reports to his teachers and/or bringing them home. No word from home.

APRIL & MAY: More of the same.

JUNE 17th: Joey turns in his final exam, which he had a week to work on, two days before the last day of school. At first, I'm impressed that he turned something in, until I realize that…well, I'll let the note I placed on the online portal speak for itself:

"I am sorry to report that [Joey's] essay was a collection of unrelated, PLAGIARIZED pieces from various websites; as a result, he received a zero for his final exam."

---

(20) Note to self: Buck and the Enablers! Future name for my punk band side project when I get fired for writing this book.

(21) Clearly the DAILY updated online parent portal and bi-monthly Emails weren't enough. Hey whaddya gonna do? Kangaroos are notoriously non-tech savvy.

JUNE 27th: I'm about to walk into the gym with my youngest son Frankie and I get an email on my phone from Buck, which I reproduced here, as best I could, to maintain the "grammatical integrity" while still avoiding throwing the Buckster under the bus:

"hello, this is to Joey Kangaroo's [father Buck kangaroo] I am writing this email in ref towards my so grade for ur class..I noticed that the report he turned in has no grade attached to it, I checked it on GENESIS ...understanding I know he has a low averuge in ur class but I would of expected to see something ... can u email me back thx [sic]

June 27th and you send me this? I would have loved to have fired off a response Email, but I followed the "if you're angry count to ten and then respond" advice; so, I worked out, counted to 100,000, and went down the Shore for a few days, where a storm promptly knocked out our power for a few more days. And so, properly cooled down, I sent the following pithy reply a few days later:

*Sorry for the delay, we just got power back at my house, and I just received your email. I left a comment attached to the grade on Genesis; it reads **"I am sorry to report that Joey's essay was a collection of unrelated, PLAGIARIZED pieces from various websites..."** The zero grade was actually generous, as plagiarism—stealing someone else's work (in this case, several people) and claiming it is your own—to this degree sometimes carries a more severe penalty. In college, plagiarism of this type can result in anything from academic probation to removal from the program. It didn't seem prudent to add insult to injury since Joey was already failing for the year. He knew it, and I believe you knew it (based on our meeting and the grades/comments in Genesis this marking period,) but he failed to do anything to rectify his situation. He stopped giving me the weekly progress reports [that he was supposed to bring home to you] two weeks after our meeting with Mr. Platypus, and every time I gave him extended time to finish a project, I received nothing or very half-hearted work in return. Joey's a good kid, and he's* *honest, so I am sure he'll tell you that I afforded him every chance (and then some) to save himself, but he just chose not to take advantage of those opportunities. Please let him know that he can still approach me next year about help with his papers when he needs it, although he will no longer be in my class.*

I received two emails shortly after the aforementioned correspondence, one very short, and one very long. The first one read, and I quote:

"I only ask about my sons grade, I dint ask for attitude I know he didn't turn in some work but now, cause of you, he's going 2 summer school. ur a racist." [Sic]

The second one, which arrived in my Gmail inbox a few hours later, was the second longest piece of writing Joey Kangaroo ever submitted to me. It began:

"Dear Step, I am so sorry for my Dad's email…"

So am I, Joey, so am I.

Even though this story was a lighter shade of pathetic—again, let me implore you, parents of all hues, shades, tints, colorations and pigmentations, chill out on the haphazard tossing out of the 'racist' accusation, ok? I mean, have you SEEN the average teacher's paycheck? If I had aspirations of keeping black and brown people down, or if ANY teacher of ANY color wanted to "stick it" to (insert demographic of your choice,) I'm pretty sure we could find a way to do it that didn't involve shitty pay, limited influence, and built in hypertension.

So, let's get to that final story I promised you.

I've got a million of 'em, but this one so perfectly exemplifies the race card conundrum that I simply had to save the best for last.

Warten, er ist nicht schwarz?

Taliyyah Taffysticky must have liked my class. Apparently, she talked about it all the time when she was home. She even dropped some knowledge on her Mom, Tameeka, the night Trump got elected, explaining the Electoral College when Mom wanted to know how the hell Hillary had more votes but was still losing. (We had talked election stuff every day in between English stuff leading up to the election, and Taliyyah was on point.)

T2, as I affectionately called her, told me all the time about how she and her Mom would argue when Taliyyah would spoil movies by predicting everything that would happen in advance (mainly because she paid attention in class when we talked about how all stories are related and follow, essentially, the same patterns.) T2 also turned in one of the best presentations of the 2nd marking period, a hilarious comparison of *The SpongeBob Movie* to Joseph Campbell's archetypical Monomyth.

Sounds like nothing but unicorn farts and *Hello Kitty* cupcake dreams, right?

Tameeka told her daughter that I was a...

No, not a racist, not *that*; well *not **exactly** that.*

But I'm gonna tease you a little longer with this one because the payoff is priceless.

Over the course of a two-week period, I got blindsided by a hastily scheduled meeting requested on behalf of Tameeka Taffysticky, which (not gonna lie) concerned me because Taliyyah had been noticeably *not* herself in class of late. When I pressed her on this, her increasingly agitated answers were just a variation of how her mom was "unreasonable," or "so annoying," or "a bitch," and she was making cryptic comments about how "[she] should have never talked about this class," but she got so upset when I pressed her for more information that I just let it go; although I was, very uncharacteristically, nervous because I couldn't imagine what T2's Mom could be upset about.

Finally, Taliyyah blurted out the problem, right in the middle of an animated classroom debate: "My Mom thinks you shouldn't be telling us this stuff."

The kids were used to T2 talking about her battles with her Mom, but a few knew about "the big meeting" (which was scheduled for the next day,) so it got very quiet suddenly in one section of the room and, teenagers being teenagers, the awkward silence spread until…

"Uh, I don't tell you all anything. Topics come up, we talk about them, from as many sides as we can…"

Taliyyah responded, albeit very sheepishly[22] "Yeah, but…"

"…AND I'm pretty good about keeping my opinion out of it unless you specifically ask me, right?"

T2 and the class responded in a cacophony of agreement and defense and (to be fair) side conversations ran amok. I waited a minute or so (I like a little organized chaos) and then regained control, but when I tried to resume our conversation, which, at the time, was about whether our desire to associate with people like ourselves is primitive in origin, acquired over time, or other—Taliyyah burst in again: "Y'all don't get it, she don't think you should be…you

know how you do the devil thing?"

"Devil's advocate?"[23]

"Yes, that. She don't think that a black man should be saying any good things about _____, or talking about _____,[24] You know, stuff like that."

Wait, I'm confused.

Are you confused?

We were confused.

Actually, Ashley Zoboomafoo wasn't confused; she gave voice to what we, collectively, *thought* we heard, but couldn't have *possibly* heard:

---

(22) In fairness, I should have been more aware of T2's awkwardness and backed off. If I had had any idea whatsoever what was coming, I would have backed off; clear mistake on my part, despite the amazing chapter that resulted.

(23) Very often, I will play "The Devil's advocate" (deliberately taking the "other side") during debates/discussions to hone my students' skills at counterargument and to help them substantiate their assertions.

(24) My editor thought that leaving the blanks here sounded awkward, and I apologize if it does, but the full, unedited disclosure of what we talk about in my class is for my students and my students alone. They deserve that much.

"Why did you say a *black* man? You still got that Black Lives Matter conversation on your…?"

"No!" Taliyyah finally dropped the hammer: "She thinks Step is black and…"

It would impossible for me to properly relate what happened in my class after those last six words were exclaimed. Suffice to say that both Taliyyah's voice and my own were temporarily drowned out by the reaction of twenty-five students to the [now evident] fact that Ms. Taffysticky thought I was not only black but, evidently, an "Uncle Tom" as well.

Try to imagine what an incredibly diverse group of two dozen plus teenagers, who have been encouraged to find humor in the incredulous, and speak openly (and LOUDly) when they have something to say, would sound like when one of their own dropped the bomb that her mother was angry at her daughter's white teacher for—T2's words now—"not being black enough."

Yeah…it sounded just like you think it would sound.

Only louder.

Once I regained control, yet again, I had to ask the obvious, didn't I?

"Why, exactly, does your Mom think I'm black?"

The threatening-to-resume cacophony was cut off *immediately* with a look and a slashing motion across the throat that would've earned me a 15-yard penalty in the NFL.

"I don't know. You just sound like a black guy I guess."

"And you, uh, never thought to mention that I wasn't?"

"Nah, I figured if she was gonna be all extra, let her find out for her damn self!"

I would love to tell you that I was mature about this, that I told Taliyyah to go home, tell her mother what was true about my hue, give her a hint about my tint, rectify her consternation about my coloration…

One more?

I feel like one more would do it.

…tell her that my pigment was a figment,

but I didn't.

No, I didn't, and I didn't for two damn good reasons and one gratuitous reason: One, I thought this was a teachable moment; and two, I wanted, I **needed** to see Tameeka Taffysticky's face when she found out that her [no doubt well-practiced] reprimand got moved from the Apollo Theater to the Vermont Theater of Performing Arts.[25]

And hey, let's be real, this was going to make an **indispensable** story for the next book.

The day of the meeting

I don't know that I've ever been more excited for a parent-coming-to-yell-at-me meeting in my life. (And I've had more than a few. Believe me.) Seriously, when my wife tells me she's going to make special "Avenger" waffles for me on my birthday, and I wake up to the smell of butter, batter, syrup and superheroism in the air...

I was *that* kind of excited.

Of course, there was a more rational part of me thinking: her mom doesn't *really* think I'm black, and if she does she's not *actually* coming here to yell at me for being—what?—I don't know? Not black *enough*??

Taliyyah *surely* told her by now, and, if that is the case, what the hell is this meeting *about*?

Suddenly I felt 50% like a kid on Christmas morning and 50% like a naked guy in front of a packed auditorium who forgot his notes.

I'll spare you the boring parts, but when Tameeka Taffysticky entered the room, the look she gave my principal, a man who, let's just say, looked like she thought I was *supposed* to look, bounced me right back into 100% this-is-gonna-be-great mode.

I wish you could have seen the introductions. In keeping with protocol, administrators, legal/union types, and counselors introduced themselves first, and my principal finished with (what *should* have been a simple, pedestrian) "and you know Mr. Stepnowski."

No. Based on the confusion (and, dare I say panic?) that flushed Ms. Taffysticky's normally arresting features, (she was, in fact, a charismatic woman,) she most certainly did NOT "know Mr. Stepnowski."

She looked to Mr. Atlas (nope, wrong guy sweetheart,) and back to

---

(25) Not sure if such a place exists; I just went with the whitest state I could find for a cheap shot at humor.

me, (yeah, I can see it starting to sink in,) and around the room with a combination of dignity and desperation that was as unique as it was impressive, but then the desperation part started spreading across her face like a fast-moving Florida rain storm.

Mind you, the only people in the room that knew the "little secret" were me and my diminutive union rep, Barbara Badass, (who I had only told mere seconds before the meeting so as to absolve her of any wrongdoing.) Barb knew instantly that I had been telling the truth, and, within those few awkward seconds of "most-of-us-are-educators-here-and-we-know-SOMEthing-ain't-quite-right," I started to feel badly for Momma T.

Damn my empathetic bones.

So I stopped looking at her the way a king cobra looks at a one-legged mongoose and extended my surprisingly beige-colored hand and offered to shake hers. She accepted, albeit limply, and I suggested that "[we] work together to see what we [could] do, moving forward, that [was] in the best interest of Taliyyah."

I smiled. Tameeka's "representative" smiled.

Barbara Badass looked at me like I was Saint Francis of Assisi.

Five other people's faces took on various versions of "okaaaaaaaynot-sure-what-just-happened-but-that-sounds-like-something-we-can   get-behind-and know-how-to-facilitate-so…"

But T2's Mom, for some reason I will never comprehend, (maybe she felt like she had a speech ready and didn't want to waste it, I don't know,) took my olive branch as a sign of capitulation and adopted a tone and a body posture most decidedly NOT in keeping with someone who came to her child's school swollen with misinformation and misplaced racial accusations. She let it be known that "[She] don't know about all that, but [she thought] there might be more going on with Taliyyah's grades."

As one-eyed Odin and his ravens are my witnesses, I looked her directly in the eye and said, *"yes, situations like this **are never as black and white** as we expect them to be. Now, how much do you want to go into here? Because I have Taliyyah outside."*

Taliyyah was outside. I made sure of that.

"No, we're good," Ms. Taffysticky acquiesced, "you can call me."

I concurred: *"Yes, ma'am,"* while thinking to myself: *"Boy, it's a bitch when you chase a cobra into the hole and the hole opens up, isn't it, ma'am?"*

Sadly, I think you know I could write a whole book, a *few* books, actually, of similar stories. Truth be told, many of them would be a lot less funny, and a lot more disturbing, So, let's just get to the bottom line and wrap up this here chapter, shall we?

Allow me, if you will, to hearken back to those not-so-lazy days of 2008 when I was writing my first book, *Why Are All the Good Teachers Crazy*. I included a chapter called *The Race Card*, wherein I offered the following advice which, if I do say so myself, seems pretty prescient:

> There are racists in the teaching profession, as in every other profession, but they are so nearly non-existent as to not even warrant mention; suffice it to say that nobody goes into this business with the intention of using their platform to keep anyone down. Those people go into politics. Besides, you [students] aren't failing because the teacher hates you because you're white, or black, or tan, or purple; you're failing the class because you aren't doing the work necessary to pass the class. Stop looking for excuses. Grow up. Learn accountability instead of weakening yourself hiding behind a fictional shield that you run behind when anything goes wrong. (Stepnowski)

I've had professors who tried to make me feel guilty for *being* white and parents accuse me of failing their kids *because* they were black. I've had Hispanic parents give me standing ovations, and white parents try to get me fired. I've been invited to former students' weddings and funerals and baptisms. One of my former students told me that he actually gave his son the middle name Francis in my honor. I've had gay students ask me to be the moderator of their club *in the same month* I was accused of being homophobic by one disgruntled student that happened to be a member of LGBT community. And now we can add being accused of "not being black enough" to that ever-expanding list

I treat 'em all the same, folks.

And to quote my father: "Opinions are like assholes; everybody's got one."

Oh, and just in case you're one of those people that think, because I'm a white, 49-year-old, middle class male, that "that's easy for me to say…"

Well—you can probably guess my response to that, but since we've already referenced my first book, go ahead back to *The Race Card* chapter if you want to hear my rebuttal in all its politically incorrect specificity.

And so, I leave you in the hopes that, at least in the educational community, we stop perpetuating the "us" versus "them" nonsense that seems to divide us now more than ever. Let us teach each other to be unafraid to have the hard conversations about a difficult subject out loud and up close, but, always, respecting "them" in the interest of improving the collective "us."

ANTS IN THE PANTS

The ants go marching ten by ten. Hoorah! Hoorah!
The ants go marching ten by ten. Hoorah! Hoorah!
The ants go marching ten by ten;
The little one stops to shout 'The end!'"

—*Children's song*

Wow. That last chapter was heavy, huh? Can't talk about race without gettin' a little intense. Let's lighten it up a bit.

Got into my classroom at the usual 6:15 A.M., hit the lights, put down my bag, got ready to put my coffee down on my—WHOA!

A couple hundred ants were actively looking…uh, active all over my desk, the floor, and all around my room.

So, after disposing of as many of the little space invaders as I could with what brutish methods were available to me at the moment, I called maintenance and told them that *"we've got a pretty sizable ant problem here in room 666."*

"Yeah, we know."

*Yeah, you **know**?* What kind of response is that?

Normally I have got the patience of the Saints and Apostles all bundled up on Xanax. However, the aloofness of the response, combined with the fact that my rooms are kept pristinely low maintenance (to the point where I actually repair things *myself* so as not to bother the custodial staff,) irked me a bit, so I responded: *"Great. Any chance of* ~~getting off your ass and~~ *doing anything about it,* ~~you useless slugs,~~ *or is your schedule full* ~~what with all the bitching about doing your freakin' jobs?~~*"*

I edited my response, of course, but my pissed-offness, as the ants made their way toward my coffee and explored my attendance binder, was approaching throat punch level. The hostility must have been palpable because, in the middle of my homeroom, the maintenance team's finest, (a pair that looked like a chubbier version of Ma and Pa from the "American Gothic" painting) arrived with a vacuum that looked like it was made some time just prior to the invention of the light bulb and started—I shit you not—*vacuuming up the ants one at a time.*

While not exactly shocked, I was surprised. *Really? Personalized ancient suction?* **That** *is the infestation protocol here at ol' Dafuqisdat High School?*

RRRRreeeeeeeerrrrrrrrrr "Yep." rrrrrreeeeeeeerrrrrrr "We're getting' a bunch of them." rrrrrrrrreeeeeerrrrrrrrrrrrrrrrrrrrrrrrrrrrrrrrrrrrrrreeeeeeeeeeeee eeeeeeeeeeeeeeerrrrrrrrrrrrrr...

At this point, what could I do but embrace the insanity of the moment. *"Well, I'm sure the formicidae"* (Thank you, Discovery Channel) *"appreciate the one-on-one attention."*

My snarky comment was greeted by the kind of laughter that I imagine comes from being blissfully oblivious to anything remotely resembling common sense. The 'suck it' tag team finished their fun time with formicidae just as my homeroom kids came streaming into the room in a wave of white earbuds, khaki shorts and bad decisions.

There were about a hundred ants visible by the time the students had settled in and seated themselves, which my Freshmen, astute little cherubs that they are, noticed immediately (and loudly) in a variety of reactions, one more hilarious than the next, until the realization settled upon them like the soothing sound of a pre-1870s vacuum cleaner...

"Wait, Step, was **that** what they was doing in here?"

Mmm-hmm.

"You told them there was ants up in here?"

Mmm-hmm.

"And those old heads showed up with a Flintstones vacuum and thought they was gonna suck them up one at a time?!? [Laughter] That is some messed up shit, Step."

Messed up shit indeed, I agreed, flicking a pair of particularly brazen ants off of my binder so I could start taking attendance.

I would tell you about how I went out and purchased ant traps at

Rite-Aid during my lunch break, which I then put all around my room, only to have the building maintenance czar walk into my room three (generally ant free) days later and—without so much as making eye contact—start picking them up, grunting "you can't have these" like he was just going to take $20 worth of ant traps and walk away with them. I would tell you how I quietly closed the door and explained to him about how it's funny the things we don't know, like *I* didn't know you couldn't have ant traps, and *he* didn't know about what I generally *do* to people who are rude to me and touch my property in the same day,

but you don't want to hear that story.

Instead I'll tell you about how, an hour later, a group of 11th graders filed into my room, starting working on their essays, each one occasionally flicking their papers to clear them of ants. Neither the ants nor the children were pleased. Fire up the vacuum! Seriously, you c(ant) make this shit up.[1]

---

(1) Ba dum BUM! Chhhsssh!

ROOM FOR IMPROVEMENT

"Home is where the heart is."

—proverb

What the hell happened to my room?

OK, I'm going to breathe. I'm not going to kill anybody. I'm not even going to hurt someone semi-permanently. I can make this work for me; yeah, I'm going to turn this into a chapter in the new book…yeah, I'll turn a pig's ear into a silk purse and all that. Yes…breathe. It's time to do some metaphoring. MetafortheloveofGod, Montresor![1]

Suppose you were a lawyer, and on the day of trial, your briefcase opened up on your way to the courtroom and some of your important papers blew away, then you realized someone stole your cell phone while you were on the train. *Then*, while you were scrambling to recover with your team, somebody messed with your visual aids so that you were unable to pull up exhibits A through F. Oh, and by the way, you're representing *yourself.*

BANG! Goes the gavel, and the trial begins, but your hard work has been undone…

Or let's imagine you are a surgeon, and on the day of surgery, you find that your instrument tray has been messed with, and your normal assistant (the one you perform all of your surgeries with) has been replaced at the last minute, and oh yeah, almost forgot, this is the operation where you will be observed by the acting chief surgeon of the hospital. You're already behind schedule, and the powers-that-be don't want to hear your excuses!

Start cutting!

OK, you get the point; and, lest you were thinking, during my

(1) Sorry, couldn't resist the Edgar Allan Poe allusion. (2)
(2) It's from The Cask of Amontillado; great story, way better than the crap you seem to enjoy reading.

rampant metaphoring: "well, those are *important* professions, they decide life and death and all that"—**then you are part of the problem** with education in this country.

Yes, you are; and no amount of self-justification changes that.

Teachers are the ones that *create* the lawyers, surgeons, engineers, and every other professional that will someday affect your life, so treating us like anything less than the white-collar professionals that we are is, if you'll pardon my French, balderdash.

Spontaneous rant over. This is what I walked into on the morning in question: (I'm sure, as with so many of my stories, *many* of you out there can relate.) I sauntered into my room at 6:20 A.M. and found that:

- my board notes had been erased,
- my computer had been logged into (and left on, corrupted in some way, so that I was unable to log in,) and
- there was trash throughout the room,
- there was scribbling where my hastily erased board notes **used** to be (the PLEASE DO NOT ERASE sign nowhere to be found,) and
- the desks had been rearranged.

I found out later (**during the observation my Supervisor sprung on me that day,**) that other things had been tampered with as well.

Yes, I could have postponed the observation, given obvious reasons why my lessons wouldn't be all they could be (uh…because I have no access to my computer, or my SMARTboard, my &@%$!? notes are erased, my copies are missing, etc.) but that would run contrary to my lifetime "open door at any time" policy and, against all previous evidence, I would expect a supervisor to be reasonable, given these serious issues, and take them into account by not slamming me in his/her observation…

The kicker about the violation of my professional space was that NOBODY seemed to know who was in my room over the weekend. Seem like simple questions: Who was in the building over the weekend? Did the Lacrosse team need the room? Did any of the maintenance people bring his/her kids with them? Did the CIA set up a temporary black site to waterboard possible ISIS informants?

Nope. Nope, and nope. Nobody knows nada. Apparently, a Poltergeist uniquely interested in napalming all of my prep work made a parapsychological cameo in ol' room 666, and nobody knew nothin', no sir. Again, if something of ANY similarity happened to a doctor, lawyer, engineer, etc., there would have been a DEFCON 2 level response, but hey, *I'm only teaching kids*, so shrugs, frowns, "no big deals" and "I don't knows" are perfectly acceptable.

Of course, and you probably knew this, in the pie chart of WHY I was pissed off, the supermodel-with-the-eating-disorder-slice is "because somebody messed with my stuff," the *regular* slice is "because someone else's irresponsibility compromised my professionalism," but the *Pac Man*-shaped slice of the chart was "because it compromised my ability to teach my kids effectively!" I only get 188 days with these kids and every minute of every day counts, so when ANYthing comes between me and my cubs...

Suffice to say I wanted to execute a Mortal Kombat fatality on somebody.

But I wrote this chapter instead.

See that! Writing as therapy! We could have saved a lot of money on that shock therapy if we had only known about this sooner, huh Mom?

And now for the heartwarming plot twist.

The kids knew something was up. I mean, the fact that nothing was on the board was a dead giveaway, so they inquired and I told them the truth. Those kids are normally good for me, but you do get the occasional sleeper, the occasional "put the phone away, Lucas," and not everyone wants to participate, these are the realities of teaching teenagers—but those kids put on a show during my observation like they were a group of exchange students from Finland that were given the chance to be taught by Beyonce'. They were borderline hyper engaged, sweet enough to turn swamp water into soda, and showed—even the normally quiet ones—that they DID, in fact, retain all of the stuff we had been discussing over the last few weeks. Halle-freakin'-lujah!

After my Supervisor left, they were full of self-congratulation and the need for recognition: "We did well, right Step?'

"She never even noticed the board or the computer!"

"You're gonna get good scores, right Step?"

"Did you hear all my answers? I knew everything you asked!"

On and on until the bell rang and they filed out, smiling like a bunch of proud piggies in fresh mud. Me? I sat in the room for a while, in silence and smiled, with big (albeit very manly) tears brimming in my eyes. If you care, and they *know* you care, the kids will come through for you.

Without your eloquent board notes,

without your carefully planned handouts,

without your brilliantly incorporated technology,

and without fail, *they'll come through*, **because they know that you will, too.**

Listen, it's bad enough we're GRADED and EVALUATED on the condition of classrooms: A) we share with other people, and B) that people have access to during after school hours when we're not there. But this year my place of employment has taken it up a notch: We have moved to block scheduling, and, without going into the finer details, I'll just tell you that after January 27th, the three classes of Freshmen I teach will be mine no longer. They will go on to their "2nd semester" schedules, and I will have to abandon the room I've been in for 5 months and teach three classes of Juniors in a classroom that is, literally, on the other side of the building.

This is pure malarkey, and why, every year, I offer to chair the "clusterfuck committee," dedicated to anticipating future…well, you know. Every teacher in the building has to teach the equivalent of "the last day of school" to our current classes on **Friday**, move ALL of our materials (when, exactly?) to another room (that was previously inhabited by God knows who teaching God knows what) and be ready to start fresh with 60—100+ new kids on **Monday; a**nd be ready to be evaluated on the *condition* of that classroom on day one.

Nothing like consistency and a sense of "home" to foster quality education, right?

But you're not supposed to feel 'at home,' and neither are they, because you're just a teacher, and they're only your students, and there's always a room for improvement.

O CAPTAIN! MY CAPTAIN!

Mr. Murdoch stood on his desk and sang a song,
his students loved it, and so they sang along.
He made them love Spanish, he made them love school,
So the man in charge chastised him, made him feel like a fool.
You could've hurt yourself,
and then we'd have to pay,
the guitar thing is "unprofessional,"
and that's all we have to say.
Mr. Murdoch was disappointed
and his students were bummed out, too
everybody lost a piece of themselves when they heard about this
and I'll bet you did, too.
But that's our educational system for you,
teachers and students told how to teach and what to know,
state test scores trump love and creativity,
and heartless boring bureaucrats running the whole goddamned show.

Yes, that's a true story, and no, I'm not going to name actual names.

Not because I'm afraid; believe me, I'd love to publicly shame the heartless pricks that contributed to the Khmer Rouge-ing of our educational system, but rather out of respect to the

real person that I chose to call Mr. Murdoch. Let me tell you a little bit about the young man that got creatively curtailed by the powers-that-be in the name of "professionalism."

Matthew Murdoch is one hell of a teacher, by any definition or criteria. In fact, he fulfills what I will arrogantly call "Step's Unholy Pentagram of Educational Realism:"

1. He knows his subject matter well enough to explain it simply.
2. He is willing to try different approaches to reach the students

that didn't "get it" the way he taught it the first time (no matter how simply it was presented.)

3. He believes that it is, in fact, part of his JOB to stay relevant [to his students] by knowing them: *what they watch, what they listen to, what they (if they) read, who they live with/date/hang with, etc.* and then relate the material he teaches TO them, which brings me to…

4. He believes wholeheartedly (and practices regularly) the belief that **loving** your kids trumps bullshit abstract concepts like pedagogy and what the bean-counter-of-the-week calls "best practice."
   and, finally…

5. *His students* (even the ones that do poorly in his class) *respect him*, despite the fact that he pushes them continually out of their comfort zones.

Matthew Murdoch does all of these things, AND he plays a mean acoustic guitar, singing homemade songs that stick in your brain like a highly motivated mariachi earworm and force you to learn the Spanish he teaches. I swear to the paella at Tortilla Press and all other things holy that *si tuviera este tío en la escuela secundaria, sería un hablante más competente del español hoy, mi amigo.*

I almost forgot (silly me) that Matt Murdoch won a very prestigious tristate 'Teaching All Stars' award during his teaching tenure. I'll also pretend to almost forget that, *shortly after receiving that prestigious honor*, Matt got RIFed[1] by a spectacularly unappreciative school board.

Matt also battled demons, both personal and professional, never allowing either to diminish his love for his students or his craft. In short, Matthew Murdoch's journey as a teacher was never an easy one, and yet his students continue, to this day, to refer to him as the one of the people that profoundly changed their lives and made them like school. Probably because he did things like take the kids for fake

---

(1) RIF = Reduction in Force. As per opm.gov, "an agency is required to use the RIF procedures when an employee is faced with separation or downgrading for a reason such as reorganization, lack of work, shortage of funds, insufficient personnel ceiling…"

military style "marches" around the soccer fields chanting Spanish lessons, had inflatable ball catches where students answered questions in Spanish, performed a mock trial about illegal immigration using *Dora the Explorer* as the fictional defendant, reviewed vocabulary using a Nerf Gun (pitting his students against Google Translate,) and incorporated recording software so that students could hear themselves and their peers speaking Spanish about various topics throughout the year. Oh, and he would occasionally stand on the desk and sing original songs designed to make lessons stick in the minds of his constituents.

But we don't want that. Or, more specifically, the people that want to strangle creativity out of education don't want that. Maybe if Matt had his kids on Microsoft laptops, on Common Core sponsored websites, prepping for standardized tests by doing mind-numbingly repetitive exercises, he would have avoided the wrath of the titans.

OK, that was a little off topic and unnecessarily snarky. Let's focus on the real problem here: **the strangling of creativity out of a profession that now, more than ever, depends on that creativity to reach an increasingly anesthetized, apathetic student population.**

Could Matt have fallen off the desk while he was singing?

Yes.

Could he have (conceivably) fallen on a student while doing so?

I guess, if he did some sort of prime-time comedy prat-fall.

Would he, or any of the students in question—the same ones that posted the video with comments like *"Mr. [Murdoch] is the best teacher ever!"* and walked around the halls *listening to the video* **to LEARN the lesson he was singing(?!)**—sue the school if such an accident occurred?

No, I believe with every fiber of my being that they would not have done so.

Nonetheless, Mr. Murdoch was summoned to the halls of power and rebuked. He politely declined to share the exact details of his official letter of reprimand with me. (To his credit, he is a *far* more forgiving individual than I,) but the general consensus is that he was told to include, in painstaking detail, every moment of classroom activity (from playing guitar, to writing on the board, to farting audibly,) in his posted lesson plans. He was also told, of course, to keep his feet planted firmly on the ground and teach in a way commensurate with what those in power deemed "safe" and "risk-averse."

Keep his feet firmly planted on the ground.

That's the kind of shit that makes me blow the fuse on the encephalogram.

Keep your feet planted firmly on the ground, while perfectly applicable (and even pragmatic) in certain situations, sounds a lot like, in this instance, the Siren's call of similarity that, if heeded, is destined to turn our already bleak educational landscape into the sort of gray, Big-Brother-esque dystopia that would make corporations proud and our children prey.

In the immortal words of Three 6 Mafia: "Fuck that shit."

Sing on, Mr. Murdoch! and (summoning James Brown now) "Geet on UP-ah" on those desks if you must! I, for one, WANT my kids being taught by someone that brings passion, innovation and LOVE to his students.

I wonder if you, reader of this book, want the same?

So, (James Brown again, really rolling now) "GET ON UP! GEET ON UP-AH!! Get on the desk ageen! Like a sex machee..."

OK never mind, got carried away there, the Godfather of soul has that effect; but you get what I'm saying. How in the hell can we teach our kids to reach for the stars, break the glass ceiling, soar to new heights, or any other sappy poster slogan if their feet are *firmly planted on the ground?*

I know Matt Murdoch, inside the classroom and outside, and I know that he is all that is good, decent, and desperately needed in this profession. He is, to continue, the manifestation of one of my greatest fears; namely, that they are stifling the heart and creativity in our good teachers in much the same way they are demanding compliance and uniformity in our children.

I opened with an original song, so let me close with a line from a Billy Joel song, *No Man's Land*, that haunts me as much today as the first time I heard it.

RETRIBUTION

"I've seen these children, with their boredom and their vacant stares,

God help us all if we're to blame for their unanswered prayers."

God help us indeed.

And so, I implore you,

Get back on the desk, Matt.

`WHAT LESSON INDEED?

"Few things are so deadly as a misguided sense of compassion."
— *Charles Colson*

One of the requirements of my job as Dean of discipline for the 9th grade is that I have to, in addition to my teaching responsibilities, address some of the disciplinary infractions of my Freshmen and deal with them accordingly. Whether that be just a heart to heart talk (you'd be surprised how effective that can be if the kid really thinks you're *listening to*, and not just hearing, them,) a detention or two, or—in more serious or recidivist cases—in-school suspension.[1] I actually like the gig; it gives me a chance to see the administrative side of things and affords me the opportunity to get to know (and hopefully help) some of the more troubled kids. Alas, it also occasionally leads to exchanges like the one with which I'm about to regale you.

Once again, I leave it up to you whether I was in the wrong, the right, all of the above or none of the above.

I knocked at Betty Boxarox's door in search of a young man named Samuel Sopascasi, in the hopes that we could discuss why he blatantly ignored Ms. Themyscira's simple request to stop running around (*with* his phone out) in Wood Shop. And by discuss, I mean give him an in-school suspension, as this was his THIRD referral of the year for inappropriate behavior, SIXTH for cell phone usage, and TWENTY FIRST overall disciplinary write up (most of which, I came to find, were disrespectful acts toward female teachers.)

Alas, when Ms. Boxarox answered, she was simultaneously thrilled to hear that Samuel was going to be held accountable for his behavior (apparently, he's been a bit of a problem in *her* class too,) and disappointed that he wasn't there to receive it because he was on the

---

(1) My jurisdiction doesn't allow me to administer out of school suspensions; those are reserved, rightfully so, for the VPs and principal.

bus to participate in a very famous track and field meet held every year around this time.

While I'm always happy to see any of our kids get chances to engage in one of a kind experiences, I wondered, as did Ms. Boxarox aloud, what kind of priorities we demonstrate when we allow athleticism to trump decent behavior,[2] and I verbalized my agreement on the way out of the room as the classes emptied at the sound of the bell.

This, apparently, did not sit well with one of our administrators, Mr. Façade, who happened to be in the hallway at the time.[3] "Excuse me, Mr. Stepnowski, I couldn't help but overhear your comment about the young man that went to (insert famous track and field meet,) and I have to ask you a question."

"Fire away."

"If we were to tell that young person[4] that he could not attend [this event] simply because of some poor decisions, what message would we be sending?"

"Let me make sure I understand your question. Are you actually asking me what message we are sending if we hold kids account…"
Mr. Façade interrupted me: "Yes, can you think of one legitimate reason to…"

I returned the favor: *"Actually, I can think of about ten million* (air quotes done deliberately with my middle fingers) *'legitimate reasons.'"*

"Well that's obviously hyperbole."
"No, I am deadly serious. Ten. Million. American. Dollars. That's about what they figure Laremy Tunsil lost last night in the NFL Draft because

---

(2) I'm not a Puritan, folks; in fact, I tend to err on the side of empathy when it comes to these things, but twenty-one write ups and a pattern of misogyny? Methinks that ain't cool.

(3) Must've been coming out of the bathroom or something, because his normal modus operandi is to be a ghost when kids are in the halls, because he might have to actually discipline one of 'em.

(4) Be advised: Any person in a suit that refers to any of our kids as a "young person," is almost always out of touch with the heart and soul of our kids.

of a simple video of him smoking pot and allegations of taking money from a coach[5] *surfaced a few minutes before the draft. Now, before you speak to the justice, or lack thereof, in that outcome, the bottom line is that lack of accountability **earlier** came back to cost that young man **later**, both financially and emotionally, as what should have been the greatest night of his life turned into a public embarrassment for both him and his family."*

(Insert Façade's best attempt at a smarmy, know-it-all voice) "Well, that's an extreme example. I think we need to be a little more realistic when speaking about these young people."

(Insert you're a fucking idiot that's about to be logically eviscerated voice.) *"Realistic how? Realistic in the fact that we have a plethora of kids in this building, like our boy Sopascasi, that have been told they're 'D1 material' but couldn't **spell** Division One, let alone maintain the academic and physical requirements necessary to fulfill that promise and go to the next level, so they'd better, even more so, focus on their grades and character in the present? That kind of realistic?"*

"That sounds very negative, Mr. Stepnowski. Are we sure we want to say that about our young men and women?" (See footnote 4.)

Well, since he asked:

*"You know, I will never quite grasp how some people interpret reality as negativity. To use your words, is that what I want to say about our kids? NO, but it is the reality, as evidenced by 13 years of tangible, ever reoccurring truth from our own building. We're never going to **repair** the problems that exist here until we **acknowledge** them, no matter how uncomfortable that might make all of us in the process. So, to your point, am I helping our students by enabling them into believing that, because they can run fast, they can outrun accountability, thus diverting*

---

(5) This was, for those who remember the incident, seemingly the only news story, sports or otherwise, the following day.

their attention away from evolving themselves tangibly and realistically in the here and now? No, I am not."

> With impressive speed, Mr. Façade lived up to his name: "I think you have a very negative attitude toward our young people, and I don't understand the confrontational nature of your comments. This young man had a unique opportunity and I can't for the life of me see why he shouldn't have been allowed to experience it."

At this point, I should have realized that I was trying to teach Plato's cave allegory to the wall of the cave, but, undaunted, I gave it one more shot: *"My attitude is the* antithesis *of negative. On the contrary, I believe in them enough to hold them to higher standards, and the way my students respond to me unequivocally proves this. If you don't see why insubordination and borderline misogyny take precedent over a sporting event, then I don't know where to go with that. As far as being confrontational, I will only say the same thing to you that I say to the aforementioned students: anyone that interprets a difference of opinion as confrontation didn't have a good argument to begin with."*

Mr. Façade simply frowned, shook his head at me and walked away.

While that great humanitarian Joseph Stalin believed that "it took more courage to retreat than to advance," I saw this as simply the lone course available to someone with both a one-dimensional argument and a glaring lack of awareness of his constituency.

How unfortunate (for Earnest Semper Façade,)

how exculpating (for Francis Felix Thomas Stepnowski Jr.,)[6]

and yet how predictable (for Samuel Sopascasi) that, less than two weeks later, I would have to be involved in the removal of the aforementioned sexist speedster from his math class (also taught by, you guessed it, a woman) because he cursed her out for demanding that he put his phone away and then threatened another student for telling him to "just put the phone away, bro, you gonna [sic] get written up."

---

(6) I am well aware that referring to oneself in the third person is uniquely douchey; alas, I am a slave to parallel structure when it comes to writing.

You might think that, given my usual attitude, I would have been happier than a wolf at the annual crippled sheep parade to see Mr. Façade standing nonplussed while Samuel loudly flung vulgarities and threats of every shade at everyone within earshot, but I cannot say, in all honesty, that I was anything but embittered.

I felt simultaneously angry at, and sad for, Sam, who was well on his way down the self-destructive path on which so many of our kids find themselves. I also felt—as Sam greeted Mr. Façade's anemic request to "just calm down, young man" with a noticeably spicier "Suck a dick, you peanut head mothafucka!" [sic]—annoyed and embarrassed for Vice Principal Façade, who, in the immortal words of William Shakespeare: "[felt] his title hang loose about him, like a giant's robe upon a dwarfish thief."

I will openly confess that I approached Samuel an hour after this outburst for the sole reason of being able to bring this chapter to a satisfying close.[7] I promised myself, that I would record the EXACT nature of our exchange, without "editing" it to fit my personal narrative. In short, I wasn't going to try to paint a turd, but I wasn't going to hide a trophy, either. Here goes…

Mr. Sopascasi rolled his eyes and exhaled loudly enough to wake the dead when I entered the in-school suspension room and asked to speak to him in private. (Uh oh, not exactly off to a good start.) Once we got out into the [thankfully empty] hallway, he softened up a bit. I introduced myself, offered my hand, which he shook tentatively,[9] and asked if we could just talk about what happened earlier. He made it clear that he knew who I was, and thought I was just coming to lecture him about "doin' dumb shit," (As you may have discerned, being a sagacious reader, "dumb shit" is a bit of a reoccurring problem in high school) so I tried a little humor:

---

(7) Most effective educators, and good parents, (8) will note that this is sensible; you simply cannot talk to a kid right after a confrontation, as the 'heat of the moment' often makes them inaccessible to logic.

(8) And aren't they really the same thing?

(9) Any educator will tell you that this is common. Parents—please teach your children how to shake someone's hand, look them in the eye, and carry a conversation; it's a dying art in an increasingly detached world.

"Well, your performance at the [very famous track & field meet] was good shit, but that outburst was some dumb shit, so, mathematically, you're kind of at neutral shit right now."

He smirked, laughed a little and asked "whatchu wanna know?"

Amazing what a little H&P[10] can accomplish with an angry teenager.

"Well, for starters, you can tell me why you treat women so badly."

(Pause, look away,) "What do you mean?"

Did you catch what happened there? You probably would have if you had been there, and you definitely would have if you were an educator that can discern very subtle changes in a kid that indicate whether you've entered a kid's emotional minefield. The change in eye contact from street-perfected stare down to unconscious look away, the subtle shift in body posture from false relaxation to guardedly defensive, the change in diction from the pretend ignorance of "whatchu wanna know?" to the decidedly more formal "what do you mean?", along with an avalanche of other subtle indicators that let us know that my inquiry about his misogyny put Samuel Sopascasi on thin ice, psychologically speaking.

I know I promised you a verbatim account of our conversation, but, as you may have guessed, our talk ventured into the deep waters of things that don't *excuse* but certainly *explain* a healthy distrust of adult women, and those things are not for public consumption, no matter how titillating or "sales producing" they might be.

I wish I was fabricating the next part, and I would, if I were in your shoes, call bullshit on me because the event that followed my tense conversation with Samuel fits a little *too* perfectly into my little anecdote; alas, as any teacher will confirm, *you simply* (say it with me, you know the words!) ***cannot*** *make this shit up.*

Mr. Dillon, a man I both respect and admire (and who happened to be covering ISS at the time) came out into the hall. "I'm sorry to interrupt, Mr. Step, but they want Sam down in Mr. Façade's office."

---

(10) Humanity and profanity, two great tastes that taste great together, and the reason why Samuel L. Jackson is so beloved.

Samuel glared at me: "Who dat?"

I couldn't resist: *"That would be the gentleman you inappropriately referred to as peanut head motherfucker."*

"Oh THAT dude." (insert loud sucking teeth sound and agitated body language) "What that nigga want now?"

As much as I wanted to fan the flames. (Yes, I'll *admit* it, I wanted to slap the agitated honey badger before throwing it into the cage,) my professionalism prohibited me from doing so. *"I don't know, but I'll walk down with you, and I would STRONGLY suggest that you refrain from calling him peanut head, motherfucker, nigga, or any other term that might get your ass bounced out of here. Now wait here a second while I make sure the teacher covering my class is okay."*

The teacher in question was *not*, in fact, okay. She had an issue with the teacher's aide, who is one of those "it's 8:15, and my break starts at 8:15, so I'm leaving even if the kids are on fire" kind of people, so, for legal purposes, I had to stay with my class. It didn't matter, because Samuel didn't wait for me anyway; he stormed down to Mr. Façade's office, whereupon our erstwhile invertebrate decided that, after about 40 better opportunities for intervention, *now* would be a good time to "get tough" with the speedy, simmering Samuel Sopascasi.

The announcements over the loudspeaker:

"Officer Nathan to Mr. Façade's office!

(Vice principal) **Mr. Brunson to Mr. Façade's office!**

The National Guard to Mr. Façade's office!"[11] **told me everything I needed to know.**

It sucks to be right sometimes, but a little more in-your-face accountability BEFORE these kids go off the rails, and a little more love and compassion WHILE they're working through whatever adult SNAFU-ishness[12] *made* them hostile and distrusting, might prevent the

---

(11) Kidding about that last one, of course, but you get the picture.

(12) SNAFU—Situation Normal, All Fucked Up

look I gave Façade when I caught him talking tough the next day about "how he put that insubordinate young man out for five days."[13]

I wonder…

If we were to tell that young person that he could not attend school simply because of the decision to confront an administrator *that only held him accountable when his own personal ego was at stake,* what message would we be sending?"

What lesson indeed?

Peanut headed motherfucker.

---

[13] How convenient that there were no important sporting events during that suspension window.

MINUTIAE IT AIN'T SO

"It's not that teachers don't want to be held accountable.
It's that they want to be held accountable for that
which matters to students."

—*Amy Fast Ed.D.*

Minutiae (mɪˈnjuːʃɪˌiː) *noun _ sing: minutia*—small, precise, or trifling details

I am tired
of spending an inordinate amount of my time
proving to people,
many of whom I don't respect,
that I am doing my job.

Sorry for the dramatic opening, but this shit is getting out of control. The amount of time that I have to spend, (time that COULD and SHOULD be spent teaching and planning,) is being wasted on mandatory minutiae like:

- Creatively stifled, micromanaged "lesson plans" that, by their nature, lack creativity and flexibility. Of course, your plans must be created and submitted using the software (that you must learn and master on your own time,) that the district purchased THIS year, (which replaced the software that we purchased *last* year, which replaced the year before that, which replaced...)
- Bi-weekly (but cryptically undefined) "benchmarks" that are supposed to measure student progress, but are "encouraged" to be short, simple and to contain some multiple-choice questions. (So much for deeper reading, higher order/creative thinking, formal writing, and anything else remotely resembling the type

of approach to text that these kids are going to get hammered with in college.)

- Oh, and the aforementioned benchmarks MUST:

1. Follow strict guidelines,
   REALITY: *These guidelines will be changed periodically and arbitrarily throughout the year, and you will be informed via email, memo, or some other cowardly method of "we-ain't-admitting-to-this-in-person" by the Great and Powerful Oz from behind the curtain keyboard.*

2. Be similar to all other benchmarks that your peers are giving.
   REALITY: *What? You don't have time to contact, and collaborate with, all of your peers? Figure it out!*

3. Adhere to the NJ standards (and you must LIST the standards that each benchmark adheres to, and *quantify* that the kids MET *each* of those standards, or you must include them *again* in the NEXT benchmark, *along with your **new** standards!*)[1]
   REALITY: *Yeah, I'll teach some valuable, deep shit in 5 days, expect them all to get it, test them on it, grade and edit those tests, conference with each kid, make note of which kids didn't "prove" their mastery, and customize their benchmarks as I make up the next round, which is already overdue because of the fucking insane timeline requirements of the **first** round.*

Additionally, the *grades* of these mandatory monoliths of micromanagement need to be recorded on spreadsheets that have to be specifically designed, specifically color-coded,[2] and updated at specific times, to record the aforementioned benchmark scores so someone in an office can prove to their masters that the software the district spent

---

(1) If I may, a word about standards: TOTAL BULLSHIT. Sorry, that was two words. I promise I'll get back to this biblical plague of micromanagement before the chapter is over.

(2) RED for passing, GOLD for failing. No, I'm not making that up and yes, that goes against every conceivable "color = grade" logic you've ever heard. (3)

all that money on is being correctly used. Serve the **software**, not the **students**.)

> **REALITY:** *These spreadsheets are, according to the suits, supposed to "measure progress," but that, my children, is* (I'm running out of synonyms for bullshit so insert your favorite here.) *How, exactly, am I supposed to "measure progress" when benchmark 1 was about characterization, 2 was about symbolism, 3 was about including pertinent quotes in writing, 4 was about fictional analysis, and 5 was about the size of a blue whale's balls? Answer: I can't, but I'm not worried because I know that all these benchmark requirements will change as soon as the wind blows (aka: when our glorious "leaders" lose faith in the newest flavor-of-the-month pedagogy* and go looking for the next shiny new model.)

"Oh, and if you [the teachers] could go back and:

- evaluate how successful last week's lessons were,
- and how accurately your benchmarks were administered,
- and what the price of tea in China was at 7A.M. and
- <u>write all that down and record it in</u> the "teacher self-evaluation" section of last week's lesson plans,

that'd be great! But that's not all! We'd also like you to:

- make sure you contact **all** the parents of **all** the kids that are struggling in your class, and offer them additional help,
- contact the kids that AREN'T struggling in your class,
- give those parents a shot of encouragement,
- upload pictures of yourself at school events (to prove to us that 'you're invested,')

---

(3) Or does it? When kids being set up to fail = more profit for SOMEone…maybe gold for failure does make sense.

And make sure you record additional classes and professional development that you should be taking and doing (on YOUR time and YOUR dime) that'd be great, too, because we, your supportive administration:

A—Know that you have an abundance of free time,

B—don't trust your *word,*

C—and need you to check off all of these boxes so we can check off all of *our* boxes, so our corporate overlords can check off *their* boxes, so they can justify giving us the federal money that somehow results in the kids still having old ass books and computers that don't work."

This reminds me of a line from the Alice Cooper song *Inmates, We're All Crazy:*

"It's not like we ain't on the ball. We just talk to our shrinks
Ha, they talk to *their* shrinks. No wonder we're up the wall..."

(Author's Note: In the interest of fairness, there is NO WAY the admins can actually navigate their crumbling kayaks through these ever-intensifying rapids of ridiculousness because, again, the "serve-the-software-not-the-students" shit traveling downhill piles up on ALL of our plates.) As usual, I could go on and on, but you get the point.

Actually, *this* time, no, you don't.

There is **no possible way** for me to properly convey how ludicrous and infuriating this slowly tightening noose of useless activity is, and how much it compromises my ability to teach your kids properly, without boring you senseless or bludgeoning you with a monstrous chapter of examples, but I *will* TRY to give you a *glimpse* into this disheartening (it is, figuratively, taking the heart out of a profession that I love) attempt to ensure "teacher accountability"[4] and "student progress."[5]

---

(4) My interpretation: "set them up for failure and then punish them."
(5) My interpretation: "set them up for failure and then privatize them."

First, no chapter on the minutiae maximae that teachers endure would be complete without explaining the all-powerful, ne'er to be questioned standards, which are supposed to guide every. single. moment. of our teaching but are, simply put, an impossibly massive list of "what the kids should know." These sacrosanct standards were supposedly "field tested" **(no proof,)** grounded in research **(uh... no proof,)** and were allegedly benchmarked against international standards, **(but...well, you know.)**

Oh, and the federal government had a major hand in their implementation, and we all know ***nothing*** says "how to properly educate-your children" like FEDERAL GOVERNMENT INVOLVEMENT!

Even with my ability to spin a tale, I can't possibly explain the sheer volume of this violation. So please, take a moment away from reading (you were looking for an excuse to get away from this book anyway, admit it) and search for

"Common Core Standards PDF."

Here's the URL: http://www.corestandards.org/assets/CCSSI_ELA%20Standards.pdf

First, you'll get an idea of the Sequoia tree on steroids *size* of this Encyclopedia Britannica of bullshit (this is just the English/Language Arts section; we've got 'em for Math, too—with History and Science comin'!) Second, you'll treat yourself to such arbitrary nuggets of nothingness as:

Demonstrate command of the conventions of standard English capitalization, punctuation, spelling and writing. [For example] a. Use a semicolon (and perhaps a conjunctive adverb) to link two or more closely related independent clauses.

Riveting, ain't it? There are thousands. Go ahead, check 'em out, I'll go grab a cup of tea.

...Hey! you're back! That didn't take tOolong![6]

---

(6) I know, I know...lame tea joke. I'm sorry that I steeped to that level. Again! BAD author! I'm sorry.

I'm guessing, like most people, that you were overwhelmed by the sheer size and—let's be honest—boring and repetitive nature of the list. You are not alone, trust me. Your kids[7] (and most of their educators) agree with you heart and soul. Listen folks, I hate to sound like the mockingbird of malice here, but there is absolutely no evidence that this Encyclopedia Satannica of Common Core standards benefits kids (in fact, I see nothing but evidence to the contrary,) so ANY time I (or any other teacher) spend searching though this voluminous list to try to play "match up" with dynamic, evolving lesson plans is—simply put—ridiculous and takes valuable time away from creating meaningful lessons. While I *do* attach standards to all of my lesson plans,[8] I simply assume, and you can do likewise, that my students engage ALL of these standards at one point or another at some point in my class, very often moving from one to another fluidly and dynamically depending on about a million different factors that change from minute to minute—you know, **like what happens when you teach actual humanoid beings in an ever-changing environment.**

OK, enough about THAT monolithic mountain of mandatory, money-driven minutiae, let's talk about P.D.Ps. No, not P.E.Ds (performance enhancing drugs,) *those* are performance *enhancing,* while P.D.Ps (professional development plans) are really just T.W.Ts—total wastes of time—and they actually *inhibit* performance!

Basically, near the end of every year, we have to turn in (on deadline, of course,)[9] a specific plan of how we plan on improving our performance next year. On the surface, this sounds like a great idea.

So does Communism, until you introduce, you know, *real life* into the equation.

You want me to plan, in painstaking detail, (and defend my reasoning,) how I'm going to improve on what I did THIS year when I have no idea what I'm going to do NEXT year, especially when…

---

(7) We used to have to POST the standards we were covering every day on the board; and the kids paid as much attention to them as a Siberian Tiger would to a block of tofu.

(8) I'm an iconoclastic prick, but I'm not an idiot; and I can be outspoken without being insubordinate.

(9) Now, will the person that's supposed to review this deadline demanded document show the same sense of urgency in meeting with me that they did in demanding the document? In a word: NOPE.

Well, let me read to you directly from the introduction I wrote on a previous P.D.P.:

While I understand that the purpose of this P.D.P. is self-evaluation, and that I am being asked to prepare, in preemptive strike fashion, my plan for improving on this year's teaching performance, please understand that everything I write hereafter will merely be a compendium of comments from various administrators, from my three post-observation notes, not that I think any of you remember what you wrote, given: A) the volume of observations and B) the fact that we never, not once, revisited your observations/recommendations. I'll rely on your input because, after all, I don't have any idea: **who my students are**, what **grade**s I'm going to have to teach, what **levels** I'm going to have to teach, what **room(s)** I'll be in, **whether I will have an aide** in any of my classes, **whether the budget will approve any of the materials** I request, whether the copier use will be limited [again,] whether I'll have a student teacher assigned [again,] and/or whether we're going to have the same class schedule, grading system, discipline system, and painfully inadequate WiFi system, *as changes to all of the aforementioned have been the only constant in the past decade*. That being said, here is how I plan to fight the good fight; however, in the surprisingly prescient words of Michael Gerard "Mike" Tyson: "Everybody's got a plan until they get hit in the mouth."

Before you ask: The single solitary member of the powers-that-be that was *supposed* to review this and actually *did* read it was mildly amused. I didn't care either way because, despite being snarky, everything I said was 100% Grade A **TRUTH**.

Once we complete these glorified shots in the dark, an administrator will get around to approving them, and that's the absolute last we will ever hear about them. There will be no "follow up" whatsoever to see whether I hit any of my imaginary targets with my pretend sniper rifle; as such, there will be nothing close to the "accountability" or "professional improvement" (aka: someone actually assists/educates/enlightens/improves/encourages me in any way whatsofreakingever) that is promised.

This is what is commonly referred to as a THEME.

Theme—THEEM (noun)

1. a subject of discourse, discussion, meditation, or composition; topic: *The need for world peace was the theme of the meeting.*
2. a unifying or dominant idea, motif, etc.,

Talk to just about any educator that you know and they'll tell you that, like the P.D.Ps I mentioned, most of the time-consuming trivialities that they are forced to put in print are simply requested so (AGAIN) somebody incrementally up the food chain can check a box (AGAIN) to satisfy somebody incrementally up the food chain from *them* (AGAIN). It's almost all busywork, and if any of it somehow benefits the kids then it's usually by accident, like a broken clock being right twice a day.

Actually, it reminds me of those "Lifelock" commercials, you know, the ones where people just "monitor" things, alerting you to problems without actually doing anything to fix them? Yeah, most of these nonsensical niceties are like that, just paperwork to fill somebody's "outbox" so they can eventually wind up in the same mysterious, never-seen-again realm to which all the missing socks go when they disappear from the laundry.

Got time for one more? 'Cause, in the words of Steve Rodgers: "*I can do this all day.*"

Want to know the three letters that can nauseate a teacher faster than eating a month-old oyster left out on a hot sidewalk?

S. G. O.

S.G.O., otherwise known as Student Growth Objectives, (even the name sounds fucking dystopian,) are, by definition, long term academic goals for groups of students set in conjunction with their supervisors. In conjunction with their supervisors? Really? Apparently that conjunction junction forgot to function in my little corner of the world, because I received about as much training and assistance in writing S.G.Os as baby snakes get from their mom. Of course, when I checked out the NJDOE website, they clearly but cryptically state that administrators have to take part in annual S.G.O. refresher training, but—and I quote— "districts have discretion in how they will conduct this training."

Mmm-hmmm.

Like most of this crap, it would be impossible to fully explain S.G.Os to you without boring you to death, but I will tell you that they involve a lot of claptrap where teachers are supposed to establish some kind of baseline for every single kid so as to (quoting AchieveNJ now) "ensure that each student receives the best possible education, by being able to measure their progress *from* that baseline." **However, any teacher with an ounce of intelligence can, (rather than suffer death by minutiae,** aka: get fired for failure to comply,) **set the baseline low and then use voodoo math to ensure that their kids make "adequate progress,"** *which totally flies in the face of the alleged goal of S.G.Os.*

Actually, the difference between what's *promised* and what's *delivered* lends itself to a good metaphor for these things: I'm sure you can think of more than a few products in the supermarket that claim to be "natural," "robust," or "fat free," but when you check the nutritional information you're assaulted with an unholy avalanche of xanthan gum, polysorbate 60, propylene glycol alginate, artificial colors, fructose, sucrose, dextrose, and satanic goat assholeose[10].

Well—the people that promote these black holes of uselessness (often the same coven of candy-asses that love standardized tests and one-size-fits-all curriculums) tout them as "methods by which teachers can improve their practice!"[11] and proclaim that they "promote reflective and collaborative teaching practices!"[12] so as to "ensure that each student receives the best possible education within their school environment!"

---

(10) Ok, I may have made up that last one.

(11) Wrong, S.G.Os do nothing but take time from my ability to do exactly that.

(12) The only time most teachers collaborate on SGOs is to ask each other what in the name of Harry Potter's scar they're supposed to do (because, again, no clear guidance except for "have 'em done or else.")

But take a look behind the curtain and you'll read all about median student growth percentiles, assessment design modules, diagnostic pre-assessments, teachers' summative ratings, and scoring and *tracking* tools (conveniently, these are Microsoft Excel-based "resources," so I wonder what billionaire Common Core cheerleader has a hand in this?) Seriously, how did teachers ever figure out what they were going to do with their students and if those students made progress before these dildos of didacticism were unceremoniously thrust ~~into~~, I mean *upon* us?

We probably just got to know our kids, worked with them, tested them at crucial junctures, and kept notes on what to work on because, you know, we CARE.

How primitive.

Incidentally, ALL of those S.G.Os have to be aligned with that massive list of capricious standards I told y'all about a few pages ago, so there IS something of a "unified nature" to all of these time-wasting requirements. You know, kind of like how 6 major corporations control 90% of all the media in this country? Yeah, THAT kind of unification; and for the same reason.

SO SING WITH ME!

All the teachers sing:
We all scramble to scrabble S.G.Os and P.D.Ps
While drop down menu lesson planning kills our creativities
The reformers count their money and fiddle with themselves while Rome is burning
But we've got mandatory benchmarks to measure how well we taught what ain't worth learning
All the "people in charge" sing:
Learn all the new technologies and tests that next year will be the first thing to go
But use them NOW because we paid for them and that's all you need to know

*Dead forests worth of paperwork to prove that you do your jobs
proficiently*
*I won't really look at it; I'm too busy giving thanks that you don't get to
evaluate ME*
And all the kids sing:
We still got tons of emoshunal issues and problems unresolved
But the teachrs are 2 mired in minutiae so I guess their all absolved
We ain;t two good at nothing that matters and we ain;t aloud to rest
*Don't really do nothing meaningful in class nomore but we sure is good
at them tests!*

Listen folks, I might not speak for everyone, but I know I speak
for a hell of a lot of teachers nationwide when I say I'm tired (literally,
mentally fatigued) from checking off boxes, filling out spreadsheets,
entering data, completing pre-conference and post-conference notes,
and learning whatever the flavor-of-the-month "learning pedagogy" is
THIS time around…

You know what else I am? (and I suspect that, again, I speak for
a whole hell of a lot of teachers here) *Smarter than the puppets and
pretend leaders that espouse this shit.*

MY WAY WORKS, period. And it works **because I know my kids
better than any of them, and I sure as hell CARE about them more
than they do.** My results are proven, day to day, week to week, year
to year, with not only grades and test scores but also student reflection
and parent endorsement. I don't change my way of doing things
every time the wind blows because my focus is always the same—on
making my kids smarter, more independent, and better than me in
every conceivable way. This is in direct contrast to our (ever-changing)
power structure, who, if I may quote Navy SEAL commander Mark
Divine:

"Lack a foundation in their own character development [so they
seek] career advancement without the means to become better
people…they adopt a particular model from a training event or book…
[thinking] 'All I have to do is apply skills and act as the experts say,
and things will be better.' When their results fall short of the model's

promise, these [budding] leaders [13] lose faith and go looking for the next model.[14]

Boy *that* sounds familiar.

The same (ever changing) administrators that gave me a quarter century of ringing endorsements via their "observations," *are the same people that continue to tighten the screws on me because they don't trust that I'll continue to 'produce' if they don't keep their eyes on me.* On behalf of all the good teachers out there, myself included: Fuck off, worry about yourself, and be glad that WE don't evaluate YOU.

Please, just leave me alone and, I *promise*, I'll make my kids better informed, more inquisitive, more literate, and maybe, just maybe, if you stop worshipping at the altar of data mining and chill on the "we don't trust teachers" surveillance, I'll be able to TALK to them, LEARN about them, and CREATE with them; I can teach them about character, courage, communication and commitment, *and make them better people along the way.*

Or we can do it your way: Focus on test scores, data collection, arbitrary "standards," and what *you* call accountability and *I* call an exercise in inefficacy. However, as David Guerin so astutely observed: "If standardized test scores are your school's top priority, then your mission is more about adults than kids."

Or we can let the parents and kids decide. But you wouldn't dare leave it up to them, would you? Because we both know that your mountain of minutiae would crumble faster than a house of cards on Barrow island during Tropical Cyclone Olivia.[15] Sorry if I sound fatalistic. I'm just worried, folks. **Worried that this obsession with micromanagement in the name of "productivity" is going to turn our kids into the emotionally stunted, non-inquisitive product of assembly line education.**

---

(13) I will not call them leaders. I've had a toddler-sized handful of administrators that were leaders over the years, and they know who they are because I thanked them, often and emphatically, for living up to that title.

(14) Oh yeah, don't ever doubt that your kids are being used as the guinea pigs for some aspiringly upwardly mobile administrator who needs to pad his/her doctoral dissertation with data.

(15) 253 mph hour winds. Fastest winds ever recorded; you're welcome for that invaluable piece of trivia.

I recently discovered this quote by Gottfried Wilhelm Leibniz:

Suppose that there be a machine, the structure of which produces thinking, feeling, and perceiving; imagine this machine enlarged but preserving the same proportions, so you could enter it as if it were a mill. This being supposed, you might visit inside; but what would you observe there? Nothing but parts which push and move each other, and never anything that could explain perception.

I don't know if he was talking about the modern compulsory school system, and I didn't look it up because I want so badly to believe he was, because this quote perfectly encapsulates my belief that we have too many moving parts, and none of them are working together to facilitate actual PERCEPTION, only meaningless PRODUCTION. Einstein, another pretty smart cookie, was dead on target when he observed that "any intelligent fool can make things bigger and more complex...but it takes...a lot of courage to move in the opposite direction."

I think we need to move toward simplification. Less moving parts and more beating hearts, if you will. We need to start SEEING our kids and stop just looking at them. I worry that, as good as I am at "doing the right thing" (and I am **damn** good at it,) that this seismic sea wave of micromanaging is going to overwhelm even me.

The only promise I can make you—and you can pull this book out, stick it in my face and quote me on this—is that I will walk away when that day comes.

Until then, these violent delights have violent ends, and I'll kick, scratch and fight dirty to make sure I dot enough **i**s and cross enough **t**s to keep the minutiae militia off my back so I can actually teach your kids to the best of my abilities.

THE LYRICS PROJECT: HEARTBREAK, HEALING, HOSTILTY and DAMN, I'M OLD.

"One good thing about music, when it hits you, you feel no pain."
—Bob Marley

"Geez, Step," you righteously complain, "AGAIN with heaviness and diatribes against the robotization of education in that last chapter?"

"Well, yeah!" I emphatically reply, *"Did you notice the subtitle of the book you're holding?"*

But it's not all rage and ridiculousness—as *this* chapter will no doubt demonstrate.

As I may have already mentioned, every year around March I give all of my students a project to do. It is the same project, with the same directions, every year. Remember that this is coming from a person who throws most of his assignments away after two years and *almost everything* away after three (in the pursuit of relevancy and to avoid becoming stagnant,) so you know if I keep something for over two DECADES, it's a winner winner chicken dinner.

It's pretty simple, really, you have to report on a song that speaks to you, moves you, etc. because of the *lyrics*. I don't want to hear about how the beat is bangin' or the drums make you want to dance; this is Language Arts class, so I'm interested in the WORDS and why they resonate with you.

The student plays part of his/her song, possibly putting the lyrics up on the Smartboard behind them. Then, on command, "DJ Stepdoggiedogg" fades the song down and the student tells us why the lyrics mean so much to him/her. I specifically wait until around the middle of March because, by then, most of the students have developed some comfort speaking in front of a group, and now that the kids know and trust each other (and me,) we get much more profound—sometimes very powerful—responses.

Usually, by the end of the 3-4 days it takes to get through the project, I am spent from hearing the heart wrenching stories of what my kids bring to school with them every day, and I am equally inspired by their resilience and honesty. Occasionally, I feel old.

I have heard stories of rape, abandonment, abuse, and neglect. I have heard stories of resilience, empowerment, pride and self-determination. I have watched some of the "hardest" kids in the school system (KNOWN gang members and drug dealers) give a girl with cerebral palsy a *standing ovation* and comfort her when she broke down crying at the end of her presentation. I have watched barriers destroyed as kids got up and physically held/hugged others and helped them get through tear-filled monologues.

I have written long, emotionally exhausting letters that I gave privately to students telling them that I feel for them, respect their strength, encourage them to keep going, and to tell them I'll be there if they really need someone.

And yes, I have had to put my money where my mouth was on more than one occasion.

I will not tell you those latter stories, as they are private and this is neither the time nor the place, but I will tell you three quick anecdotes that will make you cry, smile, and laugh—*and then I'll tell you the flinch-inducing "punchline" that, unfortunately, is in keeping with the theme of this whole book.*[1]

---

(1) Disclaimer: Lest you think it's all "the Oprah show" here: I'm not super teacher by any stretch—I had a few kids that blew off the project completely (several of whom knew they were failing for the year, one of which just said "I didn't feel like doing it.") It happens; you deal with it.

Tuesday

"Reaching out to each other, is all that we can do
Here we stand trying not to fall.

There's no need to worry, love will conquer all."
— *Lionel Richie*

First day of presentations. One young lady, I'll call her Abby Fabulous, had been explicit that she wanted to go *second* (she said she didn't want to look too anxious but she wanted it to be clear that she wasn't afraid.) Why, besides the obvious fear of public speaking,[2] would Abby be reluctant to get up in front of the class and tell her story? Well, for one thing, she had full blown cerebral palsy, and she was in a class of 27 VERY diverse students, including at *least* one well known gang member, two [alleged] drug dealers, and a handful of what I will politely call 'discipline problems.' While they were all, to be completely honest, good kids in my class (which I then shared with a wonderful co-teacher named Barb Lion,) it still made for a nightmare audience to get up in front of and bare your soul, particularly when you have trouble with coordination and speaking, and suffer from frequent seizures.

Well, Ms. Fabulous got up, she spoke, and as she inched across the finish line, to the sounds of Whitney Houston's *The Greatest Love of All*, she shouted that her cerebral palsy didn't define her and that she would continue to fight, and then she broke down, hard, sobbing into what sounded like: "I just want people to love me the way I love everybody."

Her wraparound (an educator that follows Abby around the school and helps her when she needs it) got up to comfort her and hold her up, but she was too late—because Juan Quintana Rodriguez—one of those 'discipline problems' I told you about, got up, put his arm around Abby, and told her she was "gangster." The rest of the class, all 25 of the rest of them, got up and gave her a standing ovation as her wraparound led her out into the hallway. The last thing she heard was one of the guys yelling "We love you Abby!"

---

(2) Public speaking, which Psychology Today referred to as "The Thing We Fear More Than Death," (Nov 29, 2012) often rates near or at the top of the list of phobias.

Nobody laughed.

Many kept clapping. As God is my witness, I'm actually tearing up remembering the moment as I type this. I had several teachers look into the room to see what was going on and all I could do was give the thumbs up (with tears in my eyes,) and just gesture to the class like "What can I say? Sometimes this job is amazing."

Wednesday

"I want to conquer the world, expose the culprits and feed them to the children, I'll do away with air pollution and then I'll save the whales, we'll have peace on earth and global communion. I want to conquer the world!"

— Bad Religion

Ok, so first, *nobody* saw this one coming; secondly, I *love* when things like this happen. Mikey McFeels was that kid. Well liked but generally invisible in a diversely populated urban high school of 1500+ kids. Self-proclaimed dork in an *I-love-Donnie-Darko-and-video-game-design* sort of way, but, as some kids inexplicably manage to be, **not** a target for the insecure dickwads that often prey on the halls of high school. No, Mikey was pretty chill, but (and it took me forever to come up with just the right words) awkwardly awkward. He shook visibly when asking (every five minutes) for confirmation about whether he was on the right track (he always was) with whatever assignment I had given him. He kept to himself, our Mikey did, and when he DID venture an answer out loud, it was usually greeted by some form of "Holy shit, Mikey speaks, and he likes it!"[3]

So, when Mikey McFeels got up, and to the thundering sounds of Bad Religion's *I Want to Conquer the World,* unleashed a scathing (but erudite) indictment of everything from the criminal nature of our Congress, to police brutality, to the dumbing down of our educational system, to the horrors of Monsanto and genetically modified foods, well…

I, along with every other red-blooded American in that room, sat slack

---

(3) And he likes LIFE cereal too!…wait, is that an outdated allusion? Damn, I AM old.

jawed. Having seen the occasional shocker like this before, I recovered a little more quickly than the students (but not, obviously, quick enough to jot down all of the topics Mikey hit on in his flaming filibuster of awesomeness.) The smile on my face was positively Cheshire-ish, and believe me when I tell you, the applause and comments that exploded out of his classmates (after the perfectly understandable *what-in-the-holy-fuck-was-THAT* moment of silence that followed Mikey's abrupt end and departure from the podium) rivaled Bad Religion's screaming guitars on their best day.

Back slaps, heads shaking in disbelief, and "Aight Mike, you got this!" comments filled the room like radioactivity at Chernobyl, and Mikey, I am pleased as punch to tell you, ate it up. His parents talked of nothing else when I saw them later in the year. Good stuff right there.

Thursday

> *"Every time when I look in the mirror*
> *All these lines on my face getting clearer"*
> —Aerosmith

I'm going to go out on a limb here and guess that, if you're reading this book, there's a pretty good chance that if we were playing word association and I said **Steven Tyler** you would say **Aerosmith**.[4]

If you were a student in my class of March 2016 when Carlos Crespo got up to do his lyrics project presentation, you probably had no idea who the hell Aerosmith were.

OK, so I cheated a little on that last "assumption," mainly because of the comments that rained down after Carlos started the song he had chosen. *Dream On*, while overplayed to the point of madness-inducing is, by any definition, a classic; and it was refreshing to hear a 17-year-old kid pull some 'Classic Rock' out in the midst of a tidal wave of artists with only one album, song, or, in some cases only one mix tape to their

---

(4) For those of you considerably younger than me: Aerosmith is a Rock band formed in 1971 that were kind of like America's answer to the Rolling Stones; their list of contributions, accomplishments and awards could probably fill a Wikipedia page. Steven Tyler is their [admittedly] loud-mouthed singer.

name.[5] But when I heard my students recognize Steven Tyler, (who *MY generation* knows as the singer from Aerosmith:)

"Oh that's the *American Idol* judge dude!" "No, it's the guy from the Skittles commercial." "Is it? I thought he was in a Dr. Pepper commercial?" "No, you right, he was a judge on *Idol,* but I heard he was a singer way back in the day, too, like before iPhones and shit."

Before iPhones and shit...

Seriously. How do you **not** laugh?

I think the kids started to realize what was happening, and while they certainly didn't have anything to apologize for, got a weird sense that they should. I got a stream of comments that all translated roughly into "Our bad, Step, we didn't mean to make you feel older than dirt." I assured them that one of the fun things about getting older is that awkward shit like this happens, and that they would remember this silly class and their goofball teacher someday when it happened to them, but—if y'all don't mind—Carlos has a presentation to do...

C.C. finished his presentation, and it was truly uplifting and inspiring despite starting from a dark place. Carlos promised himself to "dream on" and achieve his goal of being everything that his biological father *wasn't* for him and his sisters. The usual awkward look-aways, head nods, affirmations, and scattered applause indicated how many of his classmates understood his pain.

That happens a lot during the lyrics projects; they all *kind of know* that they share similar shadows, but when they hear out loud just how much they share in common with each other (and their admittedly screwed up teacher[6]) my kids, all veterans of the psychic wars, become a little closer to family than just classmates.

I want to end the chapter right here, with fond memories of laughter, tears, anger and pain and my Grinchy heart growing three sizes in one

---

(5) No disrespect intended. In fact, the size and diversity of my iPod library expands considerably every year thanks to this project. Nothing like teaching teenagers to assist in one's social awareness and musical relevancy.

(6) Oh yes, I do my presentation first, and I talk about everything from my suicide attempt to the death of my son and everything in between. That usually opens the door to honesty on their behalf and lets them know that there won't be any judgment from me because, hey, I'm ugly on the inside too.

day and all that; alas, I would be doing a disservice to my brothers and sisters in the teaching profession if I neglected to point out that I had an administrative "walk through" on day two of the project presentations. I thought "Holy sheep shit! For once the timing is perfect, (s)he's gonna see how powerful and life changing this class can be!" I was so excited I used the word "gonna" in my head and didn't correct it!

I was told that my lesson was "less than proficient" because I hadn't posted my objective anywhere and several students weren't actively engaged because they were writing (the students are encouraged to make notes so they can talk to/ask questions to the presenter *after* they're done) during the presentation, and I remained seated the whole time.

But, she noted, I WAS doing what my lesson plans said I would be doing, so that was nice.

All this insight after the administrator, who I'll call Katerina Kuntwaffle, spent a whopping five minutes in my class, half of which she spent staring (here we go again) at the drop-down menu on her tablet. She *needs* to drop down and...

no, no...BAD author! Mustn't go there.

But come ON! You understand my anger, don't you? It is righteous anger, is it not? All the amazing stuff that happened between those kids over three and a half days and all her fucking automaton eyes saw through her corporate software fucking tunnel vision was what her suffocatingly robotic assessment model *allowed* her narrow fucking mind to see.

Fuck fuck fuckity fuck her and her narrow-minded fucking out of touch ass!

Sorry, I'm a little angry.

I'm [more than] a little angry[7] because this is so indicative of how teachers are seen now. The things that make our job NECESSARY:

- Teaching kids to work through adversity,

---

(7) And yes, more than a little profane. I'm sorry if I went all Reservoir Dogs on you for a moment; I just want you to feel my pain. In fact, if you get in your car, find the song The Demon's Name is Surveillance by Meshuggah, blast it at maximum volume, and growl/yell the "fuckity fuck" line at the top of your lungs, you can recreate the scene from this chapter! Interactive fun with your ol' buddy Step!

- Helping them to think critically and recognize logical fallacy and blatant propaganda in an increasingly dumbed down, consumer-driven country,
- Providing role models for empathy, civil disagreement, and intelligent discourse in an increasingly fractured society,
- Showing them *how* (and *why* they should not be afraid) to be loving, humane individuals in an increasingly hostile world, are being SYSTEMATICALLY ERASED by:
- constant testing,
- weekly benchmarks,
- corporate-driven curriculums,
- teacher evaluation systems that reward dog-and-pony show "performances" but aren't designed to assess real teaching,
- and an ever-growing list of magical "standards" developed by people that wouldn't have a Blue's clue what to do if they were presented with a warm-blooded human being and asked to actually TEACH it something

Caveat: I'm sorry if I sound like one of those emergency warning system TV tests, (testing sucks, standards are bullshit, administrators are corporate puppets, etc.,) I really am, but this shit is like a rash that you think is going away, only to flare up at the most ill-timed moments.

You know what *else* is making amazing classroom moments like my Lyrics Project die in frightening numbers like honeybees across this country? The kind of heartless, antiseptic computer tablet "iEvaluations" that Miss Kuntwaffle and her perfunctory peers just fucking LOVE *because they don't have to actually get to KNOW **their** teachers, **your** kids, or **anything** about the things I mentioned on the previous page that make teachers, (when we're allowed to be,) a vital component to the future of this country.*

Damn...

After those projects and that evaluation, I feel old and angry.

I'm going to go update my iTunes library with new songs now. That'll make me happy again.

Dream on.

A 6 WORD MEMOIR FOR A TEACHER

"I still do not regret anything."
— Katie Antonsson's 6-word memoir

It was the day before Easter Break, we had just finished *Dante's Inferno*, and there were going to be shortened periods for an [extremely poorly timed] assembly, so I was doing a quick assignment with my students based on the book *Not Quite What I Was Planning; Six Word Memoirs by Writers Famous and Obscure*, wherein the students had to try to encompass their entire lives in six words and, for a little extra credit, share their life synopsis and an explanation with us. Being as it was *my* class, it was understood that extra credit almost never happens, so you are gonna EARN that "EC" in here, cupcake.

As you might expect, we got a few gems:

"F*ck my mom and dad forever." (She's adopted.)

"Like Django, I am THAT nigga." (He's Asian.)[1]

"School doesn't teach the important shit."[2]

"Koalas freak me out for real." (She's brilliantly weird.)

"This is a stupid assignment."[3]

---

(1) 100% not kidding, which made it even more hilarious. Voted #2 response by the whole class.
(2) And that was #1
(3) And you can't count to six, so let's be careful about throwing the "S" word around, ok genius?

and my personal favorite…

"I don't particularly like following specific instructions." (This kid is going places.)

After some laughter, a few tears, and the general camaraderie that can only come from a motley group of misunderstood walking contradictions (I.e. ANY high school class) exposing themselves to one another, the obvious inquiry was introduced: "Hey Step, what would YOUR 6-word memoir be?"

(Insert Boromir voice here) *"One does not simply ask a room full of teenagers a revealing question without considering one's own response to the aforementioned question,"* so…

A LIFETIME FIXING OTHER PEOPLE'S MISTAKES

The other books have afforded me the opportunity to speak to teachers of every shape and size from all over this 3rd Rock, and I have found that educators tend to be givers/healers/fixers in all facets of their often very complicated lives, so I think that might resonate with a lot of you out there.

On paper, online, in life, until death:

A lifetime, fixing other people's mistakes.

Keep fixing.

THE LAST THREE DAYS

"Nothing is impossible for the person that doesn't have to do it."
                                                      —A.H. Weiler

Cue up that Europe karaoke: *"It's the FI-nal Countdoooooooowwwwwnn!"*

Only things are a bit different this year.

As a parting gift, our departing 2015-2016 superintendent and the rest of the brain trust a'la exodus turned the end of the year schedule upside down. Allow me to elaborate on exactly *how* they turned the screws. *Then* I'll make my prediction as to how the last three days will go.

But FIRST, let me mention that, (along with the normal infernal parade of behavioral issues that accompany the final days,) we—the teachers—must:

1. Endure the final process of teacher evaluations, which synthesizes those previous bullshit observations I've grumbled about,
2. defend the results of our SGOs (student goal objectives) with a ton of "quantifiable data,"
3. verify that we achieved the goals we set in our PDPs (professional development plans,) which were hastily approved by administrators who were way behind schedule LAST year,
4. provide *evidence* of student standardized test scores, compliance with individual students' I.E.P.s (individualized educational plans,) professional reflection on the success of our lessons, learning and/or experience outside of the classroom, and enough **other** requirements to make an unprepared trip to the DMV seem like a pleasant afternoon activity.

When I tell you that, in the time vortex that is mid-June, S.G.Os and P.D.Ps and I.E.Ps turn into O.M.Gs, W.T.Fs and F.M.Ls, I ain't kidding.

THIS year we were told, *with less than two weeks left in the school year*, that we would be receiving an Email "soon" alerting us who we would be meeting with (and when said meetings would happen) regarding ALL of the end of the year paperwork / assessments / evaluations /etc.

So, let me get this straight:

ALL of the S.G.Os, P.D.Ps, Summative Assessments,[1] etc., for a staff of *hundreds*, is going to go down *in the next 9 days*? Eh-kay...

Oh, and the administrative legerdemain continued: **"Teachers, don't give 'Final Exams' anymore. We want to call them "Final assessments!"** (Imagine my right hand simulating the jerking off motion.) **You will have scheduled days to give them, but** (and I'm quoting *directly* here,) **"don't spend too much time on review."**

Are you fucking *kidding*?

What do you care how long I spend reviewing? AND you don't know shit about my class because you never show your face IN my class, so how would you even know what "excessive" review time is? But I digress... Our *final assessments* (yep, still making that jerking off motion) are supposed to be done, grades are to be entered, and failure notices are to be finalized **by Monday?!?**

That would be great, if it weren't for the fact that we have *three half days* on **Tuesday, Wednesday,** and **Thursday.**

Let that sink in. A school full of very diverse teenagers, in a building where the classrooms are not air conditioned, in 90+ degree mid-June New Jersey, FULLY AWARE that NOTHING they do FOR THREE DAYS will affect their grades IN ANY WAY.

It's probably worth noting that this was a drastic change from past practice, and that it was made with no prior warning, and certainly no

---

(1) I won't anesthetize you with a re-explanation of all that shit; suffice it to say that would be like saying to you "Hey, get your tax information ready for that audit, paperwork together (and prep) for that surgery you scheduled, and pack for that 7-day vacation and be done by tomorrow—oh, and by the way, your flight schedule and surgery schedule are up in the air, and the movers are coming "some time" this week, too! Deal with it!"

teacher input. No questions were asked, no feedback was requested, no "problem" scenarios were even considered, and no potential backfire was addressed. Just an e-mail. Get it done.

AND DON'T EVEN THINK ABOUT mailing it in, people![2] No sir, we got a pseudo-Big-Brother-meets-Miss-Frizzle email from the current (now former) <u>district supervisor of Language Arts</u> complete with a typo **and** an egregious misspelling.[3]

Our grammatically challenged D.S. sent us a not-so-gentle reminder that we should be teaching "quality" lessons on the last three days, (you know, the ones that came AFTER grades were in,) and that **he wanted to see our plans "because [he knew] there [was] just awesome stuff being planned."** Translation: You'd better be fucking doing what I said 'cause Santa Claws is watching!

He added the following caveat, which I found to be pandering, insulting, and in need of proofreading:

> "… As you know, this will be a matter of 'selling' the activity to your students because [sic] they will be in summer mode. Students can be told their product will be graded through some (quick and easy) fashion and will be added to their grade. If you choose not to count it as a grade, obviously students do not need to know this…However, this activity could help a student who is on the boarder [sic] of the next letter grade."

News flash, brother, some of these kids have been in (insert air quotes) "summer mode" since we were shoveling our driveways in December.

---

(2) As if any decent teacher would even consider this. But when you get Email reminders every other freakin' day 'reminding" you… I imagine this is how productive, upstanding Muslims of good moral fiber feel when they listen to Donald Trump: "I'm a good person, but you could MAKE me angry, radical and irrational with your bullshit."

(3) I'm not a hypocrite, folks, I'm good for a typo and/or an egregious grammatical faux pas myself now and again, but: I ain't getting paid District Supervisor money, and if I'm sending something I KNOW is going to get an incendiary reaction, I supercalifragilisticexpialidocious proofread that puppy.

But at least we didn't get fucked as badly as the math teachers.

While we in the English department were being challenged to engage kids on three days of meritless activity in the build up to summer, many of the Math teachers *already had* amazing "quality lessons" (real, kick ass, fun learning projects) set up for Tuesday through Thursday, but the mathematics supervisor suddenly and arbitrarily demanded that they all do a homogeneous, everybody-do-the-same-thing lesson to end the year.

But you wouldn't *know* what they had planned, Mr. "Supervisor," because the disconnect between (Giant, Godzilla-sized air quotes) "leadership" and the people they're supposed to "lead" is monstrous, mainly because none of US even know what YOU even *look* like because you're never actually *here.* Hands up out there if you're a teacher and you know a high-ranking administrator that pulls that kind of hypocritical *demand-the-impossible-from-the-safety-of-anonymity* ninja shit.

Wow…that is a **lot** of hands.

But, yet again, I digress. (Sorry, lots of voices, off my meds.)

So I did what any good teacher would do; I responded to the request for detailed lesson plans describing what I would be doing on the last three days with a simple *"I will be talking, and listening, to my kids,"* and if he wanted to know about what, the door was open. But he never got around to that because…well, more on that later.

Secondly, I gave the final EXAMs that I had been telling my students all year about, and I called them final EXAMS; although, interestingly, when I told my students that they were to now be referred to as final "assessments," I caught a few kids simulating the jerking off motion, which touched my soul. Then I took about 14 hours (not kidding, not one bit,) grading them (they were critical thinking[4] essay exams) and

---

(4) Critical thinking is the intellectually disciplined process of actively and skillfully conceptualizing, applying, analyzing, synthesizing, and/or evaluating information gathered from, or generated by, observation, experience, reflection, reasoning, or communication, as a guide to belief and action. In its exemplary form, it is based on universal intellectual values that transcend subject matter divisions: clarity, accuracy, precision, consistency, relevance, sound evidence, good reasons, depth, breadth, and fairness. (CriticalThinking.org) (5)

finalizing grades and failure notices, then personally contacting each kid (and his/her guardian) that was failing during my final weekend of the school year.

Finally, I sat down to write personal notes to several kids that I thought made huge leaps, academically, emotionally, or in other ways. Then I put together two days' worth of closing comments that I thought were important for young men and women like them to hear. Then it was an hour of *Penny Dreadful* and off to bed to greet the coming storm.

Monday went pretty well, yearbooks being signed, counseling appointments finalized, make up exa...assess...oh-whatever the hell you want to call them given, goodbyes imparted, (some kids saw the writing on the wall and absconded early) and gifts exchanged.

Tuesday was, by the grace of Lord Hades, so blisteringly hot and humid[6] that, deprived of air conditioning, the student population was anaesthetized, the educational staff (present company included) were spiritless, and the administrative staff were smart enough to stay sequestered in their offices. (**They** had air conditioning.)

Wednesday, the temperature dropped enough to take the standards for proper civilized behavior with it. Students cursed out teachers for "failing"them; kids wandered the halls yelling and cursing like *The Walking Dead* on fast forward overdubbed with *Scarface*.[7] For my part, I explained the methods behind the madness of WHY I did WHAT I did all year, and hoped that they understood that my high standards were the ultimate sign of respect. I told them I would have personal, parting comments for them tomorrow, and encouraged them to think of any questions or comments they had for me. Sadly, for half of my classes, I would never hear those questions or comments in person, because on Thursday, the wheels came off.

You'd think I would have known something was up when I pulled up in the morning and saw the words *Abandon All Hope Ye Who Enter*

---

(5) See also: Shit that doesn't get taught in school anymore thanks to all the stuff I've been bludgeoning you with in this here literary disasterpiece.

(6) 112 heat index. To quote the iconic rock band KISS: "Hot, Hot, Hotter than Hell."

(7) Lest any of my students read this, I feel compelled to point out that, with one glaring exception [you're an asshole, Joachim] my students were on time for class, attentive, funny and engaging right up to the very end.

Here in flaming letters above the front entrance, but hey, with an XL black coffee and a sense of humor, I can endure anything for 4 hours.

I am (at least at the time of the writing of this book) still the Dean of discipline for the 9th graders, and I teach several 9th grade English classes, so by the last day almost all of the 360+ freshmen know me in one capacity or another. So, when I saw a large contingent of freshmen congregating in the hall just prior to the late bell ringing, I thought it prudent to wander into their midst and start whispering loudly "Hey... hey, HEY..." Once I had their attention I let it be known, in no uncertain terms, what would happen if they didn't get their [little fannies] into class on time and invited any of them to be the one who got to find out—*in front of **EVERY**body*—about Mr. Step's anger managements issues...

With the hallway nearly empty[8]—you gotta love the freshmen—I told the other teachers if anyone "wandered" out of class to lock them out and we would clean up the mess. Fortunately, the men and women who taught in that wing of the building during the A.M. periods are consummate professionals who didn't need my assistance; our end of the building was subdued and sublime for the remainder of the day.[9]

...'Twas not as subdued in other areas.

Alas, as one of my favorite Facebook memes observes: *"The fact that there's a highway to hell but only a stairway to heaven says a lot about the anticipated traffic numbers."*

Three fights, (two of which were shown to me via videos being posted online by students with phones within minutes of their conclusions,) two lockdown drills and, just for a cherry on top of this shit sundae, one law enforcement intervention.

I, in fact, did not get to see any of my 11th grade students; nor did I

---

(8) One young man, Nathan Ramos, all 4'6" and 120 lbs. of him, puffed out his chest and stared me down, eyeball to midsection, and announced, "I'll take care of this guy!" Nate is a great kid, and a genius; the laughter that ensued, and amplified when I cowered away saying "you didn't TELL me Nate was here!" was just the sort of moment we needed to lighten the mood and get everyone to 'buy in' on acting appropriately. NEVER underestimate the power of the students to help make you who you are.

(9) We must've "sold" those "quality" lessons really well! Or maybe, just MAYBE the students respected us, as people, enough to actually behave like civilized adults.

get to give them my final day's heartfelt "admiration and honest advice moving forward" speech because we were in lockdown procedure through the times I would have had them in my classroom (largely due to the aforementioned outbreak of fights, one of which resulted in an experienced female teacher being taken to the hospital.)

Fortunately, many of my 11th graders sought me out in person or reached out via email before the day was out, but I (and they) started the summer with a bitter taste in our mouths, a taste that: A) could have been avoided if the powers-that-be would have consulted the people who actually had to **enforce** the rules they blindly put in place for those final days, and B) was shortly rinsed from my mouth by a combination of the aforementioned student emails (most of which were quite sincere and touching) and a few coffee porters with some of my co-workers (many of whom were both energetic and inspiring, even at the finish line.)

The three fights involved everything from gang-related posturing, to retaliation to, and I quote, "boredom." Well no shit, Sherlock, we [the teachers] could've TOLD you that putting a bunch of angry, overheated kids, who know their grades are already in for the year, into a cafeteria with no food and no access to electronics is a recipe for Armageddon.

Come to think of it, just about anybody with a semi-functional brain could've told you that. And we did, folks, we did. More teachers than I care to count—myself included—offered our predictions on what was going to happen when gunpowder and gasoline were going to be thrown together in a cement mixer with minimal recourse.

But did anyone listen?

Obviously not. Maybe they couldn't hear us over the sound of those air conditioners in their offices running on high.

Sadly, all of this is indicative of two much larger problems: One, that teaching remains a profession where our (whatever's *bigger* than Godzilla-sized air quotes here) "superiors" somehow feel that it is beneath them to listen to us. And two, many students are disenfranchised from the schools they attend on a daily basis; hence, they don't care what they do or who they do it to when they're here. When you try to talk to many of these kids about respect for their peers or their teachers or the building in general, they look at you like you have two heads, largely because they have no respect for *themselves*. But enough about that for now. It's the end of the school year.

What could possibly go wrong now?

(That's called **foreshadowing**, kiddies!)

On a personal note,

The fact that one of the fights was anticipated by a group of observant teachers who informed the administration of the potential altercation, (only to watch less than zero action taken,) made the E.R. trip taken by a fellow teacher all the more enraging.

The fact that the immediate wave of social media vitriol—particularly on a page dedicated to negative gossip regarding our school—was directed exclusively at the combatants (but not the ones who facilitated the arena)—speaks to a public that is not only angry at a system that has gone rogue, but also wildly unaware of who is taking a bat to the radio as we cruise toward the big shark.

"Higher pay grade" choices made with little due diligence and no inquiry led to injury and chaos for the people forced to do the impossible by people that don't have to get their hands dirty. The fact that it resulted in a school year that ended in incarceration, hospitalization, and further destabilization of the district is inexcusable.

But, we'll try again next year.

See ya in September!

THE FANTASY: HOPE SPRINGS ETERNAL

"Hope springs eternal in the human breast; man never Is,
but always To be blest. The soul, uneasy, and confin'd from home,
rests and expatiates in a life to come."
—*Alexander Pope*

Alexander Pope in the hizzouse!

August 31st, 2016 and hope is springing eternal. It's back to school tomorrow! I can't wait to hear about all of the improvements the administration has made in our absence and how supportive the powers-that-be will be regarding the educational staff.

Yes, I'll sleep soundly tonight knowing that my desire to truly improve the youth of America will be facilitated by a system that values critical thinking, a school that invests financially in its teachers and students, and administrators that function as educational leaders, and not just self-preserving sycophants engaged in a Faustian deal with the corporate giants who want more arbitrary testing at the cost of, well, **everything** else that remotely resembles real education.

Yes, I'm sure there will be none of that; nothing but sunshine, blue skies, and marzipan-flavored Pokémon poop popsicles in MY future.

All dripping sarcasm aside, I actually extended this book (much to the chagrin of both my editor (sorry, Ed) and my publisher)[1] because I realized that I wrote the first page two Superintendents ago, and we have certainly seen two unique personalities take the iron throne over the last four years, each with his/her own ensuing shitstorm of discourteousness and dictatorship, with the third set to put his vision in

---

[1] Actually, I'm self-published, so Outskirts Press couldn't care less about me; nice people, though.

place starting tomorrow. I want to leave an opening for a possible happy ending [2] here.

THE REALITY: WELCOME BACK

We got fucked.

But more on that in a minute; let's have our coffee, and morning ritual, first.

I'm not sure exactly what year I started it, though I think it was around my third year of teaching, but for at least the last 20 years I have started the first day of school, teacher orientation day, the same way. I wake up to the song *Welcome Back* by John Sebastian (you know, the old *Welcome back, Kotter* theme song,) get dressed, have too much black coffee, and walk into school walking the razor line between cockeyed optimism and what my friend Marc Granieri eloquently refers to as **conditioned cynicism.**

The <u>song</u> is because, somewhere along the line, I *became* Mr. Kotter (which is crazy, because I always wanted to be Juan Luis Pedro Felipo de Huevos Epstein, the wise cracking Puerto Rican tough guy who always had "a note" explaining his chronic lateness.)[3] The <u>black coffee</u> is because coffee is a wonderful, wonderful thing. The <u>optimism?</u> Despite my cynical nature, forged in the fires of my caustically anti-bullshit reality, I remain—I must remain—strong in the belief that things shall improve and we will eventually figure out that we're all in this together. The <u>conditioned cynicism?</u> Well…

You might love baseball more than life itself, but if 90% of the time you got up to bat the pitcher threw his best high cheese right at your head, you wouldn't forget your fucking helmet, would you? See what I'm saying here? Pessimism is my high cheese helmet.

---

(2)   NOTE: Not to be confused with that kind of "happy ending," folks, (you know, the "massage parlor" kind); in this case, I am categorically hoping NOT to get fucked.

(3)   This alone is an interesting topic, right? Chubby OCD white kid grows up wanting to be the perpetually tardy Puerto Rican tough kid but eventually becomes the funny but sincerely caring teacher OF the Puerto Rican kid (AND all the rest of the archetypical "Sweathogs.")

On this overcast first day of September, the pitching staff didn't lead off with the high cheese. No, sir, things started off on a very positive note: we're going to hold families accountable for truant kids, hold kids accountable for insubordinate behavior and apathy, hold the crappy teachers (and possibly administrators?)[4] accountable for half-assed work, and we're going to do all of this while fostering a sense of community and yadda yadda yadda...

At LEAST our current Super still teaches a few classes at the college level, so, unlike so many "leaders" and "bosses" these days, he has some incremental fucking idea how to DO the job he's asking us to do, a vast improvement over the past few years here on the burning plains of Mordor, where the all-seeing evil eyes just hung out in their respective towers and micromanaged the Hobbit shit out of us.

Even more encouraging, when the technology the admins were supposed to use for their "Welcome back, here's everything you need to know" presentations went in the shitter (welcome to WTF High, Dr. New Guy!) he took charge, admitted that cluterfuckery was afoot, and allowed all of us to go work on our rooms. Hmmm...admitted that the "lesson" bombed, owned it, and didn't force us to swallow an hour and a half of horseshit that we knew was horseshit, instead allowing us to work on something productive??

Holy Bane's balls, Batman! We have an actual TEACHER leading us now?!

Everybody went to organize their rooms, and then to lunch, a half day into a two-day orientation feeling cautiously optimistic, but that damned "this-ice-beneath-us-could-crack-at-any-moment" anxiety stayed right there, like that herpes breakout on your lower lip that you think is gone forever, only to break out at the most inopportune time to remind you of that ill-advised one-time make out session with that sultry Lebanese Amazon at the Dixie Pig Bar & Grill. [5]

As it turns out, that conditioned cynicism is there for a reason, my teaching brothers and sisters; it is a survival mechanism that keeps us

---

(4) Probably reaching a bit there, but Gene (Willie Wonka) Wilder just died, so allow me to indulge in a world of pure imagination.

(5) Wait, that's just me?

from throwing away common sense and our concern for our kids in the face of shiny new promises and bold ideas that are, sadly, almost always doomed to go the way of the dinosaur the minute [what I refer to as] the "unholy trinity" of external forces gets ahold of them.

What, you ask, be this unholy trinity that dooms the promises and prognostications of every new batch of incoming Superintendents, principals, curriculum directors, supervisors, department coaches, administrators, board members, etc.?

Since you were nice enough to ask, I'll tell you. All this "we're gonna fix the system by doing it my way" delusion dies at the hands of:

Harsh Reality,

Selfish Ambition, and

Mob Misanthropy.

Please, allow me to elaborate, using examples that may or may not be taken directly from my own experiences during the early days of this school year.

Strike One: Harsh Reality

OK…so ya bought a new house! It's not the first time, and, if we must be honest, there have been some past failures in the moving department, but you're sure THIS is the one. It's yours now, after all, so you want to put your stamp all over it, right? And you, sir/ma'am, have watched a **lot** of HGTV, you've done a bunch of research, and you have worked on fixer uppers before, so *you*, according to *you*:

> know
> > what
> > > you
> > > > are
> > > > # doing!

And YOU are going to demolish and dispose of **everything** but the walls holding up the existing structure. To be honest, your heart is in the right place, the house was borderline condemned, but, and this is kind of big deal,

you and your *very large and **very** diverse* family have to LIVE IN THE HOUSE during the several years it is going to take you to make your dream home a reality.

All of you. And all of your busily intersecting lives. Suddenly thrust into an unfamiliar environment (again) and trying not to look inadequate as you relearn (amidst almost DAILY changes/compromises) how to live in constant chaos without compromising your contribution (or anyone else's) to the family along the way.

For those of you that don't speak metaphor, allow me to elaborate.

I work at Average High School of America (AHS from now on) and we have returned to classes in September. The 'leadership' (Superintendent, administrators, board members, etc.) has changed, in one variation or another—again. This is, by my count, the **fifth** major paradigm[6] shift we have undergone in my last seven years at AHS. Considering that every class of kids has four short years with us, that type of instability [at the top of the food chain] and re-creation [of the way education "gets done"] is as damaging as, say, trying to live in an overcrowded, already unstable house while it gets demolished and rebuilt.

Got it now?

Sadly, this is the reality in most schools.

And I've got news for you folks, now that President Donald Trump has appointed scourge of the grizzly bear Betsy Devos, a woman born into billionaire status, who *never went, nor sent her own children,* to public school, as Secretary of Education, the BIG machines are coming to demo more than just the "houses," I promise you that.

Seriously, Trump's promising to minimize the federal government's role in education, (and that would be great,) but appointing billion-dollar baby Betsy, with her past indiscretions involving failing charter schools, indicates that we'd better get ready for Charterpalooza.

---

(6) Paradigm—(n.) a framework containing the basic assumptions, ways of thinking, and methodology that are commonly accepted and practiced by members of a community. In short—"the way we do things around here."

I understand that most people don't speak (or think) in abstracts, so here is the harsh reality in its most simplified form, but keep in mind, this type of periodic reform/ reimagining/rewhateverthehellyouwannacallit happens **all the time** in the schools where YOUR future is being taught.

While I'm hitting you with the onslaught of the first few days, just imagine if this happened to the medical staff working with you during the 9 months of your pregnancy, or the legal team representing you in your big trial in nine months, etc.

Here's my personal paraphrase of the administrative "WELCOME BACK" speech. (I'll give you the harsh reality after I'm finished.) I'd bet dollars to doughnuts that this will sound familiar to some of you:

"Welcome back, there are a few things everyone needs to get up to speed on. Yes, we know the students are coming back tomorrow, but we have faith in your professionalism, (and ability to forget that we kept you hanging for almost two years in contract negotiation,) yadda yadda yadda. So anyway… Every one of you must complete a bunch of online certification classes *(safety issues, medical info, drug and mental disorders, abuse, etc.)* over the next few weeks because hey, it's not like you'll be busy, and we don't have the time to teach this stuff to you. There's a new lesson plan system, and it runs on new software, so learn it—all—and please be reminded that you are contractually obligated to submit your lesson plans by Monday morning. (But hey, we're here to support you, not threaten you.) Also, we have a brand-new discipline system, which will turn one simple step into three time consuming, convoluted steps, but hey! we can now send notices home to the parents (something that our old system could do, by the way, but we didn't bother to check that.) Did we mention that we are now going to benchmark the students every 5-7 days, and these benchmarks, which you will create from scratch (because we will in NO way instruct you in their creation or implementation,) need to be approved 2 days in advance, and the first one is due on September 19th? Oh, your rosters will change, almost daily, for the first few weeks while we figure out where to put kids in our brand-new block schedule (which you'll get used to, because you have to, don't you?) And now that YOU pointed it out, we notice that in the Power Point we showed you, (the one that took a half hour to get started) we have five learning units, four quarters of instruction, and report card dates, and NONE of the dates match up—we'll have to get on that. Oh, and we changed the grading percentages—more on that later. (Please understand, and we know you do, that all of this will change periodically as the crushing impracticality of this dawns on us.) Meanwhile, YOU are expected to be razor sharp, eminently prepared, and please don't complain about the fact that it's 90+ degrees in your rooms—it will help build "grit!" Yes, our offices are air conditioned, but that's not really relevant to your performance, is it? As you can see, we're here to help you, but not right now because we have a boatload of new stuff to learn, too. Remember, it's vitally important to protect the illusion that everything is running smoothly and that we are all well versed in every new nuance of this new system so that the kids buy in to the program! (Because, evidently, the façade OF the house is infinitely more important that the family living IN the house.)

THE HARSH REALITY: When you give the administration, the teachers, the educational aides, the librarian, and everybody else down to the maintenance staff a bunch of new things to learn at the last minute (because this is the "new," "hot," "trendy" way of doing things,) you create a million moving parts, and when a few hundred (or, in our case, a few thousand) living beings, all with diverse backgrounds and needs, explode into the building in two days, needing stability as much, or more, than the education we're supposed to provide, all those moving parts are going to get exposed pretty fucking quickly, and when multiple parts start failing simultaneously—well, you don't want to be riding that rollercoaster when that happens. But hey, it's not really that serious. It's not *really* a roller coaster.

It's only your kids' education.

Strike Two: Selfish Ambition. (aka: From the Pinnacle to the Pit)

I just received an email, from the "leadership" that has [verbally] assured me that they "trust in my professionalism" and "have my back," reminding me to use my ID card to swipe in and out every time I enter and/or leave the building (even if it's to run to Wawa across the street for a cup of coffee,) with the Orwellian little caveat that <u>this is a non-negotiable procedure and will be tracked.</u>

You getting a supportive, trusting, "team approach" vibe from that?

Me neither, and that leads me into what I consider the second roadblock to any "educational reform," namely, selfish ambition.

I've already explained to you, ad nauseum, the BIG reforms like Common Core and how there are only a small handful of people running those clown shows, but I can tell you that when it happens on the more local/district-wide level, you'll usually find a handful of people driving all the changes that create all those liability-producing moving parts. And those people are rarely satisfied with the job they currently hold.

Very often, those people have bigger aspirations than simply educating your kids. I have received a *deluge* of emails, letters, social media messages, etc. from a veritable army of educators[7] who gave me examples of how Superintendents/ principals/ Directors of curriculum (I'm still not sure what the hell *those* people do) and other administrators have blown into town and immediately begun shaping their districts/schools around what THEY understood and what THEY are familiar with, *rather than taking the time to get to know the people IN their new district/school and figuring out what might be best for them.* I find that to be lazy and self-serving, and if I went into my classrooms and just taught the stuff I was familiar with, and forced my diverse little populations of students to comply with a single vision of "how education works in MY class," the aforementioned "leadership" would be on me faster than a Peregrine falcon with the wind to its back.

---

(7) All of whom I gave my word to that I would not quote them in print; hence, no actual anecdotes that might lead to actual lawsuits.(8)

(8) The fact that telling the truth could generate lawsuits [designed to suppress it] should concern you, greatly.

And THAT, (since I'm running out of synonyms for bullshit,) is falcon feces, folks.

Want a concrete, real example of what I'm talking about? Here you go: Fast forward to three days before Christmas break (2 ½ if we must be specific, and we must.) One of the vice principals of my building—let's call her Ms. Inutil—asked one of my peers in the Language department—we'll call him Mr. Deadpool—which day was best to observe him. (Reminder: there are 2 ½ days left, and Christmas break looms on the horizon, so not really much of a **choice** involved there, and anyone who knows ANYthing about schools knows that the days leading up to winter break are traditionally...difficult[9] ...to get through according to plan.) Deadpool, to his credit, is teachin' 'em up right up until the last bus pulls out on Friday, so he offers the following reply: "Come on in today or tomorrow; I've got my kids in the computer lab doing some cool stuff." He was told by Ms. Inutil to, and I quote, "change the type of lesson because I can't observe that style of lesson."

Go ahead. Re-read it. It gets even more incredulous the second and third time.

*Kindly alter, on the fly, your cool, engaging, informative learning process, **two days before winter break**, <u>because I am incapable of 'grading' your creativity on my little computerized menu of efficiency</u>.* Clearly, whether the kids learn anything or not is "negotiable" in the face of administrative inconvenience.

What. The. Fuuuuuuuuuuuuuuuuuuuuuuuuuuuuuuuuuuuuuuuuuuuuuuu uuuuuuuuuuuuuuuck?!?

Look, I'm just going to come out and say it. Most of the "bosses' I have encountered in my quarter century teaching went the

---

(9) And by "difficult" I mean nearly impossible. Between the anxiety (in the kids that don't WANT to be around their homes/families for extended periods of time,) stress (in the kids AND teachers to get in last minute grades to alleviate pre-holiday parent implosions,) and reality (that most of these kids are burned out and don't want to hear $#!+ you're saying because they're already 'mentally' on break;) the last few days before Christmas break are rivaled only by the days before Summer break in terms of difficulty.

administrative route *because* they couldn't hack it in the classroom. **I would say, conservatively, that 80% of the people who have ever "evaluated" what an "effective" teacher I was couldn't hold my jock for 20 seconds in front of a classroom, period.** As for the infinitesimally small number of educators that left the classroom for the boardroom for higher purposes, (a.k.a.: help even more people by accumulating even broader influence,) many of them ultimately descend that slippery slope from the pinnacle of "greater influence" into the pit of corporate compliance. Mind you, I am never against someone increasing their employment stature, and I certainly encourage making more money to support one's family, but under no circumstances should you PRETEND to be righteous and "in it for the kids" when your every action runs contrary to that; you know, like making a teacher change an effective lesson because your frame of reference is too narrow to evaluate it properly!

Or preaching the gospel of Common Core's virtues to a room full of teachers that know you don't believe *in* it but that you're getting compensated *for* it. Yes, CaSandra FAllen—I'm talking to you.

No matter what the circumstances, be ever vigilant, my informed readers! Whoever is currently in charge of the building/district where your kids learn might have ulterior, self-serving motives that are less concerned with your children's futures and more concerned with their own future profit/comfort.

(Insert sarcasm voice) Shocking, I know, but forewarned is forearmed.

Strike Three: Mob Misanthropy

Part of the title of this book came from the third arm of the "education reform" monster, and this one is particularly painful, because it lies firmly in the lap of the public.

Why, I ask you, all the hostility and disrespect toward teachers?

You'll spend your hard-earned money to support entertainers, athletes, and, with somewhat lesser awareness, politicians who make God awful amounts of money yet are greedy, toxic, abusive, arrogant, homophobic, misogynistic, or worse. Even if you're not part of the contingency that overlooks character in the name of entertainment, you can't deny that a whole heapin' lot of our public are sporting jerseys of, arguing violently online about, and spending their money on some people with whom you wouldn't let your kids spend 5 seconds alone, yet you think teachers (who often spend more waking hours with your kids than you do) are "overpaid" complainers who "aren't doing their jobs" because you are TOLD (by dubious sources) that your kids are "failing" in some way.

Folks, if you're one of the horribly uninformed, quick to judge majority, I hope some of what you've read in this book has opened your eyes to what my brothers and sisters in the teaching field are dealing with, and how misguided is your vitriol. Maybe you could take your newfound knowledge [that you're being lied to, that your kids are being standardized and dumbed down, and that teachers are *quitting the profession* left and right because they don't want to hurt their students with MANDATED "teach to the test" curriculums] and educate the rest of the population. Your children will be the beneficiaries of your newfound awareness.

I've said it before, but it bears repeating: People who undergo multiple surgeries don't think they can perform surgery, people that get a ton of work done on their homes don't suddenly think they can do plumbing, electrical, or masonry work, etc., people that have been involved in myriad lawsuits don't suddenly decide to represent themselves because they now know how to practice law...you get the point. And yet, hordes of Americans think they know what it takes to be a teacher.

You don't. You really, *really* don't.

Now, if you're one of the sympathetic minority that knew, long before you read this book, what teachers are up against, I would ask that you, too, go forth and inform the masses, because we both know that one of the reasons the quality of our children's education is being systematically eviscerated is because the adult population is unprecedentedly both *uninformed* and *uninvolved*.

And speaking of keeping you informed, it seems as though the promise of the new year came with many of the same old situations, as I shall elaborate upon in the next chapter...

6 + 6 = ENABLEMENT

"They don't care how much you know
until they know how much you care."
— *Pat Summit*

Troyasia Napkin cut my class again.

Now, that may not sound like such a big deal to you, but kids generally don't cut my class. (I caught her in the hallway yesterday because I was conducting class in the library nearby where her errant soul was wandering.) Post capture, she sat grumpily while her classmates worked on material that she was unfamiliar with, largely because, as I may have mentioned, she cut my class.

Did I mention that she earned a *23* in my class for the first marking period and a *6* for the second marking period? I didn't? Well, she did.

Before you ask—it takes a sustained, albeit misguided effort to earn 29 collective report card points over the course of five months, but my girl Troyasia was **consistent**; so much so that she had accrued a second report card gauntlet of grades that read like the numbers of an academically ineligible football line: 11, 28, 67, 66 and 23.

Yes, I met with her, several times.

Yes, I met with her counselor, several times.

Yes, I contacted her Mom, and her Dean, and her vice principal, and everyone else, several times.

Let me tell you how those conversations went.

Troyasia herself: (lots of shrugging and "I dunno"s and "it's hard"s and "whatever"s)

233

Ms. Youzlezz/Counselor: (via phone, of course) "Well, it's too late in the year to change her class and, while she's asking for a fresh start, we have to follow policy; is there any extra credit you could give h…" (click)

Ms. Tablecloth/Mom: (sounding thoroughly defeated) "What you want me to do? You know how kids this age be." *(And I thought: Yes, I do; I've got four of my own.)* "I don't know what I'm supposed to do." *(I have a few ideas, but I dare not verbalize them.)* "What CAN you do, at the end of the day? She gonna have to deal with the consequences." *(Oh, yes she will, and as for what COULD be done, if my kid brought home a 23 and an 11 in* **anything***, I'd only have three kids left…)*

Mr. Façade/Vice Principal (Round I): After telling me for five minutes how he never spoke to a Troyasia Napkin, would have remembered the name, etc., Mr. Façade pulled up her file and suddenly remembered having spoken briefly to her and asked that I keep him posted. *(Yeah, I'll get right on that, Mr. Short Term Memory Loss.)*

> *It should be noted that **Mr. Façade's Dean of Discipline, Ms. Crónicamente Ausentes**, gave Troyasia *one* after school detention for cutting my class *five times*. In what can only be described as the mother of all ironies, Troyasia cut that detention.

Praying to Gods both new and old that I wouldn't have to deal with this clown show any longer, I spoke clearly and succinctly to Troyasia: *"You haven't turned in one piece of work since November* (it was Feb. 9th) *and you just accumulated more cuts in one week than 90% of my other students since I started working here* **combined***,*[1] *so it's almost unprofessional of me at this point to pass you for the year. So show me, give me a reason to at least try to help you dig out of this crater you dug for yourself."*

---

[1] Easily 1,400 students over the course of 13+ years

She cut class the next day.

And so…

The Vice Principal (Round II): I interrupted Mr. Façade's lunch; (quinoa and grilled veggies; well done in the health department, sir.) *"Troyasia cut my class again today."* To his credit, he put his nutritious fare away[2] and had her hunted down and brought to his office, where we would "get to the bottom of this."[3] Troyasia was, true to form, expressionless; neither confrontational nor remorseful, she simply shrugged and "yeah"-d her way through a series of questions. For my part, seeing that the almost impressively abysmal grade point average in my class and 6 days of cutting resulted in only one after school detention and a suggestion that I "could be doing more for her," I muted yet another administrator in my head. There was, however, a pivotal moment during this dog [tired] and [one trick] pony show where I started to feel bad for Troyasia. Mr. Façade suggested I stay after school and help her, to which I replied: *"She hasn't turned in anything in almost three MONTHS—that doesn't warrant any extra effort on my part right now."*

"I hardly think an hour after school…" I cut him off, intentionally, with my default reply to such suggestions: *"My after-school schedule is filled with kids whose parents are glad to pay for it, to say nothing of my OWN four children, who also warrant my time. I am her teacher, not her **tutor**."*

Façade, in his best 'serious administrator' voice: "This young lady needs your help." Tired, bored, but suddenly energized, I leaned forward and—a little too loudly—gave voice to something that burned inside of me for a long time: *"This young lady, who is an **11th grader** in **your** school district, failed all four major subjects last year, is failing several this year,*

---

(2) Trust me when I tell you, a LOT of educators eat their lunch on their feet or while working, IF they eat at all; many of us survive from 6am to 3 pm on caffeine and misguided optimism.

(3) Administrative euphemism for "let's get the kid in here and avoid confrontation at all costs, even if it means throwing the teacher under the bus."

*is cutting classes, can't hold eye contact during a simple conversation, and can't give more than a one syllable answer to your questions—she needs a LOT of people's help, and needed it **long before** she got to me!"*

NOTE: I am embarrassed to say that, in the heat of the moment, I said this in front of Troyasia, who didn't react (and later, in a private conversation, told me she agreed,) but that doesn't change the fact that it was unprofessional, and I apologize publicly now as I did privately then.

None of which changes the fact that I had to suffer yet another epiphany that I seemed to be the only person trying to help yet another kid that got fucked over and abandoned by a system that seemed more concerned with enabling her into the accumulation of a worthless graduation certificate than it did actually addressing her problems and helping to fix them.

If you're a teacher, I know you know exactly what I'm talking about.

My time done with Mr. Façade and this, well, façade, I returned to class. Thank you, coach Carolina for covering for me so I could gently pressure Mr. F into (insert voice dripping with sarcasm) "getting to the bottom of this." Troyasia followed me, put her head down when we got to class, and then got up and left at the bell along with her classmates, many of whom, on their way out, gave me a very specific look that said: "It appears that you're seeking to change Troyasia's behavior. Well, get your boulder ready, Sisyphus, 'cause that ain't gonna happen any time soon." Never one to be easily dissuaded, (even by students that probably knew from past experience that I was doomed,) I began to seek advice from a plethora of other sources as to how to help this young lady; sort of a scavenger hunt for pragmatic solutions, if you will.

Head of Counseling Dept.: "Can't move her classes," *(WTF? Why??)* "and it probably wouldn't help anyway," *(Hate to admit it, but he's right there)* "so just keep doing what you're doing and try to teach her when and as best you can."

Me: *"Ok, thanks, (sarcasm dripping) very helpful".*

Asst. Vice Principal: "Sounds like a job for I & RS."[4] *Finally! Some practical advice! "OK, I've never had to do this before; where do I start the I & RS process?"*

Asst. Vice Principal: Start with her counselor.

Me: *Fucksocks! Ms. Blackhole, of the counseling Dept., where initiative and rational thought go to die. "OK, that's a start!"*

Well, it *was* a start.

Kind of like passing GO in NobodyWantsToTakeAccountabilityopoly, without the collecting $200 part. I reached out to the I & RS and was told that I was in luck because they were "almost up and running."

It was February.

Six months into the school year.

And they were *almost* up and running... Great. I guess I'll go work on another chapter, or write another book, or go read the entire *Harry Potter* series while they get their shit together. In the immortal words of The Terminator: ***"I'll be back."***

(Crickets chirping. Time passing. Readers waiting...)

I'm back.

I gave it two more months. March has come and gone and April is coming to a close with the promise of a warm, green Spring to be sprung. Yes, one's thoughts can't help but turn to resurrection and rebirth around this time of year.

---

(4) Intervention and Referral System—a "coordinated system" in each school that is supposed to plan and deliver—you guessed it—intervention and referral services designed to assist students who are experiencing learning, behavior or health difficulties. The I & RS is also supposed to assist staff who have difficulties in addressing the aforementioned learning, behavior or health needs.

Unless you're a student who has not turned in one single piece of work since our last meeting back in February.

Mom, the counseling department, several administrators and supervisors, I&RS, other students, and one individual a few steps up the pay scale, all suggested that I "need[ed] to do everything [I could] for the child."

The child who has done nothing beyond take up a space in my room?

The child **whose name you forgot** 60 seconds after I told it to you?

And who, exactly, am I supposed to call now—fucking Ghostbusters?

I may have said this before, but it bears repeating:

Welcome to the world of the contemporary teacher in America.

I finally asked Troyasia to sit down with me (I had another student in the room for security purposes, but other than that I just wanted it to be us, as these one-on-one, eye-to-eye conversations have worked wonders in the past.) I asked her, point blank, if she was fully cognizant of the situation in which she had put herself school-wise, and whether there was something going on that made her just flat out give up like this.

She spoke more in that 30 or so minutes than she did all year, and it still wasn't much, believe me, but it was—simultaneously—sobering in its honesty and sad in its predictability. While I will refrain from giving you her answer verbatim, (even though she said it was OK to do so,[5]) I will do my level to convey her reaction:

Troyasia very matter-of-factly said that she didn't care "'cause it don't matter."

---

(5) I asked her if she minded if I shared her thoughts with the people who read my next book, and she said she didn't care. When I told her that I thought her feelings were valid and that other kids might like to know that they were not alone, she actually perked up a bit. (6)

(6) Note to self: pass that on to next year's teacher; might be a pathway worth exploring here.

When I asked her what, specifically, didn't matter, her answer was a brutally simple indictment of our educational system, and society, as a whole:

"None of it. My Mom act like she care but she don't, she just tryin' to look good to school. And ain't nobody here care. I told them way back I wanted to be one of them people that work with babies..."

"A pediatrician?"

"Nah, I ain't smart enough to do all that, I just wanted to work with babies, but then they told me all that stuff about 'do good in school and you can be whatever you want.' You can be a—what'd you say?"

"Pediatrician."

"Yeah, that, but I told them nah, I just want to work with babies, maybe little kids. But they kept sayin' that doctor stuff and I was like, nigga, I got Fs in science how'm I gonna be a doctor? So, I just said 'yeah, that sounds good' and they all smiled and stuff like they job was done and they was all happy but they didn't believe all that, you could tell."

"How do you know they didn't care?" (She was right, I just wanted to know.) Troyasia just shrugged—she seemed tired from talking so much—and observed: "Ain't nobody talked to me since about none of that stuff. I been like this, right? Where they at?"

I found myself at once furious, tired, profoundly sad, and guilty; however, as I said, I could tell she was fatigued and tired of talking about this, so I tried to wrap up on anything close to a positive note:

*"You don't think **anybody** in the system cares about you?"*

"Whatchu think? You always talkin' about a systemic problem. How'd I get to all this not knowing how to read and do little kid math and stuff?"

It took me a second to recover from the facts that: A) she used the word systemic, and B) that she paid attention enough in class to remember that. Nonetheless, I pressed on:

"What can we do right n—"

"Who cares?"

*"I don't know. I can't speak for everyone. Do you think **I** care?"*

"You aight, but you know you just be happy if I left, but I get that."

"You think, after all the time I spent getting to the bottom of this…"

"That's your job."

"You think I'd be happy if you just dropped out? You really think that?"

(Shrug.) "I don't know. Not happy. But you be…I don't know"

"Relieved?"

She smiled like I got the right word and, in doing so, proved her right.

We went on for a few more minutes, but it was more of the same. I apologized for not being what she thought I should be as a teacher and left our conversation exhausted and deeply saddened but with one small glimmer of hope in this swirling vortex of irresponsibility, non-accountability, and missed opportunity.

Troyasia Napkin failed every subject last year except World History (earned a "D" by 1 point,) and Health (got a "B" in a class where 95% of her classmates received an "A.")

Mr. Façade had absolutely no idea who I was talking about when I stopped by the school in July and asked how she was doing in Summer School.

"Where they at?" indeed.

Mom (Ms. Tablecloth's) phone number was inactive and the Email address I had for her was "not found" when I tried to contact her this Summer, so I waited to tell Troyasia in person about a local hospital that was looking for volunteers to hold and cuddle with babies born to addicted mothers. Apparently, there is a screening process because overstimulating the babies can cause cardiac issues, but I told her that I would—despite her *academic* performance in my class—write a letter of recommendation for her. I thought that would at least get her some time with the babies she always wanted to work with.

EPILOGUE: The following school year

I am sincerely happy, (and relieved) to report that Troyasia Napkin is doing better in school this year. No, this isn't a fairy tale ending, she has some truancy issues, and her grades aren't exactly a shrine to the first two letters of the alphabet, but she's doing better, and according to a fellow English teacher, speaking up more and smiling occasionally.

It's a start, and I'll take it.

But what do I know? I'm just a racist, dysfunctional psycho.

THE SAD CASE OF A RACIST, DYSFUNCTIONAL PSYCHO

"A huckster, a leper, a trickster, a scourge
Maybe I don't wanna be saved
By Jesus and his lawyers,
Because you're nobody until somebody hates you."
—*Bron Sage*

Almost 8 years ago I wrote my first book; it was a series of well worn, oft repeated, but sometimes hilarious, sometimes heartwarming, oftentimes offensive stories about my first teaching gig. Any further comment would be gratuitous self-promotion, and we wouldn't want *that*[1]. The books have been one of the most gratifying experiences of my life: I've done book signings, been invited to authors' roundtables, (with <u>real</u> authors!) been interviewed by newspapers and magazines, been interviewed on radio shows and podcasts, and—most importantly—got to meet, speak to, conspire amongst, and become friends with people all over the WORLD. The whole experience, even three books later, is still surreal to me.

If you've ever thought about writing a book, **do it***; you probably won't make a lot of money, (trust me) but the people you'll meet, stories you'll hear, and friendships you'll forge will be worth it.* Again, trust me on this. HOWever…

(and isn't there *always* a however?)

---

(1) Besides, you could always just pick it up and read it yourself, Why Are All the Good Teachers Crazy, available on Amazon.com, B&N.com and everywhere else superkickass literature is sold.

you will, on occasion, have to deal with individuals who do not share your unique view of the world. On said occasions, those delicate, albeit erudite, china dolls may venture into the areas of personal insult or, at the very least, dramatic hyperbole in an attempt to poo-poo on your party.

Thus, it was with just the tiniest bit of ill-founded excitement that I woke up one nippy November morning to find a NEW REVIEW for my first book!

Oh goody! Somebody must've bought it at the beginning of the school year, devoured it in a few weeks and been *inspired.*

She was inspired all right.

I don't fixate on criticism any more than I get excited about accolades; they both have their place and both can be equally useful in one's introspection and reinvention; however, this person's scathing indictment of me as a person and a professional is a sad indication of how quick people are to judge teachers. Lest you fall into the same trap, I invite you to friend me on Facebook and see what *the actual students whose stories populate that book* had to say in response to this vitriol.

Mind you, I respect this woman's opinion (and will defend her right to express it to the death.) However, I think she ventured into unnecessarily personal attack and over-dramatization. And she employed at least 13 of the 23 most common logical fallacies in her attempt to make a point:

> Sad case. I mean really sad case. This man can't understand how destructive and manipulative he was as a teacher. I worked in a school similar to this and I know quite a few teachers who could have easily been the author of this book. His racism is rampant and masked at the same time. In the book he is openly calling a student a "Monkey'" . [sic] Just because some kids grew up and still have a connection to appreciate you as someone in their lives during there [sic] youthful age doesn't mean that you were a good role model. Most people still look to their former teachers with respect and endearment when they get older but that isn't the qualification of a good teacher. I am amazed that this was published and I plan to reference it a hell of a lot of

[sic] parents I know when asked about my views on public education. I can't imagine having a sicko like this teach my child. He is a prime example of how dysfunctional the system has become. I am not at all against his claims that some if not all of his student [sic] might have been extremely crazy but my question is who qualified this man to teach. [sic] A degree and then thrown into the room. He didnt [sic]even know you can't take kids off school grounds his first day? I thank him though for helping prove my point that under no circumstances will I be sending my child into another persons [sic] care for education. Home school is the only way, no matter what. I feel so sad after reading this. How a person can rationalize anything to convince themselves is truly amazing. I have seen this kind of situation up close and trust that what goes around come [sic] around-Karma is real.

I could make a few snarky comments about the number of egregious spelling, grammar and diction errors in this short but scathing diatribe, but I respect her honesty, and I published my first book with a few errors in it,[2] so I'll just hang onto my stones in this glass house for now. Instead, I'd like to focus on three specific comments:

1. **"Just because some kids grew up and still have a connection to appreciate you as someone in their lives during there [sic] youthful age doesn't mean that you were a good role model."**

It doesn't? The fact that many of the kids you chose to speak for are now responsible, discerning, family men and responsible citizens who regularly reach out to me to verify that they are living up to the expectations I set for them "back in the day" makes me *something* on

---

(2) I was a first-time author: wrote, formatted, edited and proofread a 500-pg. manuscript down to a 300-page book myself, and a publisher said "we'd like to go to print," so I jumped like an illiterate lemming off Mount Publication. I make no apologies: I actually LIKE the fact that the book is imperfect, as it makes a great lesson every year to my students that the "heart" of a piece often supersedes the formalities.

the outskirts of positive, doesn't it? I think that any teacher would agree that just being **remembered** 24 years after teaching a student would mean you did your job fairly well.

2. "Most people still look to their former teachers with respect and endearment when they get older but that isn't the qualification of a good teacher."

Uh, no they don't and yes, it is.

Oh, and point *3?* **"Karma is real."**
You'd better believe it is, darlin'.

You know, in hindsight, I couldn't understand why this person's words pissed me off so much. It certainly wasn't because I gave a rat's ass that she didn't like me; as the saying goes, "wolves don't lose sleep over the opinions of sheep," but this was bigger than a visceral review of a book that is, by my own admission, an acquired taste, like bitter black coffee. I went back and forth, several times, with the idea of just putting this whole chapter in my ever-expanding "save it for later" file, but I am a creature that craves balance, and something about the imbalance between the personal nature of the attack and what one would expect from a simple book review (even a scathing one) stuck like a thorn in my paw.

Fortunately for me, Androcles arrived in the form of friend, teacher, rock star and dark apprentice in my imaginary Sith Empire: Edward Trautz, who pulled the thorn from the literary lion's pondering paw with a simple suggestion: He implied that while the chapter was a short, albeit effective literary middle finger to my anonymous nemesis, it lacked the macrocosmic perspective to make it a useful cog in the machine that would ultimately be the finished book. In plain English, he thought the reader should know HOW the review represented the *"quickly and zealously crafted presumptions [that turn into] public opinion and defamation"* within the nanoseconds of the online world.

Ah…there it is.

Thank you, Darth Androcles, you brilliant bastard; I'll take it from here.

We live in, arguably, the most anti-teacher climate in the history of the United States. I would say this is inexplicable to me, but think about what has become of our culture. Said it before but it bears repeating: We venerate our athletes for playing games, deify our celebrities for entertaining us, and fight over politicians who are busy manipulating us. Then we overlook and/or excuse their horrible transgressions (everything from domestic abuse to drug trafficking, money laundering to murder,) with a laissez faire attitude that you and I would *never* enjoy. WHY? Mainly because they are wealthy, arrogant products of our media machine that you are *told* to worship.

I'll give you a minute to let that sink in and admit whether you have contributed to this insanity.

Teachers—you know, the ones who should be shaping the intellect of the forthcoming generations (and who are highly respected professionals in places like China, Greece, Finland, and South Korea)—are treated like disposable bathroom wipes by the media in this country.

WHY? Mainly because teachers are poorly paid, self-effacing people who care more about others than themselves; and yet the media *encourages* you to walk all over them and hold them accountable for every minute of their working day and—in growing instances—every minute of their lives, period. The meek won't be inheriting the Earth any time soon in this climate, folks.[3] In fact, I, as a teacher, am likely to be called things like oh, I don't know—destructive, manipulative, racist, sicko, dysfunctional, unqualified, and/or irrational *all in one paragraph,* BY A MEMBER OF THE SAME SOCIETY that handed me kids labeled incorrigible and unteachable, for the crime of writing a completely honest anecdotal record of my experiences teaching them!

Yeah, that's fair.

Sit on that and rotate while you're adding the next domestic abuser to your fantasy football team, trolling someone on Facebook for not

---

(3) Which is the main reason I continue to write books, publish articles, and post on social media; because fuck ANYbody that thinks they can paint me or my profession with a broad brush of disrespect without getting counterpunched in the mouth, quickly and unapologetically.

liking your favorite Kardashian,[4] or voting for the next politician that has openly lied to you more times than you've broken your New Year's resolution.

But you[5] won't. You'll continue to put forth the same myopic soundbites you've been told to espouse about teachers: "They have Summers off!" "They only work five days a week!" "After they get tenure, they have guaranteed jobs for life," and—a recent favorite—their union is "the single most destructive force in public education in America." THAT one came courtesy of Chris Christie, the corpulent c__t that (allegedly) made Donald Trump's $30,000,000.00 tax debt to New Jersey magically reduce to $5,000,000.00 under his watch. That 25 million could have certainly helped public education in my state, but no, he's busy doubling down on his Napoleon (the pig, not the little French guy) complex by accusing teachers of being *greedy*.

When a corrupt, bloated bag of bullshit that can't even get a 30% approval rating[6] in his own fucking STATE can shit talk teachers and get his constituents to agree with him, (trust me, I've been at enough Board meetings to know that they do,) then something is **very, very wrong.**

Which brings us back to the crux of why that seemingly innocuous book review offended me at the molecular level, because it wasn't really about *me,* it was about how "quickly and zealously crafted presumptions [turn into] public opinion and defamation" and, to continue, how quickly that sort of hateful vitriol aimed at one of the few remaining noble professions gets picked up and spread like a Roomba over a fresh pile of dog shit at 2 A.M.

Now, if this entire chapter seems like an unnecessarily ginormous reaction to a simple book review, (and I totally get it if that's what you're thinking,) take a step back with me for a minute and look at the big picture.

---

(4) Just my opinion, but those are two words that should never coexist in any enlightened, civilized society.

(5) Not YOU, dear reader, you're far too enlightened to engage in such shenanigans; you're reading one of MY books, for goodness sake! I'm talking about myopic meanies like the book reviewer.

(6) Quinnipiac University poll from May of 2016, probably MUCH lower by the time this is published.

Are you passionate about your profession?

Or, do you at least take great pride in the work you do?

Or, at the very least, do you get pissed when people that couldn't do your job on their *best* day criticize your work?

Well, I meet all three of those criteria, and it is time that couch potatoes with Dorito chip crumbs stuck in their shirt rolls stop critiquing Olympic gymnasts for "not sticking the landing" in the same way it is time for people that can't write 300 word diatribes without making double digit errors in grammar and logic to stop telling me that I'm the reason the educational system is broken.

At least that's what this racist, dysfunctional psycho thinks.

And I might be a crazy teacher, but, in some ways, I'm kinda like a doctor.[7] For the continuing adventures of the "RDP," read on to the next chapter!

---

(7) Oooooooohhh—teaser footnote!

DOCTORS = TEACHERS (& THAT IS *NOT* GOOD NEWS)

"The doctor sees all the weakness of mankind;
the lawyer all the wickedness, the theologian all the stupidity."
—Arthur Schopenhauer

"...and the teacher taught all three of them."
—Francis Akira Stepnowski (my youngest son)

Last night, I had the honor of being invited to see Dr. Daniel Dempsey M.D., M.B.A., F.A.C.S. be installed as the 155th president of The Philadelphia County Medical Society. (More specifically, my WIFE, the illustrious Dr. Dawn, got invited, and I tagged along like a well-dressed primate.)

I could fill a whole chapter listing Dr. Dempsey's accomplishments and accolades, but I'll simply say that Dan is one of the finest men I've ever had the pleasure to meet. I've been in his company many times—a direct result of Dawn being his buddy—and he is always engaging, interesting, and deferential to a fault. Interestingly, I find that leaders of his ilk are, (in addition to being very, *very* good at what they do,) authentically humble and refreshingly aware that they are part of a bigger picture.[1]

And speaking of the bigger picture...

I was enthralled by Dr. Dempsey's speech, but not so much that I didn't sneak a few glances around the room, watching a veritable who's who of the medical profession shake their heads in sad agreement as

---

(1) Unlike so many of the inefficient and/or insecure "leaders" I've been forced to endure.

Dr. D spoke, eloquently but clearly discouraged, about how **doctors** were struggling against the tide to prioritize their <u>patients</u> in a world of medical conglomerates and insurance company influence. He reminded all of the healers in the audience that they went

into medicine to help <u>people</u>, to make <u>people</u> feel better; and he urged them to continue to put their <u>patients</u>' needs foremost in their thoughts, despite the swirling winds of corporate avarice and conglomeration around them. The **doctor**-<u>patient</u> relationship should be at the heart of every decision because, lest we forget, <u>patients</u> are human beings, and **doctors** are the ones entrusted to help them get better. He concluded by asserting his belief that theirs was the most noble profession, and that every **doctor**/medical professional in attendance should continue to fight the good fight that they began, each for very personal reasons, when they entered the profession.[2]

I believe, if you substituted the word **teacher** for **doctor** and the word <u>student</u> for <u>patient</u>, that Dr. Dempsey unknowingly articulated the central issue facing educators today.

We, the people who willingly went into a profession with a shit paycheck and never-ending hours, are increasingly and depressingly forced to become pawns in a corporate attempt to standardize your children. Good teachers take the fact that you entrust us with your children very seriously, but we are struggling against the tide to prioritize our students in a world of "educational reform" conglomerates and their subsidiaries, and the influence of education publishing and assessment corporations. Every time I speak to, or write to, teachers, I urge them to remember that they went into teaching to help children, to make children feel better; and I urge them to continue to put their students' needs foremost in their thoughts, despite the swirling winds of corporate avarice and conglomeration around them. The teacher-student relationship should be at the heart of every decision we make because, lest we forget, CHILDREN are human beings, and teachers are the ones entrusted to love, educate, and evolve them.

---

(2)   This is my paraphrase. Any error in translation is purely my own, and is in no way indicative of any lack of clarity on Dr. Dempsey's behalf.

And so, as I have done countless times, and will *continue* to do until the day I die,

I urge you, educators, past, present, and future—remember.

Remember why you went into this profession in the first place, and why you endure the slings and arrows that are as much a part of this job as are pencils and paper. Remember that we are shaping *people*, people who will, ultimately, be responsible for this world. And remember, most of all, the thing that is most easy to forget—that you are a good person, and that your heart is in the right place; as such, never be afraid to put the love in your heart in front of the interests of the machine.

And thank you, Dr. D., for your wisdom and inspiration; I can only hope my students feel as safe in my classroom as your patients do in your operating room.

TEACHER APPRECIATION DAY

"If there is disturbance in the camp, the general's authority is weak."
— *Sun Tzu*

Let me preface this particularly angry chapter by saying that I never went in to this profession with the intent (or desire) to be "appreciated." But I'm not a robot, either; I like a little love and recognition as much as the next person, and if I get some "icing on the cake" along the way[1] that's awesome; but let's be real here—does ANYone go into teaching expecting *anything* overwhelmingly positive in the way of recognition and validation?

Methinks not, and I'm here to tell you that if you think you're going to get anything short of

(Takes a deep breath)

diminishing resources, apathetic children, angry parents, shitty pay, long nights, absentee leadership (that will then throw you under the bus for not knowing how to do what they never trained you to do,) and a nation full of borderline armchair quarterbacks who feel qualified to tell you how to do your job and that you've got it easy because you've "got Summers off…"

then you might want to think twice about going into teaching.

Truth be told, the actual 'teaching of the kids' part is not that bad, and just about any teacher will tell you that the daily miracles, no matter how small, and eventual accomplishments (again, size is irrelevant) of our kids more than compensate for the machinations of the idiots "in charge" of our profession. Sadly, *that* part (the **actual teaching of**

---

(1) And I do; and a little goes a long way.

children) has become about the same percentage of the daily life of a teacher as actual surgery to a surgeon; instead, we,

like surgeons (and so many other professions, I suspect,) spend an inordinate amount of time dealing with minutiae, micromanaging, and mandatory paperwork.

Somehow, in the midst of all of this bullshit, we do manage to find time to do what I consider to be one of the most important jobs in the world. So, when "Teacher Appreciation Week" comes around every year, I look at it the same way most teachers look at it, kind of the way you look at birthday presents from your kids once you're in your 40s, 50s, etc.:

Anything would be a nice surprise, and we are very much appreciative, but we'd rather hear from you *throughout the year*, letting us know (subtly and/or unintentionally) that we did a good job. But IF—and please understand that I know I sound petulant here—you're going to buy us something, put some iota of thought into it, because a *clearly-last-minute-holy-shit-I-forgot-about-your-birthday-even-though-you-RAISED-me-so-I-bought-this-last-minute-arbitrary-thing* is actually more of a slap in the face than it is a welcome gift.

Which brings us to Teacher Appreciation Day where I live.

First, I listened to my kids (this time I'm referring to my actual offspring) tell me about the things that were done for the teachers in their respective schools. Nice, very nice.

Then I heard about some of the things that were done for spouses/relatives/etc. of some of my co-workers, who are also in the profession, albeit in other districts, some simple, some elaborate, all well intentioned and well received. Finally, I turned to the dark forest that is social media and was relieved to see that some administrators across this country are really going the extra mile to acknowledge their teachers (yes, Charlie Heaton, I see you out there in Pasadena!) for the work they do.

And then there are other facilities, which shall remain nameless, that send out, on Teacher Appreciation Day, antiseptic, copy-and-paste group emails (that could use some proofreading, if truth be told) to every staff member, followed up by another email letting their staff know that a local fast food place is offering a teacher discount on Tuesday, followed by four emails letting them know that: 1. The copier in the main office is down until further notice, 2. There are two meetings coming up that you are contractually obligated to attend, 3. Lesson plans still need to be submitted in a timely fashion, 4. BUT there will be (the day *after* teacher Appreciation Day) free Oreos available in the teachers' lounge; no, seriously, don't thank us, it's the least we could do. I think I speak for almost[2] everyone I work with when I say: Please get the copier fixed, I know what my contractual obligations are, and stick your Oreos up your fucking ass. I feel like Gene Hackman, in the movie *The Replacements*, after being asked what his team needs, pounding on his chest, tears in his eyes, imploring: "Heart, we need heart."

Better yet, let me quote from the more eloquent, and infinitely more intelligent, Alfie Kohn, who asks: "How should we reward teachers?" and then responds: "We shouldn't. They're not pets. Rather, teachers should be paid well, freed from misguided mandates, treated with respect, and provided the support they need to help their students become increasingly proficient and enthusiastic learners."

What they do NOT need are cheap, sugar saturated snacks brought in a day late to placate the populace; *those* should be shoved firmly up the collective asses[3] of the last-minute lassies that thought they were a good idea.

OK, OK...he never said that last sentence, but I think it was there in spirit.

Listen, folks, I don't get paid to do my job 9/10 of the way, nor do I have any inclination to do so. There are less than 30 days left in this school year and I'm busting my tail here to find interesting, pertinent information that will keep your kids learning, evolving, and—heaven forbid—*enjoying* coming to my class, so I don't need an "appreciation

---

(2) Almost everyone. In my school (as in most workplaces, I'm sure) there are always those sycophantic leeches that will eat/drink or take ANYthing free offered to them, (usually overindulging in the free shit) even if they have to prostrate themselves in the process. Ironically, these are very often the staff members who contribute the LEAST in terms of professional effort.

(3) My editor, God bless him, suggested a different mode of violation, as "[I] had [already] suggested it go up the ass in the previous paragraph." It really isn't fair what I force this man to endure.

day" or week or whatever. It's nice, don't get me wrong, but that's not what drives me, and it certainly shouldn't take some man-made holiday for the general public or my "educational leaders" to recognize how hard my brothers and sisters in this profession are working to keep your children from being swallowed up by this wicked world. In the erudite words of Nicholas Ferroni, a young man that has used his titles as one of the fittest men in the world and Sexiest Teacher Alive[4] to spread awareness about the profession: *"We should be ashamed that we need Teacher's Appreciation Week and Mother's Day as reminders to celebrate teachers and mothers."*

I concur wholeheartedly, Mr. Ferroni.

The Morning After

OK, I went back to do some proofreading on the *Teacher Appreciation Day* chapter, and, upon reflection, considered deleting the entire thing because, at times, I thought I sounded like a spoiled brat gratuitously discrediting any effort, or lack thereof, made by my administration to acknowledge an admittedly man made 'holiday.' So, I decided to give it 24 hours and, if I still felt the same way, I'd delete the whole chapter.

Obviously, I chose to keep it, and I'll tell you why. Three things happened on the day after that convinced me it needed to stay:

ONE: Chik-fil-A-you don't say

My co-worker Sarah came back from lunch and told me the following quick story. Sarah had run to Chik-fil-A, a local fast food chain, where she was given a free sandwich. When she inquired about this gesture (she thought it was a mistake) the young man working informed her that Chik-fil-A gave any educator, teacher, faculty or staff (he saw her lanyard ID) a free sandwich on Teacher Appreciation Day. Before Sarah could point out that Teacher Appreciation Day was the day prior, the young man held his hand up and said "I know, but hardly anybody

---

(4) Now that you've Googled an image of Nick—I know, he's totally dreamy, right?—you should know that, unlike most people with HALF his looks and ONE THIRD his intellect, he remains a humble, altruistic young man that works tirelessly for both his students and peers in the teaching profession. He has also told me, off the record, that I came in, like, 273rd in that whole sexiest teacher thing.

takes advantage of it, I guess teachers aren't used to being treated nicely or getting things given to them. Have a nice day."

Nice gesture, delicious chicken, interesting insight. With K-12 teachers spending in excess of 1.7 BILLION dollars **of their own money** annually on their students (largely because they aren't given proper materials due to budget cuts,) I think that young man might be on to something more than palatable poultry.

TWO: High Expectations for the students.

For the teachers? Not so much.

I had the opportunity to speak to a young lady who teaches at the middle school in my district, (I was there speaking to the 8th graders about the academic expectations they would be experiencing in the high school next year,) and she afforded me some painful insight into what new teachers are being subjected to in their college classes. She spoke both eloquently and at length, but I can summarize the general consensus of her professors' cautionary warnings into three sentences:

Expect to be disrespected,

don't expect to be paid well, and

obey the "teach to the test" curriculum if you want to keep a job.

Damn.

Suddenly the *I guess teachers aren't used to being treated nicely* kid from Chik-Fil-A seemed pretty prescient. Jeez, it's a wonder, with our teachers-in-training being given *that* unholy trinity of distasteful reality during their formative years, that we don't attract the best and the brightest to one of the most important jobs in the World, isn't it?

THREE: The smirk

This one really pissed me off. All of the teachers had a department meeting today. (Oreo day.) For you non-educators, this is basically a meeting where:

256

1. you're required to stay after school and meet with your fellow Math, History, Science, etc. teachers and
2. listen to out of touch people waste your time with shit that could have been covered in an email
3. regarding data about what you're doing wrong and why you need to improve, then
4. you review all of the deadlines, expectations, deadlines, paperwork, upcoming tests and deadlines you're expected to meet, pass and submit.

All of this is done during time that *could* have been spent productively collaborating with your peers and exchanging ideas/lessons/etc. (No... silly rabbits, while you're REQUIRED to do that, and PROVE it in your Domain 4 paperwork at the end of the year, that's all to be done in your (stifles a laugh) "free time.")

So anyway, we're signed in (gotta **prove** you were there, Big Brother's watching, ya know) and hoping the caffeine we've been mainlining will carry us through the next 30-45 minutes, when the administrator in charge of the English department comes waltzing in, late,[5] and—just before hitting us with a packet thicker than the spike I'd like to stick in his eye detailing our deadlines, expectations, deadlines, paperwork, upcoming tests and deadlines for the coming final weeks—he asked "Did everyone get your Oreos?" and actually *smirked* when he said it.

In that smirk, whether it was intentional or not (and he stutteringly claimed, when called on it at a later date, that "the smirk" was "mocking the paltry nature of the gesture,") I saw the face of every person that views teachers as some sort of subspecies that should "expect to be disrespected."

No. No. A thousand times no.

I got up and left. Fuck you, put a letter in my file, but I won't sit here and be mocked.

---

(5) 15 minutes late, to be specific; ostensibly, his/her time is more important than ours. That shit makes me volcanically angry, when ANYbody (dentist, doctor, accountant, lawyer, etc.) does it to me. Screw you, jerkoff; my time is every bit as valuable as yours, so do your job and keep your appointments.

From what I was told, several of my peers followed suit; all I know is that I was summoned

to an office several days later to "explain my actions" because "you know, the staff look to you as a role model,[6] and that reflects poorly yadda yadda yadda…"

Such began the heated conversation that convinced me to keep this chapter in the book.

Listen, every profession likes (and, quite frankly, DESERVES) to be appreciated. I don't care what you do for a living, if you do it efficiently, or at least with passion and dedication, you damn well deserve to be appreciated; hell, I occasionally give the trash guys that collect around my neighborhood money for lunch or (around holidays or days when we put out a ton of trash from one of our many construction projects) a case of beer or something like that.[7] However, if your appreciation ain't sincere then it comes across as more of an insult, an uninspired afterthought, and nobody wants to be anybody's afterthought.

If you, as a student, are happy with your teacher,

or, as a guardian, your kids' teacher,

or, as an administrator, your employees,

a simple, heartfelt compliment via email (good,) letter (better,) or face to

face exchange (best of all,) is all it takes.

You'd be amazed what that can do.

---

(6) Ah, the old pat-me-on-the-back-before-you-stick-the-knife-in-there technique. Nice.
(7) Thanks to these simple gestures, I'm pretty sure I could put a dead body wrapped in a Power Rangers blanket out on my curb and these guys would take it with a smile and a wink. Might have to try that some time.(8)
(8) Let me verify, unequivocally, I am neither advocating murder, nor disrespecting the Power Rangers.(9)
(9) Except the yellow one—he's so lame.

...and speaking of face-to-face interaction, I've teased you throughout this journey with snide comments regarding, and impish implications about, the whole "teacher evaluation" thing. I even gave you a taste of the potentially volatile nature of it with my Lady Macbeth story, so it's high time I let it all hang out and said my peace about this uniquely arbitrary abomination before I put this, my final book about education, to bed.

And with that tawdry tease, onward we go to our next titillating titled chapter!

EVALUATION or NEGOTIATION? EITHER WAY IT'S AN ABERRATION, SO GO AHEAD AND GRAB THE LUBRICATION

"Our educational society is based on trust and cooperation, so when we are doing some testing and evaluations, we don't use it for controlling [teachers] but for development. We trust the teachers."
— Henna Virkkunen, Finland's Minister of Education,
(in response to the question:
"How are teachers evaluated in Finland?
How are they held accountable for student learning?")

"Teacher observations" have become the draconian instruments of discretionary persecution or patronization; sadly, they have also become indicative in many ways, of how far too many of you are "assessed" at your current place of employment. But, as they say: "haters gonna hate" and "teachers gonna teach," so I'll stick with what I know and keep this centered around teaching observations.

But I'm pretty sure you'll see yourself somewhere in this chapter. WHERE you see yourself will either provide some much-needed solidarity and catharsis or an opportunity for self-reflection and improvement.

I'm going to assume that you have a job, or go to school, or both. Thusly assumed, let me pose several honest questions, and, because we're friends now, I expect honest answers.

If you are employed (or an employer):

Do you know who the good employees at your job are? I mean, the really, legitimately good-at-their-job workers? I'll bet you do. How about the slackers? The ass-kissers? The sloths? The back stabbers? The quiet leaders? The indispensable, know-everything-about-this-place people? How about the do-the-bare-minimum-and-still-collect-a-check people? I'll bet you can name them all, too.

If you are a teacher (or, for that matter, a student):

Do you know who the good students in your class are? I mean, the hard-working, willing-to-do-whatever-it-takes-to-earn-the-grade-they-want people? I'll bet you do. How about the losers? The teacher's pets? The don't-care-because-they-don't-want-to be-in-school kids? The I'll-do-the-extra-credit-even-though-I have-a 99-in-this-class kids? How about the get-good-grades-even-though-they're-not-super-smart-*because-they-work-their-asses-off* kids? I'll bet you can name all of them, too.

My guess is that most people can.

So why this obsession with evaluations and observations? When did having some sort of "quantifiable data" (usually in the form of some evaluation system created by someone not affiliated directly with you or your craft) take the place of good old-fashioned opening your **eyes** and **ears**?!?!

Sorry, I have a tendency to over punctate when I'm upset; it's a character flaw.

But, to my point, I'm guessing that if you're working somewhere and your last name is NOT the one on the building, then you are subject to some sort of observation/evaluation/ humiliation/violation.

And can I guess that, in most of your cases, you're being evaluated by somebody that *never did your job* or, if they did, did it non-exceptionally, but, (thanks to a few graduate credits, maybe some proper ass-kissing, a piece of paper and a new title,) now has the "authority" to tell you what you're doing wrong? Mm-hmm. I feel your pain.

Not surprisingly, THE WOMAN WHO **CREATED** SAID FRAMEWORK FOR OUR EVALUATION IS UNHAPPY WITH HOW IT'S BEING IMPLEMENTED. That seems pretty important, so allow me to elaborate: Charlotte Danielson, creator of "Danielson Framework for Teacher Evaluation,"[1] in an April 18, 2016 *Education Week* article, implied that there should be a "rethinking of teacher evaluation."

No shit, Charlotte.

But allow me to elaborate on how bad it's gotten for me and my brothers and sisters in the teaching profession. We get observed, sometimes announced, sometimes not, sometimes for an entire period, sometimes for only *part* of a period, by administrators who, for the most part, stare at their laptops, dropping down menus of prewritten categories and scores, ignoring the actual teaching and learning the way they ignore us for the other 187 days of the year that they're NOT obligated to interact with us.[2]

Making these random, subjective "evaluations" worse is that they are often conducted:

1. With no regard, whatsoever, for the timing of/external factors regarding the actual humans (teachers/ aides/ students) involved,
2. by people who, very often, aren't qualified to appraise the people they're observing in the first place,
3. with more emphasis placed on what we *didn't* do than what we did *well,* and
4. with almost *no chance* of revisiting the observer's criticisms/ suggestions/ observations for instructional purposes.

---

(1) The 'framework' according to which I, and many of my peers, are evaluated.

(2) Not always, I've had a [very] small handful of observations over the last 25+ years wherein the "observer" actually interacted with me and actually—gasp!—spoke to the students.(3)

(3) One of my editors suggested, on several occasions, that my comments on the pedestrian nature of teacher observations rings repetitive, my having mentioned it before, about a million and a half times up to now. They're correct, of course, but, in this case, I respectfully ignored them because it is redundant, on purpose, because I want to drive the point home that I am being evaluated, most of the time, by people I don't respect, who are using methods in which they are not invested, to satisfy people that don't give a penguin fart about me or my kids. THAT IS UNACCEPTABLE; as such, I will preach on, redundantly if necessary.

With your permission, I will address all four of the aforementioned examples of *bullshitae micromanagementae* in detail.

Point one: These evaluations are often scheduled/performed with no regard, whatsoever, for the timing of external factors regarding the actual humans (teachers/ aides/ students) involved.

I understand that everyone has a schedule, and administrators are no exception, so I get that sometimes they get backed up and have to get their observations in at awkward times, but I have a list of unconscionable timing incidents that reads like *War and Peace*. I already told you about the administrator who made a teacher change an effective lesson because he *lacked the ability* to evaluate it properly, but here are a few more recent examples of what I'm talking about:

- How about a teacher observed on the first Monday *of the entire school year,* before ANY kind of repertoire or mutual understanding has been established? Before the class roster is even FINALIZED? Before anything even remotely academically meaningful has been undertaken?

What did this person THINK he/she was going to "observe?" Or… was the observer just trying to get a jump on the 'ol paperwork, with no regard whatsoever for *the subjects* of their observation?

- Or how about this gem? (I like this one because it encompasses so many of the elements that make this bullshit so bullshitty.) Math teacher was observed by the Director of Curriculum and Development (read: office dweller who is totally and unequivocally out of touch with the day to day realities of the classroom) *on the first day back from Christmas Break!* While the teacher was—as she is contractually obligated to be—at the door during change of classes, a student, one of the few students who came to school that day, (let's call her Fortune Residuos) shut down the teacher's laptop [which had visual slides for the lesson cued up.] It should be noted that this student was still in school despite **seventy-five** discipline referrals, (yes, you read that correctly,) but hey, everyone needs a second, or seventy fourth, chance, right? Aaaaaaanyway, as the teacher was getting her laptop restored and lesson back up, the D.O.C.A.D. (let's call her Fellatio Pearson,) came in the room, unannounced, again, *on the first day back from Christmas break*, and promptly announced that she was disappointed that the lesson hadn't begun yet before she took her seat and stared at her (decidedly non-sabotaged*)* laptop for the remainder of the period. The class was a fairly traditional lesson on factoring: as in "welcome back after a two-week break; we're starting clean with a new concept, so I'm-a-gonna-introduce-you-to-factors."

Fellatio told her (later of course, God forbid she actually speak to her during the observation,) that the lesson "was not rigorous" and that the teacher's score was a 1.99. (2.65 is the lowest score one can get to attain "proficiency," and if you don't finish the year with an average evaluation score of 2.65 you are subject to all sorts of nastiness, including potential plans to fuck with your **salary**.)[4] Thanks to that screw job score, which came with—surprise surprise—neither advice on how to be "rigorous" nor constructive criticism nor realistic compassion,[5] our intrepid teacher wound up with a 2.6**4** for the year.[6] It took over two weeks for the acting principal to change one of HIS observation scores from a 3 to a 4, thanks to common sense pressure from the union and someone much farther up the food chain who had known the teacher for years, and *knew* that she was "proficient." It should be noted that the principal was, allegedly, pissed about changing the score. The Math teacher's final score for the year was a [still underwhelming] 2.76 thanks

---

(4) Not officially in place in my State yet, but the rumbles have started that the powers-that-be want to start attaching teacher salaries to their evaluations and/or State test scores. If that happens, to quote the announcers from Rocky II: "Everybody better get ready for World War 3."

(5) THAT requires a heart & a brain, BOTH of which Ms. Pearson missed when the Wizard was handing shit out.

(6) Talk about a supreme dick move.

to the change in the—get ready for it—SHOWING PROFESSIONALISM category.

Serendipitously but dishearteningly, the aforementioned story brings me to my second and third points: **We are, more often than not, being evaluated by people who <u>are not qualified</u> to appraise us; people who, as a result, place (in an attempt to demonstrate their authority,) more emphasis on what we *didn't* do than what we did *well*.**

Once again, let me quote Charlotte Danielson herself, who recognizes that the administrators *doing* the evaluations are misusing the framework, largely *because* they are unqualified. She observes that:

> [F]ew jurisdictions require…evaluators to actually demonstrate skill in making accurate judgements. But since evaluators must assign a score, teaching is distilled to numbers, ratings, and rankings, conveying a reductive nature to educators' worth and undermining their overall confidence in the system.

Listen, if a teacher is unprofessional, lazy, or irrelevant, they SHOULD be evaluated harshly and, if necessary, reprimanded or terminated. I'm on record that a *lot* of teachers should get out of the profession, but let's be honest—this half-assed system shouldn't be trusted to test the ripeness of an avocado, let alone an educator's proficiency, and that is only compounded exponentially by the fact that the people wielding the weapon are often as qualified to do so as SpongeBob SquarePants is to split the atom. Allow me to elaborate, with the help of award winning author, Ph.D. in English studies, teacher, lecturer, scholar and publisher Ted Morrisey, who, in his 2016 blog, *Danielson Framework criticized by Charlotte Danielson*, ascertained that:

> In her criticism of administrators, [Charlotte] Danielson has touched upon what is, in fact, a major shortcoming of our education system: The road to becoming an administrator is not an especially rigorous one—especially when it comes to academic rigor—and once someone has achieved administrative

status, there tends to be no apparatus in place to evaluate *their* performance, including (as Ms. Danielson points out) their performance in evaluating their teachers...you oftentimes have and administrator who had only a limited amount of classroom experience...and whose only advanced degree is the one that allows them to be an administrator (whereby they mainly study things like school law and school finance,) sitting I judgement of a teacher who has spent [many] years honing their teaching skills and who has an advanced degree in their subject area. What can the evaluator possibly say in their critique that is meaningful and appropriate? ...all they can do is nitpick. They can't speak of anything of substance.

(Morrissey)

Mr. Morrisey is far more eloquent than I, so I'll put it another, more metaphorical, way: If the workers on a multimillion dollar construction site are being supervised and scolded by a supervisor that doesn't know the business end of a screwdriver from his own ass because he spent most of his life studying and working in graphic design, then the mood around the construction site (not to mention the quality of the building itself) is going to suffer quickly and quantifiably. But hey, we're not building skyscrapers here,

we're only educating children.

And since the most recent example I regaled you with involved a teacher being told that the lesson (insert jerking off motion) "lacked rigor," let me speak for a moment about just that word, since it seems to be increasingly used as the default criticism by the type of administrators to which Mr. Morrissey, Ms. Danielson, and I are referring:

(Ahem) Rigor.

A word that gets thrown around schools today like poop in an angry primate enclosure. Exasperatingly enough, the people who keep asking ME to "employ rigor" or micromanaging my lesson plans for "rigorous work" tend to have a few things in common, upon which I will elaborate. In my experiences, the rigor proponents:

1. Don't look like they spend a lot of time in discomfort, physically or mentally.
2. They CERTAINLY got out of the classroom as quickly as they could.
3. Their time spent on their craft, beyond their contractually obligated paid time, is minimal at best, and
4. they have no calluses, bruises, scars, or stories to tell that validate their intimate knowledge of that which is rigorous.

In short, most of them wouldn't know what actual RIGOR was, (in any form,) even if it approached them in plain view, from a distance, turned them around, and bit them on their-too-often-seated ass.

The End

No surprise then, that a report from the Network for Public Education states that "Evaluations based on frameworks and rubrics, such as those created by Danielson and Marzano, have resulted in wasting far too much time. This is damaging the very work that evaluation is supposed to improve." That, in itself, is bad enough, but when expected evaluation turns into *premeditated persecution* well, that's a whole different animal, isn't it?

Indeed, as Ted Morrissey correctly observes:

If administrators are using the Danielson Framework as a way of punishing teachers—giving them undeservedly reduced evaluations and thus exposing them to the harms that can befall them, including losing their job regardless of seniority—***there***

267

> **is no way for teachers to protect themselves**. (Emphasis mine)
> They cannot appeal an evaluation. They can write a letter to be
> placed alongside the evaluation explaining why the evaluation
> is unfair or invalid, but their complaint does not trigger a review
> of the evaluation. The evaluator's word is final. (Morrissey)

I, for one, have seen far too many examples of this predatory
practice; in fact, I'm pretty damn sure that my previously documented
contretemps with Lady Macbeth was a direct result of the fact that I
publicly questioned district and building policies that I thought were
untoward. Fuck her (and any administrator) that abuses their title and/or
power in naked displays of immoderate retaliation.

Again, I'm 100% certain that there are a LOT of you reading this
right now that have been fucked over by someone slightly up the food
chain, (who wouldn't have a single clue how to actually **do** your job
efficiently,) simply because—and I'll put this as simply as I can—*they
don't like you*. That might be common practice, but that doesn't make
it right; as Claude C. McDonald so righteously observed: "Sometimes a
majority simply means that all the fools are on the same side."

I think I've firmly established that [what was supposed to be the
meaningful practice of] evaluation and improvement has become
capricious claptrap, malicious malarkey, groundless gibberish, and
(one more) farcical phooey filled with meaningless, flavor-of-the-month
verbiage (rigor, best practice, pedagogy, etc.) wielded by dissonant
puppets who judge "certain behaviors that can be ticked off a checklist"
(Danielson) without offering actual insight or relevant advice.

That being said, let me address my fourth and final criticism; namely,
that **the capricious criticisms that are habitually heaped upon teachers
are given with almost *no chance* of revisiting the observer's criticisms/
suggestions/ observations for instructional purposes.**

By way of example, I offer a slice of my own particular party pooper
pizza of harsh reality: I've been observed almost *70 times* in my years
as a teacher. How many times has an observer followed up with me to
see if I improved on [what they thought] I should work on?

Four. Vier. Quatre. Quatro. Cztery, (Mad props to the law firm of

Long, Kopp, Joyce and Steer,) useful follow-ups, where the administrators in question offered pragmatic, well-informed feedback, criticism that made me a better teacher, and gave me practical tools with which to improve my performance. The rest of those Oh...so...important observations, criticisms, and evaluations?

Never saw 'em again, and nobody ever followed up to see if I implemented them.

So, I ask you, what purpose did they serve?

None, they served no purpose at all. A dog-and-pony show of the most pedestrian order.

One of the many beautiful byproducts of the first three books, and the subsequent press/social media surrounding those books, is that I've built up a pretty sizable network of educators[7] that correspond with me, and I'm here to tell you that the *overwhelming* majority of them concur that the way teachers' observations are conducted is cryptically scheduled, derogatory by nature, and educationally vacuous.

A shame, really, because (and you can mark THIS day down on your calendar) ***I actually sympathize with the administrators, to a degree,*** because the minutiae that they are forced to endure[8] forced them away from the good old days of walking the halls, talking to teachers and students, and actually *knowing* what the people in their buildings are doing, *without* having to consult some computer uploaded busywork or some awkwardly forced fortune telling, followed by some silly song and dance negotiation.

Fortune telling? Negotiation? "What have these to do with being a teacher?" you ask, in your best concerned voice. Well, since we're co-conspirators and all, I guess I can let you in on the secret *"fifth* level of Hell" that makes the teacher observation process as much fun as a root canal on a bed of nails without anesthesia while listening to Justin Bieber: the pre-and post-observation notes conundrums, or, what I like to call "the shot in the dark followed by the kick in the nuts."

---

(7) My very own KISS Army, I'm so proud! Don't laugh, I'm a soldier in good standing since 1977.

(8) To prove to their corporate overlords over there in educational Mordor that they're doing their jobs.(9)

(9) There, they're and their, used correctly, all in one sentence. Boom.

Let's talk about the PRE-observation notes, because they are, essentially, how this landslide of laughability gets started rolling in the first place. Before we actually get observed, a teacher is expected to access the 'evaluation portal" site, (ours has changed *several* times in the past few years.) Assuming that you are able to get in on your first or seventy-fifth try (the tech is often wonky at best,) you are then asked to fill out extensive "pre-observation" notes about what the person coming in is going to see.

1. I have never received any actual training/guidance on how to access these portals and/or how to fill out the pre-observation trivialities, but by now I am well acquainted with the "just learn it and get it done" modus operandi.
2. Like you, I have no earthly idea what factors may affect the lesson in question days (sometimes weeks) prior to when the "observer" is scheduled to show up, AND...
3. ...it's about a 50% certainty that the observer will cancel, postpone, or come at a different time than the one upon which we originally agreed. (But you already *knew* that, didn't you, attentive reader?)

That's fine, as long as the observer in question doesn't expect to see the lesson THEY asked ME to describe *in advance* **before they changed the *date* and *time***. Do you see the colossal ridiculousness here? That would be like a building inspector asking a foreman to predict *exactly* what *everyone* on a jobsite would be doing when he showed up at 9 A.M. on December 5th, only to get pissed because he showed up at 3 P.M. on December 22nd and didn't see what he was told he would see!

Oh, but they **will**, folks, they **will** ask to see the lesson originally agreed upon, largely because common sense and compassion would die cold, lonely deaths in the realm of "observation logic."

Alas, now that I, the teacher du jour, have been observed, I must await being summoned to my post-observation conference, which may be scheduled—based on my experiences—anywhere from a few days to infinity ***after*** *the actual observation happened.* Once the post-ob conference actually becomes a reality, I will be forced to defend everything I did during a lesson that may have been weeks—possibly months—ago using, you guessed it, POST-observation notes on the portal. An awful lot of hitting "send" and waiting in lieu of actual punctual human interaction; the entire thing smells of cowardice and detachment to me.

Because hey—to put this as succinctly as I can—**nothing says "I'm trying to help you" like an arbitrary checklist of numbers, which can be disputed and/or changed, that were filled out during a drive-by perusal, which was performed by a person who isn't held accountable for their observations, and is in no way incentivized to actually *follow up* on them.**

To be fair, most of the administrators in question KNOW that the "scores" are hastily assigned, relatively robotic, and coldly conceived, so the post observation turns into a stichomythia of legal haggling wherein I, the teacher, am obligated to itemize my hastily assigned scores and barter for an (exceptional) "4" where the observer had seen fit to give me a (proficient) "3." Or, in more serious cases, the teacher might be obligated to threaten union involvement and/or legal action unless the unengaged "evaluator" changes a (non-proficient) "2" or an even more damaging "1" to a sufficiently proficient numeral. Small wonder why Charlotte Danielson herself observed that "few jurisdictions require their evaluators to actually demonstrate skill in making accurate judgements."

Oh, and speaking of "obligation," in many districts, teachers are given lower grades in certain categories for not being able to prove that they participate in school functions *beyond their contractually obligated time*, and *for which they do not get paid*.

Listen, almost every teacher I know, *almost every one*, goes to proms, sporting events, plays and musicals to help out; many of them go to events *outside of the school* just to support their kids. They stay after school, give up lunch periods, and Skype with kids on weekends to give their students extra help. They buy materials out of their own pocket, give kids lunch money, etc. They spend hours (sometimes entire weekends) at home calling and collaborating with parents, grading papers, and revising lesson plans. They coach sports and moderate clubs, earning almost nothing if you factor the cash to money ratio of their hours and hours of service and support. In short, most of us put in a LOT of non-contractually obligated time. Therefore, to exercise punitive measures anyone whose obligations at home/health concerns/etc. take precedent over that which is above and beyond what is "contractually obligated" by giving them a lower score?

That is total

fucking.

bullshit.

While you process that, let me flash back a bit and put this whole mess in perspective by comparing the observation process with another recent clown show that we all witnessed:

As I sit here finishing this chapter on my 49th birthday, (January 21, 2017,) my social media feed is inundated with stories of protests, clashes, and vitriol surrounding our 45th president of these not-so-United States. It saddens me deeply that we continue to divide ourselves, often with increasing violence and intolerance, but what ***really*** grinds my gears is that very few of these people were as *for* any of the candidates (at any stage of the election process,) as they were *against* others and, to be honest, I can't blame them; the entire PROCESS sucks. No way you can tell me, in a country of over **324 million** people, that the shit show we handed the American public throughout this election cycle was the best we had to offer and the best we could do. Which, serendipitously enough, brings me to the issue I spoke of earlier.

Much like the old joke *"politicians are like sperm, one in a million actually become a human being,"* **so, too, does one in a million teacher observations become a useful exercise in human understanding and evolution.** The rest become the haggle and the waggle show.

But, and I sense I've beaten a dead Trojan horse at this point, the whole process is twisted, toxic, discretionary, and infuriating.

And that's why, unless the person 'evaluating' me is *legitimately engaged* and shows that they want to *collaborate* with me, *over time,* to make me a more effective educator, I sign the results and walk away, making it clear that I care as much about their opinion of me as they do about me as a person. It should also be noted that my hastily scrawled signature may or may not look like the words "fuck you" when written a certain way. (Or so I've been told. Wink Wink)

Not that it matters.

Most of the people that have "evaluated" me over the years have moved on, been demoted, been relieved of their duties, or simply faded away from the profession.

I, like most good teachers, am still here.[10]

---

(10) And always will be.

Trumpy, Happy, Bashful, Dopey, Scaredy, and one Sleepy Doc

"You know that I care what happens to you,
and I know that you care for me.
So I don't feel alone, or the weight of the stone…
And any fool knows a dog needs a home,
a shelter from pigs on the wing."

— *Roger Waters*

Trumpy

In the interest of complete honesty, I went to bed at 10:30 P.M.; I'm far too jaded to believe that either candidate would change my life profoundly, and far too evolved to care about the media circus surrounding the election process. I care about my students, and they need their teacher to be wide awake and focused at 7:00 A.M. when our school day starts; so, again, I went "night night" about five hours before Donald Trump was announced as the President Elect of America.

I'm not going to offer my half-assed political commentary, because it doesn't matter and you don't care (nor *should* you, by the way; what the hell do *I* know about politics?) Instead, I'm going to tell you about how life altering events such as this afford teachers the opportunity to be, at our best, what we were born to be—educators, protectors, and healers.

Happy

Before I was even half finished my very large and very black coffee, twenty-four former students showed up in my homeroom at 7:01 A.M. this morning. I have a 9th grade homeroom, so my 18 freshmen were surprised into silence when a double dozen of upper-classmen came in and surrounded me like they wanted my lunch money. Fortunately for me and my hunger, all they wanted was unfiltered honesty and inexhaustible compassion.

Teachers are good for that kind of stuff.

The kids wanted to know, and I'm paraphrasing now, two things: **How** this could have happened and **why** they should not be afraid. They're kids, so the first order of business was to comfort them from the blitzkrieg of vitriol, misinformation, and propaganda by which they were besieged (thanks, in large part, to the 'responsible adults' in their lives.) I tried to calm them, and I told them that I, and the rest of the people that cared about them, still loved them and suggested that they continue to love and look out for each other. Nothing super profound there, right? But they didn't want profound, they wanted comfort, so I stayed off the soapbox and focused on their needs. Many of them had me the previous year, so they were still pretty familiar with my "two Ss of death" theory: When people are scared, they make irrational decisions, when people are stupid they make uninformed decisions, when people are *both*...uh oh.[1]

Obviously, as intelligent young people, they were **conflicted**, (yes, even the black and brown and hijab-wearing ones.) They were thrilled that so many people voiced their dissatisfaction with 1% "we-don't-give-a-fuck-about-you-politics-as-usual," (they read *Animal Farm* and *Brave New World* with me, after all.) But they were, simultaneously, heartbroken that, in order to do so, they were forced to choose a candidate that—in order to get elected—exhibited behavior that would've gotten him thrown out of my 9th grade English class. And so, we talked, we commiserated, we agreed to disagree, and my twenty-four astute stepchildren left my classroom the way all kids should leave a classroom: informed and inspired, but unsatisfied and inquisitive.

They were happy to have been there, but not nearly as happy as

---

(1) And let me be clear about this, I didn't give a damn who won, but I was bitterly disappointed that the American public were, for the most part, complacent with the fact that syphilis and gonorrhea were presented as the only two viable options. "Uh, I'll take NEITHER for a thousand, Alex."

I was to have had them. Then a few of my freshmen, who were really *forced* to eavesdrop, started asking questions and, well, the conversation began again in earnest, until...

Bashful

One young lady, a very soft-spoken Freshman girl I'll call Bashful, asked to speak to me out in the hall. Amidst the chaos that was the hallway during homeroom the day after a shocking[2] presidential election, we found a quiet spot and she asked me, with actual tears in her eyes, if it was true that she would be "sent back." I assumed (I know, I know...ass out of U and ME) that she was Muslim, and was referring to the rhetoric regarding Trump banning Muslims from the country, and when I inquired about that, Bashful started crying and said "No, are they gonna send us back to Africa?" (Bashful, as you may have ascertained, is black.)

Now folks, some of you may be shaking your head, some of you may be laughing, some of you may be crying. Hell, some of you might think I'm making this up altogether, but I'm not. (I wish I was to be honest.) I only relate this little anecdote to remind you what we, as teachers, are faced with *on a daily basis:* frightened, misinformed children who are the products of frightened, misinformed parents, who are often the products of a frightened, misinformed society. These kids come to us every day—and especially on days like this—seeking honesty, empathy, safety and security *that they very often don't get at home.*[3]

Of course, we deal with a metric ton of stupidity, too.

Dopey

Oh, the chapter I could've written on just the inane, incendiary and flat out ridiculous things I heard students regurgitate all day. I say regurgitate, of course, because independent thought tends to starve in solitary confinement within the confines of the average High School.

---

(2) Admit it, you were surprised.

(3) Please try to remember that when you're spouting that "those who can't do, teach" nonsense.

Sadly, most of these kids just repeat what they hear from any number of unreliable sources,[4] and it is all-too often our jobs, as educators, to help these kids navigate the assault of information.

Witness the first questions that came bursting forth from my first period class as they burst through the door: The normal "What's up, Step?' and "Good morning, Mr. Step" were replaced with the loud, almost abrasive:

"How Trump gonna win?!"

"Most people didn't vote for that man!!"

"He got all them Mexicans to vote for him so he could get Obama out of being President!"

"Mr. Step, did you hear that Trump won?"

And those are the ones I could *remember* when I got home; there were some real winners that escaped me, I'm sure.

While that all came from a chaotic cacophony of student sound, it nonetheless contained a veritable sudoku of whattheheckareyoutalkingabout-itness, so I attacked the questions in reverse order.[5]

"Yes, I heard that Donald Trump won, and I was very surprised to hear that."

"President Obama was leaving office at the end of this term regardless of who won, because no president can serve more than two consecutive terms."

---

(4) Some of which are electronic in nature, some of which are flesh and bone and slightly larger models that live under the same roof.

(5) As you might expect, some of the NON-Walking [brain] Dead students were leaning forward in anticipation of how I would handle that onslaught of inquisitiveness.

"I don't think, as you put it, "that he got all the Mexicans to vote for him." (Several Hispanic students nodded vigorously.)

"I assume when you say that 'most people didn't vote with Trump' you mean that the popular vote showed Hillary Clinton winning, which leads me to believe that you were asleep during our entire conversation about the Electoral College. But hey! I don't take that personally, because if you think (air quotes) *'all the Mexicans' voted for him to 'get Obama out' then you've been asleep for most of the last 6 months".* (More vigorous nodding and more than a few laughs.)

And so, the day passed, and I did my best to educate my students, encouraged them not to contribute to the misinformation, (the media was doing a bang-up job of that already,) and to remember that, <u>no matter who sat in the Oval office, nobody controlled their destiny as much as they, themselves, did.</u>

Later that evening, as I sat in my home reading the wildly different reactions to the election results, my very sleepy-looking wife, (the illustrious Dr. Dawn, had stayed up all night watching the election results unfold) came in around 7:30 P.M. and, over dinner asked me how my kids reacted to Trump winning.

"Well, twenty-four former students showed up in my homeroom at 7:01 A.M. this morning…"

I NEVER REACHED THE
SUMMITT, AND THAT'S OK

*"They don't care how much you know
unless they know how much you care."*

—*Pat Summitt*

Pat Summitt died today and, for some unknown reason, I knew that her death would help me start bringing this book to a close. Of course, this ain't the first time that Coach Summitt helped me without knowing it.

My students are always surprised when, as it does every year, the subject of inspiration comes up and I tell them that my coaching and teaching idol is a woman. I'm not sure why, as I preach gender equality and acceptance of all lifestyles with Hellfire and damnation intensity; but after I finish telling them all *about* Pat Summitt, they totally understand.

Please understand, before we go any further, that I do not *equate* myself in <u>any</u> capacity with Coach Summitt. *She* was an old testament God, a trailblazing innovator that changed the landscape of women's sports, college athletics and, in her own way, the world—*I am simply an idiot, full of sound and fury,* that originally felt some kinship in our teaching styles, heard stories [about her] throughout my career that resonated with me, and decided that, at the end, as role models go—I could do a hell of a lot worse. I only use comparison in this case to: 1) bring closure to this book by emphasizing points that I feel passionately about and 2) pay homage to an extraordinary teacher.

When I got my first teaching gig, I was twenty-two years old, full of piss and vinegar. I was pushed right into the "deep end," being entrusted with the biggest and baddest "severely emotionally disturbed"[1] teenagers that the school had to offer.

---

(1) That's what they were called back then, and that is EXACTLY what they were.

All day, all to myself, with total autonomy and total accountability.

Pat Summitt was asked to take over the University of Tennessee Lady Vols basketball team in 1974, thrusting her into a world that she felt compelled, against everything society had accepted, to change. All this at the ripe old age of, you guessed it, twenty-two.

Of course, I knew how to teach English and how to control a room, but those skills were a skeletal framework that needed a LOT of meat added to its bones if I was going to be a supremely effective teacher and change what I had already determined, after a few days, was a broken educational status quo. (Yes, before you ask, I was arrogant enough, even then, to believe I could change the world.) So how was I supposed to get started? What was I to do? Where could I turn for advice? And most importantly, *WHO* could I look to as a role model of what I wanted to be as a teacher and a mentor?

I'll TELL ya who,

Patricia Sue Summitt.

I had always been aware of Pat Summitt, but, in a moment I can now only describe as fate, I saw a brief biographical program about her on TV during my first few months teaching. She took over an uneventful women's program in a male-dominated world, and although she knew basketball and hard work intimately (like I knew English and crowd control,) she knew, instinctively, that to get her *players* where she wanted them, she would have to, literally, change the *game*. By the time I started teaching in 1989, the Lady Volunteers were already a sure bet to either win the Women's NCAA Championship or be damn close to it. Far from content, she continued to push and, as her knowledge increased, so, exponentially, did her fire and intensity. She was once quoted as saying *"I think that a lot of people would perceive my style as being intimidating, [and] although I don't want to intimidate kids, I am very demanding."*

"Well there you go, dumbass," I remember thinking, "why look any further? **The man you want to be is that woman right there."**

Thus began my personal journey to emulate the best of the best.

Little did I know how steep that metaphorical mountain was going to get, or how much it would help me to define the qualities that I think a great teacher should radiate: Selflessness, introspection, accountability, adaptation, knowledge (of their craft) and, most importantly, love.

SELFLESSNESS: Word has it that when she was earning $250 a month in the mid-1970s, Summitt collected and washed her players' uniforms herself; apparently, she knew that if she didn't do it, no one else would. I have personally spent thousands of dollars on my students on everything from school supplies to hygiene products, from clothes to grocery orders, and everything in between. Why? Because in many cases, if I didn't no one else would. Lest you think that makes me unique, ask any of your teacher friends if they've spent their own money on their students; you'll be surprised how many of them say yes and how much they've spent. <u>Good teachers are selfless.</u>

INTROSPECTION: In 1999, *60 Minutes* interviewed Summitt,[2] and I remember vividly the story she told about how one of her players told her that she needed "more encouragement and less brutal honesty" or something like that. At first, Summit flatly rejected the idea, but then (before I could finish pumping my fist and saying "that's RIGHT, coach, you tell her!")

she evaluated herself honestly and came to the following realization: *"You know, sometimes I'm more stubborn than I am smart. But that time, I decided, "You need to be smart about this, and you need to give in."* <u>Good teachers are brutally honest with themselves.</u>

ACCOUNTABILITY: When asked if her moment of [stubborn] self-realization was painful, she responded that it was, but that *"[she] could hear it in her [player's] voice. She meant it. She really needed it. She was about to break. And the one thing you never want to do is break their spirit. You know, you can upset them, but when you push to the point of breaking someone's spirit, now you've got a real problem, and you never know when they'll come back. I mean, you never know if they'll ever regain their composure or their confidence or their belief."*

---

(2) After a long internet search, I found a video clip and excerpts from that very interview, at http://www.cbsnews.com/news/pat-summitt-i-am-very-demanding/; give it a watch if you need an inspirational kick in the booty.

I remember that feeling, staring at channel 3 on my little TV set in my apartment in Fishtown, feeling like Pat Summitt was personally reprimanding me, telling me what a pompous twit I had become. You see, I was about 10 years into my teaching career, and, thanks to some pretty amazing success with what many considered "unteachable" kids, I started thinking my shit didn't stink and that I knew it all. And yes, it pains me to say, but I had probably (definitely) run roughshod over a few students' more pressing emotional needs in my quest for what I wrongly defined as their "success." Since that day, I have referred to what I try to do for my students as "evolve" them. While some may think that sounds insulting, that couldn't be farther from the truth; in fact, I use that specific term to remind myself that what I am doing, ideally, is attending to and improving *every single facet* (mental, physical, spiritual, psychological, emotional, etc.) of the children I'm entrusted to teach.[3]

Of course, that doesn't mean I still don't catch myself rolling over my students' feelings like an M1128 Stryker Tank under the auspices of ensuring their evolution (and appeasing my ego.) But when I catch myself, or when the students let me know—often more politely than they should—that I'm doing it again, I own it. I apologize, sincerely, explain (but not excuse) my reasoning, and talk to the kids about how we can reach our common objectives without compromising my standards or permanently disenfranchising them from the whole process. Again, I am but one of a legion of teachers that self-evaluate, evolve and improve on a daily basis. <u>Good teachers</u> are, by nature, introspective, and they <u>hold themselves perpetually accountable</u>.

ADAPTATION: I was 36 and had just accepted a one year teaching position, convinced that if I did well, a permanent position was a very real possibility. I won't go into detail, but I had parted ways from the only teaching job I ever held because I refused to leave one of my young men to the wolves "to avoid a situation" that would "reflect poorly on the school." It was volatile, it was scary, and it was *permanent*. I was as adamant that what I was doing was right as I was uncertain what my future would hold. When this new job landed in

---

(3) It is no coincidence that the Navy SEALs often refer to their training exercises as "evolutions" for this very reason.

my lap (gloriously, late in the Summer, after I had already given my then very young children the *"Daddy's going to be a landscaper now"* speech,) I assured the then superintendent that I was exactly what he wanted, a wolf that was well seasoned in combat but still extremely, thanks to my current employment situation, hungry to prove himself. Only after signing the contract did an absolute avalanche of doubt fall squarely on my thick head, and the voices began. (And they were all in bold type, so I knew it was serious:) **Can I teach "normal" kids? How am I going to write lesson plans? I never had to write lesson plans! What the hell is a rubric? Can I follow a curriculum? What IS the curriculum? Technology?! You've got to be kidding; the only technology we had was a metal detector! Oh, what have you gotten yourself into, you idiot? You've been a teacher, but let's be honest, you've never done anything like this before...**on and on and on until sleepless nights became exhausted days.

THIS time, I actually went looking for Pat, and I found her, at Barnes & Noble, in all her autobiographic glory. I devoured *Raise the Roof: The Inspiring Inside Story of the Tennessee Lady Vols' Historic 1997-1998 Threepeat Season* in about two days and—true to form—found the inspiration and answers I was looking for. One of the quotes that stood out to me was her assertion that *"the willingness to experiment with change may be the most essential ingredient to success at anything."* Of course, I knew, deep down inside, that changing to adapt to an evolving educational landscape was necessary, albeit terrifying. I also knew that I had been granted an OPPORTUNITY, not given a punishment, and that I should embrace it as a kick in the ass to update and upgrade myself as a teacher.

...much the same way an already *massively successful* coach did on her way to becoming a *legendary* coach. Pat had a five-year run that included a championship (90'-91,') a runner up [to the championship] (99'-00,') two sweet sixteens (91'-92' and 93'-94,') and an elite 8 (93'-94'). Against that staggeringly successful backdrop (which also included two more championships) she openly admitted to having to adapt to the new era of the game and a new generation of *players*.

"What?!?" I thought as I read about her desire to experiment with

change, *"why the hell would you 'adapt' a winning formula that already won…*

> *Three National Championships IN A ROW (95—98',)*
> *the **last** of which came via A PERFECT, UNDEFEATED SEASON?"*

"Oh, that's why." I thought to myself, chagrined even though I was alone in the privacy of my home. So, I experimented. I changed. I evolved. I adapted. I learned what I knew and didn't know, admitted the latter and improved the former, and I

worked

my

ass

off until my rubrics became the ones other people used, my lesson plans became the gold standard, and my incorporation of technology… ok, I still suck at that, but I'm learning! I still suck at a lot of things, if we must be honest, (and we must) but I, like so many of my peers, am in a near constant state of self-education, professional development, and overall improvement.

Because good teachers adapt to their surroundings, and then *improve* those surroundings.

And speaking of professional development and improvement…

KNOWLEDGE (OF YOUR CRAFT) I didn't need much in the way of guidance here, as I (along with any good teacher you know) feel compelled to continually update my knowledge base and remain relevant to whatever generation of students I'm teaching. If that means acquainting myself with the new Kendrick Lamar CD, reading *13 Reasons Why*, checking out a local artist, or—God help me—watching an episode of *Pretty Little Liars*, then so be it. I'm also almost continually enrolled in post-graduate classes to keep my certification viable, my knowledge base growing, and my craft sharp. (Again, I'm hardly alone in this.)

I'm not going to go into Pat Summitt's continuing evolution of her craft; I don't have enough room here. Just Google her name and you'll get educated quick fast and in a hurry how her game evolved and her accomplishments became even more global in scale.

Sadly, as I started this chapter by pointing out, those quantifiable accomplishments are at an end, because after fighting early onset dementia, `Alzheimer's Type,' she died quietly today. I specifically said her **quantifiable** accomplishments because the most amazing thing that will remain about Pat Summitt, her greatest legacy, will be written in flesh and blood, in the memories and lives of the people she touched; her players (who I will take the liberty of calling her *students*) all speak about the icy stare, the intensity, and the brutal honesty and ever raising standards, but they all (most of them through tears) speak of WHY they endured this relentless taskmaster...

because they KNEW that **she loved them**,

and that **everything she did for her kids came from a place of LOVE**,

of wanting them to be better than her,

better than they could ever dream of being themselves.

The confidence she instilled, and the voice she planted inside their heads and hearts, a voice that they will pass on to *their* children, students and players, makes that legion of Summitt's students the living embodiment of her teaching.

As such, she remains immortal.

I'd be willing to wager that some of you reading this are doing it through a veil of tears, or behind an ear-to-ear grin, because you feel the same way about your students, and memories of the love that has passed between you never really goes away, does it? If you're not a teacher—go ask one what their fondest teaching memory is, or about a kid that they made a real connection with.

Watch their faces. We can't help it. A glow comes from us that can't be faked or manufactured, and that type of authentic love stays with our kids. I took a break in the middle of writing this to grab a bite to eat and read the answers to a questionnaire I give all of my students after the final exams are in and failure notices have been submitted. I ask for brutal honesty, ask them to keep it real, because they have nothing, per se, to lose, and so they get a chance to "pay me back" for the hell I put them through.

And pay me back they did. One letter after another talking about how they hated me at first, or were afraid of me, or felt intimidated because of what they'd heard, etc. BUT, almost every one of them came to a point, (at different times throughout the year) where they "got it;" when they realized that there was a method to my madness, and that it was all in the name of evolving them in every conceivable way. They bought in, just when they thought they were going to tap out, because they felt safe, and they felt empowered, because they felt loved.

<u>Good teachers love their students; that is as obvious as it is non-negotiable</u>.

I would like to believe that Coach Summitt would approve of me as a teacher, although I suspect she'd find a few holes in my armor and suggest that I fix them "if [I was] up to it." It occurs to me as I write this that she would have *loved* my Dad; neither of them was ever satisfied, and both of them extolled the virtues of suffering in silence (Pat Summitt endured *six* miscarriages during her coaching career, and I endured the death of my first-born son; both of us went back to work shortly thereafter.)

<u>Good teachers are never satisfied</u> with themselves or their students; there is always more we can do to help them and more they can show us, revealing more of themselves in the process.

Got that?

Good teachers are selfless, introspective, and accountable; they adapt to their surroundings (although they're never satisfied with those surroundings) and they love their kids.

Your kids.

We love your kids.

So, think about that before you speak harshly,

before you act confrontationally,

before you think judgmentally.

Speaking for myself, I may not be perfect, but I'm working to be, and I'm enduring the slings and arrows of life and this profession willingly in a never-ending battle to educate, protect and evolve *your children*.

I am more than willing to work with you in that endeavor.

I *want* to work with you in that endeavor.

However, if you feel compelled to cast the first stone, I can do that dance, too.

Either way, I'll probably never even approximate the level of impact that Patricia Sue Summitt did during her teaching/coaching career, but I'll be damned if I won't try; furthermore, I'll take solace in knowing that I did it my way, because my way has always been, and always will be, about the kids. I'd like to think Coach Summitt would've been OK with that.

TRIGGER WARNING

"Integrity without knowledge is weak and useless,
and knowledge without integrity is dangerous and dreadful."
—Samuel Johnson

*"I guess that makes knowledge **with** integrity dangerous*
on a whole different level."
—Scott "Sharky" Schopper

I hope that, years from now, when someone reads this book, that we have evolved as a species to the point where people have to ask "what is a trigger warning?" Alas, for the moment, it seems to be a word that has planted itself firmly in the zeitgeist of our current invertebrate culture. Colleges and Universities are issuing "trigger warnings' on works of art, literature, and film; more disastrously, they are *prefacing lessons* with these "you're-probably-too-sensitive-for-this" warning shots.

No. No. A thousand times no.

But there it is, yet another acquiescence to the softening and stupefying of our society; the fact that it has made its way to the hallowed halls of learning made a part of me die inside, but it set *another* part on fire.

This may be my last book about education, per se, but it won't be the last time I comment, scathingly and sarcastically, about the **S**tupidity **H**eightening the **I**rrelevancy of **T**oday's educational system. No sir, there are fictional stories, poems, articles, blogs, speaking engagements, and maybe another novel or three on the horizon; but, for now, we need to bring this book to a close so you can get busy living your life and making a difference in your own way.

So, how to bring it home? That's always the hardest part, for me anyway, when starting the writing process: Where am I going to *end*? Luckily, with the previous three books, something triggered (no pun intended) a visceral response in me that made it obvious what song would be the encore of each of my previous too-loud-for-the-crowd literary "concerts."

When I was trying to close *Why Are All the Good Teachers Crazy?* an author who is far more famous and talented than I said that if anyone made it through that book then they clearly enjoyed my "unique narrative voice," and he suggested that I just say "goodbye" in the same voice.

S.C.R.E.W.E.D. was such a radical departure, (to this day, it's my Metallica *Load* album; people either love it or hate it) and the tone was so much darker, that I felt it needed to end that way; fortunately, an anonymous letter from a disgruntled parent reminded me why I wrote the book in the first place, and helped me end book two in defiant fashion.

Ending *Teaching Sucks* was simple: I was on the beach and saw one of those airplane ads for TeachNow.org or some shit promising that you could be a teacher with only a few weeks of training, blah blah blah. In a paroxysm of productive fury, I typed the ending on my phone right there and then.

This one was the easiest of all, thanks, in large part, to our apparent dystopian love affair with keeping the incoming generation soft and stupid. Recently, hundreds of educational faculty members across the United States have been reported to a website called *Professor Watchlist*—a website launched by Turning Point USA, a well-funded, right wing political organization. The group **says** its aim is to identify teachers that "advance a radical agenda," but from everything I was able to glean it sounds like they simply want to take educators that teach kids to question voraciously, think critically, and debate successfully and put those teachers on a list of "dangerous faculty."

Thank you, *Professor Watchlist*, and all of the narrow-minded twits associated with it; you have given me my new mission statement and, no small feat, the ending to this book.

I want to be on your list.

In fact, I want to be public enemy #1.

I want to be known, according to your cowardly criteria, **as the most dangerous**

fucking teacher in America.

And so, gentle reader, I leave you to your individual endeavors. I, it seems, have work to do, force feeding the youth of America the red pill[1] and kicking the hornet's nest of anyone trying to tell me how to teach YOUR kids, in MY classroom.

Our retribution, it seems, is just beginning.

---

(1) Term popularized in science fiction culture, derived from the 1999 film The Matrix, wherein the red pill symbolizes knowledge, freedom and the sometimes painful truth of reality, (and the blue pill symbolizes falsehood, security and the blissful ignorance of illusion.)

LOUD LOVE

At the end of the day, we are all a sum of our parts; and a select few need to be mentioned in print for how they have affected my life as both a writer and a teacher.

THE CO-CONSPIRATORS

Ed Trautz—(aka Darth Trocious)—People, I simply cannot tell you, in a million words or less, how different this book would have sounded without Ed's tireless help. I am a royal pain in the ass, sending him stuff at weird hours of the morning or long past when everyone normal is in bed. To make matters worse, I am constantly changing my vision of what each chapter should be and how it should read, (usually in the middle of the editing process) and, apparently; I, am, an, absolute bugbear; when it; comes, to commas, and; semicolons. Trautz bears all of this with a patience that would make most of the latter-day Saints blush if they weren't all as dead as doornails. **Understand that, <u>unlike</u> with my previous books, I explicitly told Ed to stay the fuck out of my way when it came to the controversial stuff and to stick to improving my grammar and clarity.** Nonetheless, he continually tried to save me from myself, and I sincerely love him for it. *Please know that if something in this book really pissed you off, Ed probably tried to stop me from publishing it at some point.* Trautz is probably as sick of this book as I am after the number of edits and rewrites we collectively endured, and he (rightfully so) probably got pissed at me for ignoring his pleas for subtlety and nuance. Instead, I wrote like a redundant bull in a china shop. Like my parents, he did his best; I just don't listen; however, if my words sound coherent and clear, and if potentially sticky topics go down smoother than two fingers of Johnny Walker Blue, that's all because of the editor, people, and Oliver and Elliot's Dad / Emily's husband is the best there is, the best there was, and the best there ever will be, period.

291

Tommy Castagna—When I get the emails from my publisher about trim, bleed, kerning, font, spread, justification, baseline, gutter length and other formatting requirements, it sounds like somebody spilled the Pythagorean Theorem onto a Gordian knot to me. Thank goodness Tommy, my guru of graphics, lord of layout, sultan of specifications, has been there, since book one, to make my hastily typed documents print ready and turn my vague imagery into actual eye-catching book covers; and he does this all for kind words and hockey swag. He is, indeed, the man.

Jason Secoda—Jason created the "balloon me" for the author photo, and that is far from his most impressive work, I assure you. (Check out *Airheads Entertainment* on Facebook for more of Dr. Secoda's jaw-dropping work.) I've always looked at Jas as more family than friend; in fact, I often refer to him as somewhere between being my oldest son and the younger brother I never had. His brutally honest input on the book led to some key revisions that, upon reflection, made it more palpable for non-educators.

NOTE: While I had a great deal of help in producing the final product you're holding, I must adamantly insist that any grammatical errors, redundancies, or transgressions fall squarely on my shoulders, and mine alone.

THE VOICES

Andy Vasily is a citizen of the World. From Ontario to China to Saudi Arabia and points in between, he has preached a gospel of teaching through inspiration, perspiration, and meditation. I was lucky enough to be both a guest on his international *Run Your Life* podcast and the guest *host* (of his 50th episode.) My relationship with Andy and his lovely wife Neila continues to evolve, and I am the richer for it. Hopefully, the three of us (and Ross "the Boss" Halliday) can run up a mountain together and meditate on top when we get there.

Justin Oakley unselfishly allowed me, twice, to be the gonzo gorilla

I can sometimes be when he graciously welcomed me onto his *Just Let Me Teach* radio show. Justin is a consistent, outspoken voice that continually advocates for teachers across the country, including this one. No matter how much I push the envelope, Justin shows the love, fights the good fight, and promotes the books(!) and I respect the hell out of him for it.

Jon Harper is a vice principal in Maryland that welcomed me onto his *My Bad* radio show. Jon and his producers Errol and Jennette asked me to evaluate the mistakes I've made as a teacher and how I learned from them, a useful exercise for any good teacher. Our conversation was the fuel I needed to begin the 2016-2017 school year, and the online interview he conducted with me regarding this publication, (which I included for your reading pleasure,) reinvigorated me during the excruciating weeks of final editing. Thanks, Viper!

The *Fans of the Author Frank Stepnowski* Facebook group—700 members and growing. Don't laugh, that's not too bad for a self-published hack such as myself. My friends (sorry, I just can't call them fans, J.K. Rowling has *fans*, I have *friends*) offer constant support, encouragement, criticism and love. Contrary to the belief that I run entirely on caffeine, loud music and anger, the folks on the fan page sustain me through the darkest of days, and they are the coolest support system in the universe.

Max Pulcini and the staff at *The Spirit of the Riverwards* newspaper— it's particularly gratifying when "the old neighborhood" gives one of its own props, and the gang at the Spirit (including Maryanne, Tommy and Kathy) have always made this former Fishtowner feel welcome.

The people that write online reviews and/or **promote the books via social media**—I simply don't have enough time to list you all here, but you have no idea how important you are to me. I don't have the luxury of a publishing company to promote my books or make them visible to the public. The valuable time you spend letting others know about my books makes you all accomplices to my thought crime, and when I tell

<u>you that I appreciate each and every one of you, that is not hyperbole folks; you really do help make one man's dream of being an "author" a reality—never underestimate your importance in that regard.</u>

THE AVENGERS

My "inner circle" of awesomeness. The people who call me on my shit when I'm an asshole and call me on the phone when I'm in need. You've met Ed Trautz, (Iron Man,) now meet the rest of the team:

Nick Fury—Fred Roth. The mysterious one who, while often out of my sight, is never out of mind. Fred remains one of the few people on the Earth that gives more than he takes, and his cynicism and sarcasm have always paired nicely with my intensity and anger. Although I don't spend as much time in his company as I should, Fred is my square hammer of reality, and he is as good as it gets in the friend category.

Hawkeye—Marc Granieri. My compadre' in coffee consumption and love of literature, G is the one constant in a swirling sea of uncertainty at my job, and his accuracy in knowing exactly what to do and say when I need it earned him his marksman title. Father, husband, coach, mentor, athlete and scholar—he is, truly, a man's man, and I aspire to be more like him in many ways.

Thor—Billy Staab. A 40+ year friendship that has survived 3 wives, 8 children, over 200 live concerts, and too many work hours to count. Nobody on this Earth handles adversity with a smile better than my long-haired brother from another mother. Here's hoping we're still able to sneak sushi lunches and live metal shows into our schedules well into our 90s, brother; I have no doubt we will.

Hulk—Pete Nardello. As physically intimidating as he is sincerely loving, my partner in the silverback & rhino tutoring company, (and occasional Iron Hill date,) is a brick wall with a warm center. Our friendship seems destined for lifelong status; and I look forward to watching him parent Annie, Lena, and Claire, and love Kristin all along the way.

Black Panther—Bobby Ellis. The smartest guy in the room, no matter where the room is. Whilst juggling an amazing wife and three exceptional children, Bobby has always made the time to be a godsend to my family, and his unique brand of humility and humor are places of sanctuary that I never tire of visiting.

Scarlet Witch—Kim Morgan. A free spirit and ferocious wit, she doesn't have to waste her time checking on an old fart like me and promoting my books, but she does and she does. Kim's love is genuine and her magic is strong.

Quicksilver—Richie Castagna—A much overdue shout out to my brother-in-law. The shit doesn't hit the fan often in my house, but when it does, it does so in epic proportion, and Richie is always there, providing stability, composure, and the kind of legal advice that would normally cost me a mortgage payment or five. Fortunately, all we have to do is keep him stocked in Guinness and running shoes.

FLESH OF MY FLESH, BLOOD OF MY BLOOD
My Mom, Mary Wilson—Mom turned me on to books and lyrics at a very young age, and her encouraging literacy without pushing is probably why I continue to read voraciously and write unapologetically to this day.

My Dad, Frank Stepnowski—For instilling me with a warrior ethos. I wish I could've been a little better at the construction stuff, Pop, but my head and my heart were always into building things that had a pulse. Please know that, in your spirit, I do no harm but take no shit.

My sister, Molly—One of the founders of the "Fan" page on Facebook. For reasons beyond my comprehension, Mol is a tireless promoter of her tyrannical, half-assed amateur author brother.

My wife, Dr. Dawn Stepnowski—I often joke that Dawn hasn't read of any of my books. She hasn't. She doesn't have to; she *lived* them with me, and shared in all the sadness and euphoria that accompanied them. It takes a special kind of person to tolerate my under-slept, over-caffeinated, intolerant OCD ass; and it takes a one-of-a-kind woman to make me want to be a better man. I'm continually thankful I tricked her into marrying me.

My in-laws, Butch and Norma—Writing these books often involves blasting music of a sort of which they are not fans (although my mother-in-law's Meshuggah impersonation is classic) and periodic bad moods that roll in like dystopian dust storms. They tolerate this, and my generally surly mood, as well as anyone could hope for.

My stepson Brendan—Part of the reason that I'm so hard on you is because I don't want you to wind up like many of the kids that show up in my books. I know you won't, and maybe—someday—I'll let you *read* those books.

I would be remiss without a shout out to **Ozzy (the "black rabbith,")** who sat faithfully by my side while I wrote and revised, cursed and cajoled, edited and evolved. He's partial to sarcasm, Motörhead, and raw spinach, so we're kind of simpatico. Here's hoping his 4 lucky rabbit's feet translate to good sales.

and last, but certainly not least, YOU, THE READERS.

I still have a hard time believing, after all these years, that anyone would take time out of their lives to read something I wrote, let alone discuss it and write about it online. One of my favorite writers and thinkers, Neil Gaiman, famously remarked of himself: "I don't think I'm mainstream. I think what I am is lots and lots of different cults. And when you get lots and lots of small groups who like you a lot, they add up to a big group without ever actually becoming mainstream."

I like that concept. I'm pretty self-aware, so I know that my books are an "acquired taste," and that I'll never be "mainstream," but you know that, too—and yet you stick with me, forgive me for my faults and walk with me along this weird journey.

For that alone, I am sincerely, and eternally, grateful.

The acclaimed director Christopher Nolan made what I thought was an eloquent and accurate commentary on the role of the audience. He asserted that: "The audience tells [him] what the film is...Audiences seeing the film—that's the final piece of the creative process." He goes on to admit that "[Film is] an imperfect medium...every film is imperfect...The impetus is to try to do better on the next film."

I feel the same way about my books, and this one is no exception. You, the reader, make this formerly inanimate object come alive with your engagement and reaction. If this book motivated, infuriated, vindicated, or stimulated you in any way, I consider the entire writing process worthwhile. Are there flaws? Surely. Will I always endeavor to do better on the next book? Of course. That being said, I stand by what you hold, and I thank you, again, for being the final—and most important—piece of my creative process.

And hey, no matter *what* you're reading, keep reading,

and I'll see you next time.

BONUS MATERIAL
Interview with Frank Stepnowski

"The devil hates a coward."
—*My Dad (Frank Sr.)*

Several weeks prior to publication, Jon Harper, host of the *My Bad* radio show, conducted an online interview with me regarding this book. Having had early access to the material, (and having interviewed me before for his show,) Jon was uniquely qualified to orchestrate this exchange.

His questions were authentically inquisitive, and gloriously devoid of bullshit. Some of his inquiries made me slightly uncomfortable, and one of them made me downright angry; in short, they were perfect.

We hope you enjoy the interview as much as we did.

If there are any questions YOU want answered, reach out to me on:

Fans of the Author Frank Stepnowski on Facebook
or via **@Frankstep1** on Twitter,
and I promise I'll answer you as honestly and expeditiously as possible.

If you'd like to hear more from Jon, you can hear his work and/ or connect with him by checking out:
The #MyBad radio show http://www.bamradionetwork.com/ my-bad/
or via **@Jonharper70bd** on Twitter,
you will not be disappointed.

JON: Right off the bat, I want to know, what were you afraid to put in this book? Don't bullshit me and say nothing! I *know* there were some things that even big bad Step, in hindsight, edited out because you were afraid, what were they?

STEP: Nothing. I ain't afraid of shit. (Laughs)

JON: Unacceptable! I know you were afraid to publish some things!

STEP: Oh no, of course you're right, I'm just stalling for time because you hit me with a question right out of the gate that's making me uncomfortable. I love it. Hmmm…what was I afraid to publish? Probably not enough (laughs) because my wife swears that every book is going to get me fired! But, in reality… (extended pause) Obviously, I don't care about coming after the superpowers: Chris Christie, Bill Gates, David Coleman, Betsy DeVos, Pearson Corp., by name, but for the more anecdotal stuff, I changed names, dates, genders, races, et cetera to acquiesce to my legal advisors so I obviously don't want to get sued.

JON: Do you have an actual legal team?

STEP: Yessir, and I am well advised and *very* well protected, I assure you. Oh! I know! There were several times, in this book in particular, where I promised the audience exchanges between myself and students verbatim, but, upon reflection, I was afraid to violate the "what happens in Vegas" rule of my classroom. I'm sorry if that isn't as exhilarating an answer as you had hoped for, but as far as being afraid of reactions to what I say? You know me, brother.

JON: A great deal of your stories involve kids that our society labels as disadvantaged, disturbed, problematic, etc., and many of them are black and brown. Last I checked, you're a middle class white male, so *who are you* to be telling their stories?

STEP: That question, as it is posed, is narrow-minded in scope and racist in nature, but you are absolutely correct that people have, and will again, ask it in a variety of ways. I'm the guy who has been sitting next to them, teaching them, learning *about* them, listening *to* them, trying to understand them, helping them through their problems, polishing their strengths and improving their weaknesses. I'm the one responding to their texts and emails and posts throughout the day and into the wee hours of the morning and during my alleged weekends and summers "off." I'm the one editing their papers, correcting their work and helping them with their projects, even if they aren't for my class, and for 25 years running, I'm one of the *first* people they mention when they're asked who made them the person they are today. I've been invited to, and attended their family dinners, graduation parties, weddings, and funerals; I've sat in hospital rooms and prisons waiting to talk to them. I am the godfather of their children and, if they allow me to be, support system for their guardians. In short, I don't have time to worry about what they *look* like because I'm too busy working my ass off giving them everything I can of myself so I can rest a little easier when they leave me knowing I did everything I could to help them. I'm the one, as you so eloquently put it, *telling their story.* That goes for *all* of my kids. They're not my black and brown and yellow and white and whatever kids, they're just my kids, and the idiots who ask questions like that are, I find, usually seated on their ass somewhere passing judgment from a non-engagement bubble, safe behind the fact that any accusation, however subtle, of racism, must be treated with kid's gloves and, as such, exonerate them from their *lack* of involvement. Ta-Nehisi Coates, in a visceral passage from *Between the World and Me*—if you haven't read it, you should, by the way—recounts a friend who was killed, portraying him, hauntingly, as a collection of the love that was poured into him, and the time that was invested in him, from a variety of sources, which made his death all the more tragic because it ended this intricate, ever-growing web of interpersonal relationships made manifest by one beautiful, singular entity into which flowed many rivers of succor and support. That scares the shit out of me because I look at all of my students that way; as such, and I live in constant fear that any of them will be cut short or fail to achieve their potential. How could anyone who really feels that way be unqualified to tell their story? Again, Jon, I know *you* understand that, but it gets tiresome hearing that pedestrian shit from people that think because they **look** like my kids that they have a right to question my engagement **with** those kids. Fuck them, after what I've done (and continue to do,) for my students over the last quarter of a century, I don't have to answer to anybody.

> **JON: Your last statement is a perfect segue into the next question. I've seen your Facebook profile, we've spoken several times, and I've read your other publications: Why all the profanity in the books and the "alpha male" stuff online? *I* know you've got a prodigious vocabulary, and *I* know you're an in-shape dude, but I also know the "Step behind the scenes;" and, (in trying to put myself in the minds of other readers/ possible fans,) I need to know: We're reading about education from the mind of an author, so why the hell should we care about the tough guy stuff, and why all the cursing?**

STEP: Thank you, first of all, for seeing past the surface and trying to understand what Captain Ahab, in *Moby Dick*, referred to as "the deeper layer." I've addressed both of those issues many times; in fact, there's actually a chapter in this book called *On Profanity and Profundity*. But for the new readers just coming on board, (and welcome, by the way,) let me summarize: I neither invented expletives, nor do I require them to speak effectively. However, as both a linguist and a realist, I am acutely aware that my job is to educate and edify as effectively as possible, and imprecations, whether they're sprinkled in occasionally or dropped on you like carpet bombs, do the trick in that regard. I wrote my entire third book without one lick of foul language, none of my articles contain profanity, and I'm currently writing a children's book and a novel, neither of which require curse words, but, up until now, I write about what goes on in education, and A) I'm extremely passionate about the subject, so my language reflects that and B) I don't know if you've walked the halls of most schools in America, but it's a little disingenuous to tell the stories of our students without authentically replicating their verbiage, and that verbiage, more often than not, contains profanity.

As far as what you refer to as the "alpha male" stuff, you're smart enough to know that any of that kind of posturing comes from a place of fear. I have a wife, children, a stepson, and legions of students and people that I legitimately love and care about; unfortunately, the world is becoming a more and more dangerous and damaging place and—laugh if you want to—but I consider it my solemn duty to be an effective barrier between them and the world that would try and harm them. If the people I'm entrusted to protect know, not *think*, *know* that I can do so, that helps grease the wheels and facilitate trust and a safe learning environment, and that is priority one. Actually, I heard a fantastic response to a question the other day from former SEAL, and one of the baddest men on the planet, Jocko Willink, that answers the second part of your question briefly and eloquently. He was asked "What motivates you to train so hard when you can already walk through a wall and beat up 99% of the population?" His answer? "Really thick walls and the other 1% of the population," so there you go, if you're truly dedicated to your calling, you're always focused on what you can't do, and you try to rectify that.

JON: Fair enough, but for someone who seems so precise and deliberate in the care of his body and mind, you come across as imprecise, if not borderline reckless regarding your verbiage; how do you reconcile that?

STEP: (Laughs) Reckless? With my verbiage? Oh man, you couldn't be more inaccurate with your analysis if you tried, regarding both propositions, actually. That is a fantastic question, though, because I can totally envision people thinking exactly that, so here goes: Six months ago, I underwent surgery to remove my gall bladder, repair a major hernia, and remove 80% of my stomach via a gastric sleeve procedure. Just prior to that, I had surgery on my hand to rectify several issues, and just prior to *that* I had cortisone shots directly into my left shoulder and left knee. ALL (with the exception of my gall bladder,) were direct results of my, and I'm making air quotes that you can't see, "precise and deliberate care of my body." Granted, I never smoked or did drugs, I barely drink alcohol, and I ate pretty healthy, albeit tons of food, so none of the obviously bad shit, but my physicality was reckless; for no good reason, I pushed my body hard enough, through unnecessarily ridiculous workouts and ravenous, unhealthy eating, that it, literally, started breaking down.

Whereas with my verbiage, I have always been, and I am, with each passing year, more and more surgical, particularly when I write. Diction, clarity, and syntax are sacrosanct to me; if you knew how many times this book was rewritten, your head would explode. Somewhere, my two editors are shaking their heads and rolling their eyes, but this book went from a 450+ page manuscript to a 300 something publication that looks *nothing* like it did in its infancy.

I'm guessing, by reckless with my verbiage you mean either my redundancies or my profanities, or both. I think I covered the profanity issue in the last question, so let me address the superfluity. Look, I get that I sounded repetitive: Standardized testing sucks! Common core is evil! Most of the people in charge don't give a shit about your kids! Parents too often blame teachers for their own inadequacies! Good teachers are leaving the profession because they're forced to abandon why they went into the job in the first place! Yadda yadda yadda, all too often I wind up sounding like an angry teacherosaurus with Thesaurus, but that's only because, and please hear the next five words in all caps, THOSE THINGS ARE FUCKING IMPORTANT! See, a little profanity helps get the point across with just the right *je ne sais quoi*! All kidding aside, it's a shame that the most interesting and noteworthy stuff I write about happen to be the most visceral and unsettling, but don't get it twisted, the way I write about them is a million miles from reckless, I stand by everything I say and how I say it.

JON: Again, your answers lead to more questions…

STEP: Good answers should, should they not?

JON: Who's conducting this interview?

STEP: Sorry (laughs.)

JON: You mentioned that the most interesting stories are often the most visceral and unsettling, so why should I buy your book? I mean, the cover screams angry and depressing. If every time I turn on a screen I'm already assaulted by stories and news flashes that bum me out, why should I buy this book, which seems committed to pissing me off?

STEP: I hate to sound like a social media meme, but if it doesn't *challenge* you, it doesn't *change* you, and people simply need to change their awareness regarding this stuff, period, so I need to shock them to get their attention, and anger them to facilitate their follow-through. It is not anything close to conjecture to say that we are at a tipping point in the battle for control of our future generations. The increasingly corporate enterprise that is compulsory education is treating our children more like little automaton consumers that need to be told WHAT to think and less like beautiful, unique human beings that need to be reminded HOW to feel. In an age where we are being increasingly divided, this dumbing down is no longer just infuriating, it's terrifying, largely because of the nightmare scenarios that are starting to unfold as a direct result of collective fear and stupidity. If we allow our children to be raised angry, disengaged, disenchanted, and self-centered, then what future have we wrought for ourselves?

I *have* to keep hammering away at the injustices and insensitivities I see because our children's lives are at stake. While I am formally walking away from writing books about education, I will continue to work as passionately as the day I started (perhaps more so?) to improve, at least, the quality of the education I bring to your children. By the way, I know, unequivocally, that I speak for legions of good teachers in that regard. My man Henry Rollins astutely remarked that "if you're not pissed off, you're not paying attention." If you're one of MY target audience, you're already pissed off. If you want to stay asleep, I can't help you, and my books aren't for you.

JON: And that brings us to our final question. This is your fourth book that focuses on the subject of education, is that fair to say?

STEP: Certainly.

JON: And you swear this is your *last* book on that subject?

STEP. Correct.

JON: Then how is this book different than the others? Why should I read it? And how can you be sure—given the passion you claim to feel about education—that you'll never write another book like this again?

STEP: That is *three* questions, Viper,[1] and ***damn***, dude, are you trying to get people ***not*** to buy my book? (laughs)

JON: (Laughing) You said "no holds barred!"

STEP: True, true. OK, in keeping with my mild OCD, let's address your final assault on my book sales in chronological order:
This book is *significantly* different from the other three. *Why Are All the*

---

(1) John and I are both fans of Game of Thrones, both the HBO series and the novels upon which it is based. During one of our conversations, he playfully referred to me as "The Mountain," and I to him as "The Viper," largely due to the massive disparity in our sizes. The nicknames stuck, although I would never, under any circumstances, crush his head like a ripe melon...unless he asks me another question like #2

Good Teachers Crazy being a funny, flawed, anecdotal and—ahem—*alleged* autobiographical romp through my first decade teaching hardcore special ed., *S.C.R.E.W.E.D.* was a fictional catharsis as much for me as it was intended for my readers, *Teaching Sucks* was an intentionally toned-down conversation between me and the people who send their kids to school every day. This book, *Retribution*, is an intentional and unapologetic throat punch, from someone still in the field, thrown *at* the people who shit on teachers, *on behalf of* those teachers. In this book, I very intentionally set out to be my peers' righteous instrument of cruelty. I think, I *hope,* a decade later, that it provides a fitting book end to the first book.

I can't tell you why to read this book, but I can tell you, if you're an educator, that I'm putting my ass on the line defending you and my signing my name to it. We are a profession under attack, and I think we should support each other in general, online, in print, and, when possible, in person. If you're *not* in the educational field, your children still go to school, and if you don't have kids, you're still living in a world where your future is going to be intimately affected by the kids coming through our educational system, so you should "know thy enemy," so to speak, and my books are a lot more accessible than, say, the really textbook-y type books of this genre. And if you're just the kind of person that likes a little adversarial thinking, I'm your man. Way back in the late 1800s, Bayard Taylor warned "Let no iconoclast invade thy rising pantheon of the past." Well Fuuuuuuuuuuuuuck you, Baynard! Consider your pantheon invaded, violated, and everything in between. Only now do I realize I should have made that the epigraph of this book! (Laughs.) Finally, I make no promises that I'll never write about education again, I'm starting a blog as soon as this book hit the shelves, and I have a few potential periodical deals in the works, but no more books. It's all fictional novels, short story collections, and kids' books from here on.

JON: Before we wrap this up, some of your previous answers made me think of another question.

STEP: Fire at will, sir.

JON: I know that you're your own person, and that you don't really give a crap what *most* people think, but you've written three books prior to this one, and I know you've gotten feedback from people you *do* care about. What is something different about this book that is a direct result of input from the people you are about?

STEP: Finally, an easy one. As I mentioned back when you asked the "reckless verbiage" question…

JON: You're not gonna let that go, are you?

STEP: Nope. So I told you about how massive an undertaking it was reducing, revising, rewording and re-editing this particular book. Most of that is the result of two men who I love very much, and respect tremendously: Ed Trautz and Jason Secoda. Both gentlemen are like brothers to me; hence, they are brutally honest when it comes to telling me when my writing sucks, when it shines, and, most importantly, when my words don't accurately convey what they know I'm trying to get across.

Ed has been an invaluable resource since day one of my first book, he's the inexhaustible fountain of focus I drink from when I hit the wall. On this book, in particular, his ability to keep me *coherent*, over the course of three years and, literally, close to a hundred potential chapters, was invaluable. And, as I mention in the acknowledgements section, he did, despite my warnings, keep me from overindulging in what I will politely call literary assault and battery; I am absolutely certain that this book is more professional than it would have been because of him

Jason wanted to be a part of this book, and, because he's not an educator like Ed and I, he critiqued the manuscript in a very different way. He

307

suggested I make certain parts more palatable for the layman reader, and he challenged me to improve my clarity of expression and qualify some of my assertions. His advice, when heeded, resulted in key changes that made this book infinitely more accessible to non-educators.

JON: Excellent. This has been a fun exercise, I like getting you to think, and pissing you off. I find it a lot safer from over 3,000 kilometers away! Any final thoughts?

STEP: First of all, thank *you*, so much, for doing this. I can't believe you took time away from your beautiful family while you were in Aruba to listen to me babble incoherently about my next piece of subpar literature. Actually, one of your questions made me think of another answer. Way back at the beginning you asked me what I was afraid to write about, and then you asked me about the race issue in a later question. I wish I was more comfortable writing honestly about racial issues without having to concern myself with how every single word would be micro analyzed and hyper scrutinized, so I guess I left some good stuff on the table in the name of preventative measures, but I'll work on that, with the help of my students and friends, and we'll see if I can't evolve a little in that area.
As far as final thoughts…

JON: Whaddya got?

STEP: Well, to whomever is out there listening to this or reading this, we currently live in a country where 7% of the population thinks chocolate milk comes from brown cows, and we seem to have an increasingly large demographic of people that claim to hate other cultures that they don't understand, and couldn't find on a map if you spotted them a key and a clue; so just because *I'm* done writing books about the importance of teachers and education doesn't mean **you** can't do it. Start your book today, you'll have a surplus of material to work with on a daily basis, I assure you. Then, maybe Jon or I can interview *you* someday.

CPSIA information can be obtained
at www.ICGtesting.com
Printed in the USA
LVOW09s1511240917
549877LV00010B/66/P